GEORGE NEAS
HIS
POWDER HORN
DEPICTING
THE ARMS OF GREAT BRITAIN,
AN EARLY MAP OF HANOVER
AND SUNDRY OTHER
SUBJECTS.

PERIOD: LATE 18 TH CENTURY
DRAWN BY: JOHN M. SHEFFER

# Encounter at Hanover

## Prelude to Gettysburg

STORY OF THE INVASION OF PENNSYLVANIA
CULMINATING IN THE BATTLES OF
HANOVER AND GETTYSBURG
JUNE AND JULY, 1863

*with*

A BICENTENNIAL VIEW OF THE TOWN
FOUNDED BY
COLONEL RICHARD MCALLISTER
IN 1763

*Originally Prepared and Published by*

The Historical Publication Committee of
The Hanover Chamber of Commerce

1963

White Mane Publishing Co., Inc.

First Printing, 1962
Second Printing, 1985
Third Printing, 1988


ISBN 0-942597-07-9 (previously ISBN 0-932751-04-0)


This White Mane Publishing Company, Inc., publication is printed
by arrangement with
Beidel Printing House, Inc.
63 West Burd Street, Shippensburg, PA 17257


In respect to the scholarship contained herein, only acid-free paper has been used in this book to insure permanence and durability.


For a complete list of available publications
Please write

White Mane Publishing Company, Inc.
P.O. Box 152
Shippensburg, PA 17257


PRINTED IN THE UNITED STATES OF AMERICA

# FOREWORD

Commissioned in April 1961 by the Hanover Chamber of Commerce, the Publication Committee worked diligently to compile and publish this hard-bound book featuring the Centennial of the Civil War Battle at Hanover, Pa., and the Bicentennial of the founding of the Borough of Hanover.

Members of the Publication Committee are as follows: Philip W. Bange, Edward H. Blettner, William M. Collins, Thomas Y. Cooper, Charles S. Diller, C. Homer Meredith, John M. Sheffer, Harry C. Stonesifer and Jacob S. Wirt.

## ABOUT THE AUTHOR

Originally prepared and published for the Civil War
Centennial by the Historical Publication Committee
of the Hanover Chamber of Commerce, most of the
research and basic narrative history for this book was
by historian George R. Prowell, (1849-1928). A
native of York County, Pennsylvania, Prowell based much of his research of the battle on actual interviews with participants and eyewitnesses. A graduate
of Millersville College, Millersville, Pennsylvania and
the University of Wooster, in Ohio, his varied career
included service on the staff of the Philadelphia Press,
associate editor of National Encyclopedia of
American Biography and as superintendent of public
schools in Hanover. Other books by him include —
*The History of York County, Pennsylvania; History
of Wilmington, Delaware; and the History of the 87th
Pennsylvania Volunteers.*

## ACKNOWLEDGMENTS

Grateful acknowledgment is made to the following companies, organizations, publishers and individuals for permission to reprint photographs and material belonging to them and for the help given the committee in preparing this book:

ANSCO HISTORICAL COLLECTION—Photos of Generals Custer, Grant and Hancock

ALLIED PIX SERVICE, INC.—Photos of Winebrenner Home

RUSSELL W. BOWMAN, Seven Valleys, Pa.

MRS. MARGARET C. CLARK—Historical data

WILFRED C. CLAUSEN—From Photographic Collection

MRS. NANCY E. CROUSE—Typing

THE LIBRARY OF CONGRESS—Photoduplication Service, Photo Collection

EDMONDS STUDIO—Photo Collection

EMMANUEL UNITED CHURCH OF CHRIST—Collection

THE EVENING SUN—Photographs

MRS. C. F. EHREHART—Collection

J. E. FLICKINGER—Photo Collection

NAOMI FUHRMAN—Mary Leader Photo

LEWIS D. GOBRECHT—Photo Collection

A. P. HETRICK—Photo Collection

HANOVER PUBLIC LIBRARY—From Historical Department Collection

MRS. GRACE T. HIMES—Historical Data

DR. FREDERIC SHRIVER KLEIN—Photos and advice

MRS. DOROTHY W. KLING—Volunteer typist

MALCOLM S. MESSINGER—Proof Printing

MT. OLIVET CEMETERY ASSOCIATION

S. DONALD MICHAEL—Material from Heber Michael Collection

WM. WOODBURN POTTER—Photo and Material Collection

STANLEY E. ROSER–Seven Valleys, Pa.

JOHN M. SHEFFER–Map and Drawing

ST. MATTHEW'S LUTHERAN CHURCH–Historical Dept. Collection

THE SUNPAPERS, PHOTOGRAPHIC DEPT., Baltimore, Md.

MRS. HELEN E. BOLLINGER TRONE–Photo of Kitzmiller's Mill

THE VALENTINE MUSEUM–Photo of General Stuart

MRS. C. P. WOLCOTT–As Advisor

# TABLE OF CONTENTS

## PART I

## TABLE OF CONTENTS (Continued)

TABLE OF CONTENTS (Continued)

# PART I

## POWDER HORN MAP

It is a privilege to present as our frontispiece a masterly reproduction of the engraved powder horn containing the earliest known map of Hanover. The splendid drawing is the work of John M. Sheffer who was able to study the horn at close hand when it was being exhibited in 1956 at the Hanover Public Library. This valuable piece of early Americana was owned at the time by a New York collector.

In Mr. Sheffer's opinion the horn is one of the finest examples of its kind and was without doubt engraved by a professional, probably an itinerant artisan, who visited Hanover and thus was able to execute the map with extreme accuracy from actual observation. The map does not need the word Pennsylvania to prove that it is our particular Hanover. The five main streets converging in a public square with a stream shown at the end of Carlisle Street leave no room for doubt concerning the locale.

Only one church is shown, the first German Reformed, correctly placed on the plot now known as "Under the Pines." It is a log structure with steeple built in 1766. Seven of the buildings show a flag or sign identifying them as inns or taverns. Prior to the Revolution according to Prowell there were seven inns conducted by the following: Daniel Barnitz, Andrew Etzler, Alex Forsythe, Charles Gelwix, Francis Heim, Peter Winebrenner, and Henry Welsh. The Richard McAllister residence, surrounded by a stockade, is at the junction of the Baltimore pike and Monocacy road and faces the latter. Another building with stockade is probably the Mathias Neas tannery.

Attention is called to the Arms of Great Britain, engraved with masterly detail, as pointing to a date for the horn as prior to the Revolution. No loyal American would want a powder horn with this insignia or a pictured ship flying a British flag after 1776. Colonel McAllister laid out Hanover in 1763 and devoted himself to public affairs. The date for the horn should be during the colonial days sometime between 1763 and 1776.

The cartouche bearing the name of George Neas poses the greatest challenge in dating of the horn. There were two Hanover citizens of that name. The most prominent of these served as postmaster from 1798 to 1810, was a delegate to the General Assembly, made an ocean voyage to Germany and back in 1802, and was engaged in the tannery business. A son of Mathias Neas, he was born in 1769 and died in 1829. If the horn was made in colonial days, he was too young to qualify as owner. The other George Neas is listed as a taxpayer in 1783. He may have been a brother of Mathias Neas or even his father, and Mr. Sheffer thinks the most likely original owner of the horn. The hunter, his dog, the antlered deer, and the fox are stock figures used on horns of the period.

*Early Scene in Center Square—This is one of the first photographs taken in Hanover. It was made by Plumbe National Daguerrian Gallery of 136 Chestnut Street, Philadelphia, in the year 1845. The Central Hotel is shown as it appeared in those days while other early structures in the northwest angle are also shown. The building on the right has been recently razed to make way for the new Wenger Building.*

## A TOWN NAMED HANOVER

Richard McAllister or M'Calister, of Presbyterian Scotch-Irish descent, settled on a tract of land he purchased in 1745 from John Digges who had obtained a grant for 10,000 acres from Charles Calvert, Lord Baltimore. Digges' Choice was at that time believed a part of Maryland. The McAllister tract lay six miles north of what afterwards became known as the Mason and Dixon line, dividing Maryland from Pennsylvania. The fertile lands were covered with a dense growth of hickory, walnut and oak trees. McAllister erected a log house and operated a store and tavern at a crossing of the heavily-traveled Monocacy trail and a road leading from Baltimore north through a pass in the Pigeon Hills.

Other settlers in this section were mostly of German Palatinate origin. In their home country they lived in villages and farmed tracts of land on the outskirts. When the Scotch-Irish frontiersman decided in 1763 to lay out part of his farm in town lots he shrewdly counted on their custom of association to draw them together. They called it "Hickorytown" in fun, and as McAllistertown it grew steadily but slowly. When Michael Tanner (Danner), a county commissioner, suggested he name the place in honor of Hannover, Germany, the village population increased more rapidly. They had their barns and stables in the town and cleared farm tracts in the suburbs. They had their Lutheran, German Reformed, and Mennonite churches in good measure, but to this day you will not find a Presbyterian church in the place. For many years Conewago Chapel, three or four miles away, sufficed for Catholic settlers from Maryland and elsewhere.

Five main streets radiated from a square or diamond. They led to York, Baltimore, Frederick, Carlisle, and the Pigeon Hills. The most direct road to Gettysburg lay through McSherrystown. The idea of the Public Commons as a breathing place and playground was British.

Colonel Richard McAllister commanded the Second Pennsylvania Regiment of the Flying Camp which consisted of eight companies, six of which were composed of recruits from York and Adams counties during the Revolution. Adams did not become an independent entity until 1800. Hanover had a population of five hundred by 1776-80.

Fifty-two years after it was founded and twenty years after the death of the founder, Hanover was incorporated as a borough March 4, 1815, by charter granted by the Legislature of Pennsylvania. The New and Universal Gazetteer in 1800 described Hanover as "the second town in York County for size and wealth. It contains about 260 houses, many of brick." By 1820 the population was 946, and the 1860 census placed it as 1,638, with 600 houses in and about the borough. The population of Gettysburg then was considerably under 3,000. The town was not laid out by James Gettys until 1796.

Gettysburg lies 14 miles northwest of Hanover; York, 19 miles northeast; Baltimore, 41 miles south by the turnpike; Frederick, 40 miles southwest; Westminster, 16 miles south; Harrisburg, 36 miles to the north; and Carlisle, 30 miles northwest.

Both Hanover and Gettysburg reeked with obscurity. In the minds of outsiders Hanover has been confused with Hanover Junction, and it has been only in the last few years that a

*Richard McAllister residence at corner of Middle and Baltimore streets, built of logs encased with brick. Tavern and store adjoin on the north side. Benjamin Franklin was a guest of McAllister in 1755. Razed in 1950.*

Brady photo listed in the government archives under Hanover Junction, Virginia, was accidentally identified as really Hanover Junction, Pennsylvania.

Oddly enough the story is told of Hanover getting credit in one instance as location of the Gettysburg battle. It appears that when news of the battle reached Washington it bore the date line of Hanover because of telegraphic transmission by Danny Trone from Hanover of news of the great struggle. The ambassador from France in haste to get off the news of the event placed in his diplomatic pouch the account dated from Hanover, and for some weeks at least with the slow movement of documents by ship at the time Paris residents read in their newspapers about the crucial struggle being at Hanover instead of at Gettysburg.

Hanover is located in an unrivaled and well-drained plain which extends from the Maryland line north to York and westward to Gettysburg. The town stands 601 feet above sea level, 229 feet higher than Continental Square, York, and 220 feet lower than Maryland line south of Hanover.

## Kept Livestock in Back Yards

The residents here still kept cows, horses, swine and poultry in their back-yard stables in Civil War times and considerably later. Cows were driven out to pasture in nearby fields from barns just off Center Square.

The nineteen coachmaking shops, seventeen smithies, and twelve cigar factories of that period give an idea of industrial employment here, not to mention the clock makers, coverlet and carpet weavers, and iron molders. Then as now Hanover was a trading center for a large area. The war had dealt the town a heavy blow in depriving the carriage workers, especially, of their Southern market.

Four churches provided for religious activities of the town: Emmanuel Reformed Church, on Pigeon (Abbottstown) Street, the Rev. W. K. Zieber, pastor; St. Matthew's Lutheran, West Chestnut Street, the Rev. M. J. Alleman, pastor; the Methodist Church, Baltimore Street (where St. Joseph's Catholic Church now stands), J. S. McMurray, presiding elder, and A. W. Guyer, pastor; and the United Brethren Church, Pigeon Street, the Rev. Martin Lohr, local preacher.

Hanover was noted for its many excellent taverns with yards for accommodation of the teamsters and Conestoga wagons which came through here from Baltimore to Carlisle en route to the West. A Turnpike Company formed in 1808 improved the original Maryland road of 1735 to the Conewago settlement. The East Berlin and Hanover Turnpike Company was formed in 1810. The Monocacy road was extended by Lancaster County from Wrightsville through York and Hanover in 1739.

The first railroad in York County, which forms a part of the Western Maryland, was laid from Hanover Junction on the Northern Central Railway to Hanover. The first train pulled into Hanover September 29, 1852. The depot at the Hanover end was placed on the Commons.

## Hanover Branch to Gettysburg

The railroad was extended a distance of seven miles to New Oxford, and the line to Gettysburg was completed December 16, 1858. The seven-mile Littlestown Railroad was laid by November, 1856. Captain A. W. Eichelberger was president of these lines at the time of the Civil War. The Frederick and Pennsylvania Line Railroad and the Bachman Valley Railroad were included in the management of the Hanover Branch.

Borough officials in 1863 included: Burgess, Joseph Slagle; councilmen, Cornelius Sarbaugh, William Trone, Dr. Henry C. Eckert, Moses Esterline, Henry Wentz, C. M. Renaut, Jacob Bender; constable, D. S. Tanger; auditor, Allowies Smith; assistant burgess, C. M. Renaut; secretary, L. F. Melsheimer; treasurer, Daniel Q. Albright.

From the early pioneer days, while Adams County was still a part of York, there was always a spirit of rivalry between the Scotch-Irish settlers of Gettysburg and the Germans of Hanover. When Adams County was set up as a separate county in 1800, Gettysburg as a county seat and later the home of a college and theological seminary gained the ascendancy in culture and prestige. At the time of the Civil War its population was larger than Hanover, but thanks to the thrifty and diligent character of the Pennsylvania-Dutch residents of the fertile area chosen

Richard McAllister's first home in Hanover was a farmhouse of log and stone erected about 1745 on a 100-by 270-foot tract in an angle 250 feet in the rear of the lots on Frederick and Baltimore streets and next to where the Hanover glove factory now stands. A one-and-a-half-story brick dwelling was built to the rear of the original log structure. This property was sold to Henry Welsh, grandfather of the late Roy Spangler, in 1763 for 49 pounds, four shillings, and ten pence. It was at this time, 1763-64, that McAllister built a brick-enclosed house at the corner of Middle and Baltimore streets, and later a two-story house adjoining on the north side for use as a general store and tavern. These buildings were razed in 1950.

by Richard McCalister for the town he founded, Hanover forged ahead in agricultural and industrial wealth.

Even prior to the Civil War Hanoverians had a saying in their popular dialect expressing their advantage over their neighbors to the west:

> "Och, Gettysburg, du arme stadt,
> Alle Dawg Buchweatze Kuche
> Un dee net sott."

Freely translated the sense would be as follows:

> "O Gettysburg, you threadbare town,
> Living for you must be tough;
> Every day buckwheat cakes,
> And of those not enough."

### Model for Battle

Architects in ancient times not infrequently built a small size model of the structure planned, mosque maybe or temple, and it remained for comparison alongside the main building when that was completed.

Hanover like Gettysburg is situated on a plain between two ridges. Both are easily approached by roads from all directions. Hanover had its Plum Creek and Gettysburg its Willoughby Run. It is frequently pointed out that Lee approached the field at Gettysburg from the North and the Union army came from the South. At Hanover the approach was reversed. Stuart attacked from the South and Kilpatrick after countermarching and re-forming came in mainly from the North.

Otherwise when not in close conflict both forces occupied rising ground, with the towns more or less in between. Stuart planted his artillery on Cemetery Ridge which in the case of Gettysburg was occupied by the Union armies, with Bunker Hill and Seminary Ridge the opposite elevations.

In both battles the new Spencer seven-shot repeating rifles were put to use by the Union cavalry, marking a decisive change in cavalry tactics. With these rifles dismounted cavalry were effective against infantry as well as against cavalry. Pleasonton used artillery at Chancellorsville effectively. Saber battles had seen their day, that at Brandy Station one of the last and most impetuous. General John Buford startled the enemy with Spencers the first day at Gettysburg as Custer did at Hanover. In both encounters the Confederates had the advantage at the start of the conflict, and the Union forces held possession of the field at the end.

When it is a matter of local personalities who helped make history Hanover has its exemplars to compare with Gettysburgians. The Adams County seat points to Wesley Culp who had come north as a Confederate soldier to die on the patriarchal acres of Culp's Hill, while Hanover can boast of Corporal John Hoffacker of the Eighteenth Pennsylvania Regiment whose fate it was to be shot and instantly killed in defense of practically his home town when his regiment met the first charge there of the enemy. He was born and brought up on a West Manheim farm just south of Hanover.

A parallel to seventy-year-old cobbler John Burns of Gettysburg who, armed with rifle, attached himself to a Wisconsin company marching up the Emmitsburg road to battle to the air of "The Campbells Are Coming," will be found in a John Doe of the Hanover area, according to the account of Cavalry General David M. Gregg. Carrying a rifle and in civilian clothes this anonymous character rode up on a farm horse and asked permission to join his troopers. Referred to an aide he continued with the division to the scene of battle. Concerning his further achievements and ultimate fate neither history nor tradition provide an answer.

Hanover cannot match Jennie Wade, only citizen to be killed at Gettysburg, but it is a big wonder that none of the women and children on the streets met death when Jeb Stuart's cavalrymen charged up Frederick Street to Center Square that Tuesday morning, June 30. Large numbers were engaged in bringing food and refreshments for the resting Union soldiers.

However, it developed eventually that a Miss Lizzie Sweitzer, a domestic employed in the family of the Rev. M. J. Alleman, of St. Matthew's parsonage, Frederick Street, claimed she did suffer a bullet wound on that occasion. And what is more she returned to Hanover thirty-five years later seeking evidence on which to file claim for a pension. She was then a widow, Mrs. Lizzie Waltz, and needed the aid of a crutch when walking. She was helping to distribute food among the soldiers, and before she could reach a place of shelter was struck in the ankle by a pistol or carbine ball, inflicting a serious wound, she said, from which she had never fully recovered.

The Hanover Spectator in its issue of September 12, 1862, told of the excitement prevailing in town when word was received of Lee's invasion of Maryland. Crowds gathered in the streets and workshops to hear and discuss the news. Rumors turned to reality, the paper said, "when refugees from Frederick and Carroll counties, Maryland, came pouring into town, some on horseback, others in carriages and wagons, each and all declaring that the enemy had crossed the Potomac and that 'Stonewall' Jackson was in Frederick." Not many days later, on September 17, sounds of cannonading were heard in town from the direction of Hagerstown. The fiercest battle of the war was taking place on Antietam Creek. The anxious citizens knew that some of their own kin might be involved. Company C of the 130th Pennsylvania Regiment was commanded by Captain Joseph S. Jenkins of Hanover, who was seriously wounded in the battle.

The rising tides of war had flowed close to Hanover then. Less than ten months were to pass when it too would be engulfed in those flood tides.

### Editor Leader Voices Appeal

The following editorial appeared in the Hanover Spectator, June 19, 1863, W. H. Leader, editor, expressing the apprehensions of the public as rumors of Lee's invasion spread and giving assurance that the patriotic fervor of Pennsylvania citizens would not be found wanting in the great crisis:

> "Our town has been in an intense state of excitement during the last few days. A thousand and one rumors are circulated in the course of the day of such a conflicting character that it is impossible to give a correct statement of the actual condition of affairs.
> "From what can be gleaned from the reports it is certain that rebels are on this side of the Potomac, in some force, variously estimated at from six to twenty

thousand, mostly Cavalry and mounted Infantry. The latest dispatches state that about two thousand are in Chambersburg, throwing up entrenchments. Several have been captured, on whose persons dispatches were found calling on the main rebel army for reinforcements. This would indicate that they are fearful of their ability to maintain their hold of these places, and hence move forward cautiously and slowly.

"The people throughout the State are, we are happy to learn, aroused and are responding to the call of our patriotic Governor, as promptly as the nature of the times will admit. New York and the New England States are sending their noble, loyal sons with promptness to our defence. Major Jenkins started for Harrisburg on Tuesday morning with some fifty young men the flower and pride of our town. Others were making arrangements to leave in a few days. From all parts of our good old Commonwealth her heroic sons are flocking to her rescue. This is as it should be, and none should stand back from selfish or political motives, as the blow is aimed at us all without distinction."

## THE PUBLIC COMMONS

The sketch of the Public Commons was made by Benson J. Lossing a few days after the battle here when he was en route to Gettysburg. It appears in his Pictorial Field Book of the Civil War. He wrote that bullet marks were visible on the fences and buildings in the vicinity. He continues as follows: "Stuart led a

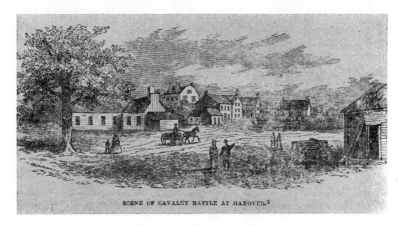

SCENE OF CAVALRY BATTLE AT HANOVER.

desperate charge in person on the flank and rear of General
Farnsworth's brigade on the Common near the railway. A severe
battle ensued in the town and its borders, when General Custer
who had advanced to Abbottsville (?) returned, and the Confederates were repulsed with the loss of a flag and fifty men.
Farnsworth lost about one hundred men. The gallant New York
Fifth Cavalry led by Farnsworth and Major Hammond bore the
brunt of battle and won high commendation."

[EDITOR'S NOTE: — The invaders penetrated as far as the railroad yards but the main clash occurred in the southwestern end
of the town.]

Borough council took legal possession of the Commons in 1859.
Property owners adjacent to the Commons included Samuel
Fitz, John Barnitz, David Bixler, Charles Barnitz, and the Eichelberger heirs. George Young & Sons (John S. and Reuben) started
shipping grain by railroad to Baltimore in 1852. Samuel Fitz
erected a five-story Penn Flouring Mill at a cost of $30,000 in
1863. He had established a foundry to the left of Abbottstown
Street in 1840, and also manufactured threshing machines. Conrad Moul moved shops near the railroad on Abbottstown Street
in 1855 for making reapers and in 1857 had plants on the Commons. The Hanover Junction, Hanover and Gettysburg Railroad
also had its shops and station there.

## LEE INVADES NORTH

President Abraham Lincoln issued the Emancipation Proclama-
tion January 1, 1863. The war between the North and South had
about reached the half way point. General Joseph Hooker was
assigned to the command of the Army of the Potomac January
26, 1863, succeeding General Ambrose Burnside. The Union
army was encamped on the north bank of the Rappahannock,
near Fredericksburg, Virginia, with General Lee's forces on the
south side of the river. Hooker made efforts to stop desertions,
call back absentees, and restore discipline and morale to his
army. The cavalry was consolidated and placed on a higher
state of efficiency, the commander, George Stoneman, being
given sick leave.

In the three-day battle of Chancellorsville, May 2-4, Lee and

Jackson outmaneuvered Hooker and had things pretty much their own way. Howard's Eleventh Corps was badly mauled. With the use of three regiments of cavalry and twenty-two pieces of artillery against Jackson fighting almost into the night, Pleasonton helped save the Potomac army. Hooker was stunned May 3 by the concussion of a shell against a post near which he was standing, the command devolving upon General Couch. Pleasonton was placed in charge of the cavalry corps as major general of volunteers. "Stonewall" Jackson lost his life in this battle, Hooker lost the battle, and Lee lost his right-hand man. It meant the end for Hooker and a hollow victory for the South.

The Confederate forces a month later were gathering in preparation for Lee's invasion of the North, the infantry in three corps under Longstreet, Ewell and A. P. Hill; and the cavalry in three divisions under Hampton, Fitzhugh Lee, and W. H. F. Lee, with Stuart commanding. A Grand Review of the twelve thousand cavalrymen took place June 5 on the level plains at Brandy Station with distinguished guests from Richmond followed by a moonlight ball and another review three days later for General Lee. Stuart's headquarters were at Fleetwood homestead on a hill near Brandy Station. Stuart little expected that Pleasonton's cavalry in two columns under Buford and Gregg were near enough to have been invited to these reviews. They appeared at Fleetwood uninvited June 9 for what is considered the greatest saber fight of the war.

Pleasonton's men charged three times up Fleetwood Hill, each time at a walk, then a canter, and finally at full speed gallop, and although dislodged in the final charge came off with renewed confidence and audacity in whatever lay ahead. Stuart lost five hundred men, Rooney, Robert E. Lee's son, among the wounded. Important secret information was secured as a result of which Lee abandoned previous plans and removed the bulk of his army to Hagerstown by way of Williamsport, and from thence to Chambersburg through the Shenandoah Valley.

Pleasonton's successful raids at Aldie, Middleburg, and Upperville were offset by the overwhelming defeat of Major General Robert H. Milroy's Union infantry at Winchester before Lee moved north.

Advance of cavalry units generally indicated infantry would

follow. Jenkins' cavalry preceded Ewell by a week into Pennsylvania, serving as a screen and collecting horses and cattle en route. Imboden's brigade rode twenty miles west of Chambersburg guarding Lee's communication line. The brigades of Jones and Robertson remained to guard entrances to mountain passes. They took no part in the battle that was to follow. To Imboden afterwards went the dubious honor of escorting the ambulance train during Lee's retreat.

### Lee Reaches Chambersburg

On the 22nd of June Ewell, who had one wooden leg and used a crutch, crossed the Potomac at Williamsport and Shepherdstown and, marching through Hagerstown, reached Chambersburg on the 23rd. On the 25th Ewell ordered Early to march through Gettysburg to York and Wrightsville. On the 26th Early's advance west of Gettysburg was delayed by the presence of the Twenty-sixth Pennsylvania Emergency Regiment, under Colonel Jennings. On the morning of the 28th, Early's forces en-

GENERAL ROBERT E. LEE

tered York and Gordon's brigade, passing through York, reached Wrightsville on the afternoon of that day, but the bridge across the Susquehanna was burned before the Confederates could reach it. On the afternoon of the 29th, Early received orders to return to Gettysburg and in obedience to this order, reached East Berlin by the afternoon of the 30th, and Gettysburg on the afternoon of the 1st of July.

Meanwhile, Longstreet and Hill, having crossed the Potomac on the 24th and 25th, reached Chambersburg on the 27th. On the same day, Ewell, with Johnson's and Rodes' divisions, entered Carlisle. The advance of Jenkins' cavalry was then on the west bank of the Susquehanna opposite Harrisburg. The Confederate cavalry, because of its injudicious movements, failed utterly in that most important office of cavalry to keep General Lee informed of the movements of the opposing army. Lee, late on the evening of the 28th, or early the 29th, by the chance arrival of a Longstreet hired scout, learned, for the first time, that the Union army was at Frederick and not, as he thought, still south of the Potomac. Believing that the Union commander would attempt to cut his communications with Virginia, Lee moved east of the mountains, so that by threatening Baltimore and Washington, he might keep open his line of retreat. All the component parts of the Confederate army were now ordered to concentrate on Gettysburg, and during the next few days, all except Stuart's command moved in that direction.

It is claimed that Lee's orders to Stuart were discretionary. His principal tasks were to guard Ewell's right, keep in close touch with him, and harass the Army of the Potomac's rear and flank. If he cut around the Union army he was to join Early as soon as possible at York. Several tricks of fortune prevented Stuart from carrying out these orders. In the first place he was delayed when Reynolds' First Corps got on the road leading north before him or maybe he delayed in getting on the road; then Meade fanned out his troops in a wide arc, making it impossible for Stuart to communicate with Ewell with the Union army between them; and to top it all he picked up a white elephant straight after he crossed the Potomac into Maryland. The question is raised whether Lee may not have been less than thoughtful in not advising Early to be on the lookout for Stuart.

### Stuart Captures Wagon Train

After being on the road without pause three days and three nights, Stuart finally crossed the Potomac far behind schedule at Rowsers Ford and within a few hours' ride of Washington. He rested and grazed his horses that Sunday, June 28. He was living off the country. No wonder he regarded it as a stroke of luck when Fitzhugh Lee captured at Rockville a supply train intended for Meade. There were 150 heavily-laden white-topped wagons in the train, but in the mad scramble the Federals made to escape twenty-five of the wagons were wrecked or escaped back to Washington.

Stuart passed up a play-to-the-gallery temptation to ride down to the Capital just for the devil of it; he destroyed some canal boats, and after a night march, scattered a small troop of Union men at Cooksville, and took time to tear up B. & O. tracks at Hood's Mill and burn the bridge at Sykesville en route to Westminster.

From Union Mills he took the "back" road to Hanover. There was some tough pulling ahead with the handicap of the captured wagon train, especially on that steep grade known as Conewago Hill after crossing Indian Run in the valley leading to Gitt's mill. But after the hill was surmounted the mule-skinners happily soon came to a cleared field on the Gotwalt farm east of the Westminster road a couple of miles from Hanover. First settlers found this bare spot on which nothing grew. Screened by woods it was an ideal spot to park the wagon train after the road through Hanover was found blocked by Union cavalry. Tradition has it that the last Indians camped in this section before their migration from this area. The treeless tract may have been a ceremonial assembly place for the Indians.

---

## PIPE CREEK-UNION MILLS LINE

General Hooker began his movement to cover Washington on June 15, the day Longstreet left Culpeper. As Hooker moved northward, east of the Blue Ridge, Hill and Longstreet moved up the Shenandoah Valley and Hooker crossed the Potomac at Edward's Ferry on the same day that Hill and Longstreet crossed at Williamsport. On the 28th, Longstreet and Hill were in Cham-

bersburg with their two corps, composed of six divisions, and of
Ewell's three divisions, Johnson's and Rodes' being at Carlisle
and Early's at York. At the same time the Army of the Potomac
headquarters was at Frederick.

General Hooker had the respect of his men and most of his
officers. He didn't like the General in Chief H. W. Halleck,
Headquarters of the Army, at Washington, and Halleck didn't
like him. Hooker was expected to defend Washington and Baltimore in addition to facing Lee's invading troops. He asked that
the ten thousand men under General French at Harpers Ferry
be transferred to his command. When Halleck refused Hooker
asked to be relieved.

On June 28 Major General George Gordon Meade succeeded
Hooker in command of the Army of the Potomac. It was a job
he didn't want, but being a good soldier he went to work. The
same day the garrison at Harpers Ferry was placed under his
command. At 2 p.m. June 28 the new commander made his first
request. He notified Halleck that his cavalry forces required three
brigadier generals. For these posts General Pleasonton nominated
Captain Farnsworth, Eighth New York cavalry; Captain George
A. Custer, Fifth New York Cavalry; and Captain Wesley Merritt, Second cavalry. Secretary of War Edwin M. Stanton O.K.'d
the appointments effective June 29.

Meade received his first piece of bad news when Washington
informed him at Frederick June 28 that his wagon train had
been captured by Fitzhugh Lee near Rockville. Washington was
instructing Major General D. N. Couch at Harrisburg to hold
the enemy in check on the Susquehanna. Meade changed his
headquarters from Frederick to Taneytown.

## Meade Plans Defense Line

The ever-cautious Meade planned a Pipe Creek defensive line
with professional military strategy. Two years of Civil War
battles had shown that a carefully selected defense line almost
always resulted in success for the defenders. He believed Lee
would now strike toward Washington. He planned and ordered
a defense line along the Pipe Creek hills, extending from Middleburg on the west near where Big Pipe Creek enters the Monocacy,

MAJOR GENERAL GEORGE G. MEADE
*Commanding Army of the Potomac.*

through Taneytown, his headquarters, through Union Mills, on Big Pipe Creek, and to Manchester on the east. On the wooded hills overlooking the Pipe Creek valley, the line formed a perfect position to meet and destroy any drive from the north toward Washington. Westminster, about six miles south of Union Mills, was the supply base, connected with Baltimore and Washington by railroad, and having roads which fanned out to each of the four units of the Pipe Creek line. Small units and stragglers could catch up from the rear, while advance units probed for the enemy. It was a perfect plan, and the Pipe Creek order was officially announced from Meade's headquarters at Taneytown early on July 1, with plans for troops, surveys, signal stations, supply and engineer units. The Pipe Creek battle, however, never took place.

Meade's official order for the Pipe Creek line issued early July 1 directed the Sixth to Manchester, Twelfth to Littlestown, Third to Taneytown, Fifth to Union Mills, First to near Emmitsburg, and Second to Frizellburg, near Westminster, as reserves.

Brigadier General Henry J. Hunt, Meade's Chief of Artillery, made a survey of the Pipe Creek, defensive-offensive plan and favored it. He was also the only general of the Army of the Potomac who understood the plan. Had Lee captured either Culp's Hill or Little Round Top, the Pipe Creek line would have saved the day—and Baltimore and Washington—for the Union armies.

Two developments spoiled Meade's plan. First, General Reynolds, with the First Corps, was near Gettysburg because of rumors that the enemy might be concentrating there, and should have received orders on July 1 to fall back to Emmitsburg, but instead he engaged in a skirmish which rapidly developed on a larger scale, and Reynolds was killed at the start of the engagement. Without other orders, the First Corps remained at Gettysburg to fight.

Second, if Stuart had reached Lee in time, with information about the location of Meade's army, Lee might have concentrated for an attack before the Pipe Creek defense line had been fully organized. But, without information about the Union army, with the Susquehanna River crossing a failure, and with a long supply line from the Valley, Lee had begun to withdraw his forces from

Harrisburg, York and Carlisle, and the numerous available roads made Gettysburg a natural point of concentration. According to Fitzhugh Lee, "Had Lee had all of his cavalry in Pennsylvania, the irrepressible conflict would not have taken place at Gettysburg, but possibly on Pipe Creek."

Instead of the carefully planned battle on Pipe Creek, the battle at Gettysburg took place, with neither commander having accurate knowledge of the terrain, the opposing forces, or the facilities for supply and communication, and with chaotic confusion for the first two days as the armies gradually organized for the final test of strength.

### Union Forces Aligned

By the evening of the 30th the Union army was spread out in a fanlike shape extending eastward and westward from Emmitsburg to Manchester, Maryland, a distance of about thirty miles. Reynolds' First Corps was at Marsh Creek, four miles south of Gettysburg; Howard's Eleventh at Emmitsburg; Hancock's Second at Uniontown; Sickles' Third at Taneytown; Sykes' Fifth at Union Mills; Slocum's Twelfth at Littlestown; and the Sixth under "Uncle John" Sedgwick at Manchester. Of the Union cavalry, Kilpatrick had that day defeated Stuart at Hanover, Buford, with his division, was picketing the roads radiating from Gettysburg, and Gregg's division was protecting the right flank of the army at Manchester. Late on the night of the 30th, after the orders for the next day's movements were already issued, Meade learned for the first time from General Couch, at Harrisburg, that Lee had already moved east of the mountains with the greater part of his forces. On the same night he learned from Buford that his pickets west and north of Gettysburg were in contact with the corps of Hill and Ewell. The Confederate corps averaged a distance of four to fifteen miles from Gettysburg; the Union corps averaged from four to thirty-five miles from that point. Slocum was at Two Taverns, Sykes at Hanover, Sickles at Emmitsburg, and Hancock at Taneytown, and the First and Eleventh corps near Gettysburg.

Indulging in the luxury of armchair speculation, one might wonder what would have happened if Stuart had been able to report to Lee June 30, instead of being intercepted by Kilpatrick at Hanover, what might have happened if he had been a little earlier or a little later. IIis course, however, barring further orders, was set to join with Early at York, and he kept to that course, driven ever farther east and away from the main Confederate forces, and he likewise kept possession of the captured wagon train, seemingly his nemesis.

Union Mills, in the center of Meade's defense line, was a little manorial community named for a brick gristmill built in 1797 by two Shriver brothers, and their homestead was located where the Westminster road divided into two forks. In 1863 the Shriver family living in the original homestead were Union sympathizers with a son in the 26th Pennsylvania Emergency Regiment; but other members of the family had built a mansion across the road and were Southern sympathizers, with four boys in the Confederate army. The former family owned slaves but the latter did not.

## Stuart at Union Mills

The family at the homestead was awakened about midnight, June 29, by invading rebel soldiers and horses swarming around the grounds. Hungry troopers crowded the old kitchen where slaves tossed flapjack batter on the hot griddles to appease their appetites.

While the troops occupied the Pipe Creek meadows, black-bearded Fitzhugh Lee found a comfortable place for a nap under an apple tree in the orchard. Stuart put in an appearance at the home across the road in time for breakfast and early morning glee session, including his favorite ditty "If You Want to be a Bully Boy, Jine the Cavalree," with Fitzhugh Lee, Major McClellan and other members of his staff joining in.

There had been a question of where "Jeb" Stuart spent the night of June 29. A letter written by Mrs. Eliza Jane LaMotte, now preserved in the Carroll County Historical Museum at Westminster, reveals that he passed the sultry June night on the pavement in front of Mrs. LaMotte's grandfather's house on East Main Street in Westminster. The cavalry leader straddled a chair as he would have a horse and rested his head and arms

*The William Shriver home at Union Mills, Md., where Jeb Stuart break-*
*fasted the morning of June 30, 1863. Cardinal Gibbons spent his summers*
*here and had a private chapel where he said masses.*

on the back of the chair. An armed guard stood nearby, and
the weariness of the troopers may be gauged from the fact that
the guard asked a member of the household to awaken him in
case General Stuart should wake up. It was about 7 a.m. when
Stuart stirred.

Self-confident and in high spirits with everything thus far
going so well Stuart may have added one chorus too many at his
breakfast musicale when the gay cavalier entertained his hosts
at the William Shriver home that fatal June morning before he
departed at 8 a.m. to attempt another of his famous rides "around
the enemy."

Villagers partial to the South told where the Shriver horses
had been hidden. The tannery was raided for leather. Confederate bills were tendered in payment.

Stuart's scouts learned during the night of the 29th that Kilpatrick's cavalry was directly ahead of them at Littlestown.
Stuart decided to circle around Kilpatrick by taking the right
fork of the road at Union Mills, to Hanover. After a gay breakfast and morning musicale with his generals at William Shriver's

home, they moved past the old Shriver mill toward Hanover, about 8 a.m. Fitzhugh Lee's brigade moved along the left, between the Hanover Road and the Littlestown Road, and Hampton brought up the rear with the wagon train, which Stuart had decided to keep, even though it delayed him.

They arrived in Hanover about 10 a.m., just as Kilpatrick arrived from Littlestown to intercept them. A bitter battle took place, and Stuart managed to get away with his wagons, diverted to Dover the next day, and missing Early at York again by only a matter of minutes. Passing through York New Salem he was possibly only a few miles from Early at East Berlin, en route to Gettysburg.

### Guide to "Jeb" Stuart

According to Robert H. Fowler, editor of the Civil War Times, the William Shriver family, living on the West side of the Westminster-Littlestown highway running through Union Mills, had four sons in the Confederate service when "Jeb" Stuart stopped

*The old Shriver homestead at Union Mills is now a museum open to the public. Washington Irving and Audubon the naturalist were among the famous who visited the place when it was an inn. Brigadier General James Barnes, U. S. A., and staff spent the night there when en route to Hanover.*

at their home for breakfast the morning of June 30, 1863. Naturally this Southern hero and members of his staff were welcomed into the home. They sang songs around the piano and quickly became good friends.

One of the Shriver boys, Herbert, just about 16, was a good rider and fond of horses. General Stuart took a liking to the youth and praised him for his horsemanship. At Stuart's request the parents permitted Herbert to ride with the Confederates as a guide.

The youth was thus enabled to be a witness of the battle at Hanover and accompanied Stuart to Gettysburg. Later he went south, enrolled at the Virginia Military Institute, and was wounded in the celebrated battle of New Market where the VMI cadets responded to a call for service and helped to block the assault of Federal forces. At one time during the struggle heavy smoke blanketed their front. Cadet Lieutenant Shriver and Cadet Noland leaped a fence and crawled forward thirty yards to get a better look at the enemy. As they rose from the ground an outburst of firing caught Shriver and sent Noland scurrying back to the rail fence. Shriver suffered a painful arm wound.

Herbert's son, William H. Shriver, Sr., residing in Baltimore with his wife, the former Hannah McCormick, told the Times how in 1905 his father, then 58, pointed out to him the exact spot near Gettysburg where Stuart dismounted from his long and futile ride around the Union army following the Hanover battle. He recalled the spot as being near a clump of hickory trees and a brick farmhouse with a side entrance to the cellar.

Incidentally Mr. Shriver is the uncle of Sargent Shriver, director of the new Peace Corps.


## Sykes' Corps on Move

Sykes' Fifth Corps arrived at Union Mills on the afternoon of the 30th about four hours after Stuart's departure. The old homestead became a Union headquarters. Brigadier General James Barnes and his staff occupied the house, and in turn Union songs brightened the evening with accompanying music on the old square Steinway still to be seen in the same room

GENERAL GEORGE SYKES
*Commanding Fifth Corps.*

and the same residence. Meanwhile the troops spread over the meadows along Pipe Creek just abandoned by the Virginia cavalry.

Sykes reported his position to Meade that evening. He said: "No enemy about. Stuart, Fitz Lee, and Hampton staid last night at the house of a Mr. Shriver who owns a mill. They left this morning between 8 and 10 a.m. some toward Hanover and some toward Littlestown, but I take it all have gone to Hanover. . . . My troops are very footsore and tired." The Shriver homestead, still maintained to this day, with its furnishings in original condition, over 150 years since it was built, is open to the public because of its historic associations.

Sykes left Hanover with two divisions at 7 p.m., June 30. The third division had not yet arrived there. Orders were left for it to follow. He marched nine miles to Bonaughtown (Bonneauville) where a brief rest was given the men. At 4 a.m. he resumed the march to Gettysburg. The march of Sickles from Emmitsburg that evening was like a triumphal procession through the countryside with the farm folk along the road to cheer him on.

MASON AND DIXON LINE

*Charles Mason and Jeremiah Dixon, British surveyors, ran the line named for them between Maryland and Pennsylvania, a distance of 244 miles from the Delaware, in 1763-67. Each mile was indicated by a stone marker bearing the letter P in a circle on one side and the letter M on the other, and each five miles by a Crown stone marker with the emblem of Pennsylvania on the north side and that of Maryland on the south side. The Missouri Compromise measure extended the line in effect westward along the Ohio, dividing the free states from the slave states. The Crown stone shown in the photograph is located a short distance east of the Hanover-Baltimore pike about six miles south of Hanover.*

Hancock transferred command of the Second Corps to his second division head, General John Gibbon, who brought that corps to the field. Before fighting resumed the second day Meade had 58,000 men aligned on Culp's Hill and Cemetery Ridge.

## CITIZENS PREPARE DEFENSE

During the early summer of 1863, all was excitement and turmoil on the Pennsylvania border. The alarm was sounded, "The Rebels are coming!" almost every day, and an unending stream of hurrying refugees filled all the roads leading northward. Horses and cattle, store goods and valuables were hidden away or hurried for safety from the spoiler to points in the happy land beyond the Susquehanna. The news of Milroy's defeat, of Lee's advance, and of the crossing of the Potomac by his army, followed in quick succession, and the formidable proportions of the invasion caused increasing dread and apprehension. That Lee intended to transfer the war with all its horror from Virginia into Pennsylvania was certain, and the records of the two years past made every one familiar with the woes they might expect to come. Rumors of all kinds of battles, of burnings, of robberies and other outrages, rendered the people restless and fearful, and only those with the strongest nerves could get sound sleep at night. No man knew what the next day would bring forth.

When Governor Curtin discovered that the enemy intended to invade Pennsylvania, he ordered the people in the southern tier of counties to remove their horses, cattle and valuable effects east of the Susquehanna for safety and protection. For several days long trains of wagons loaded with household furniture, as well as women and children, passed down the turnpikes and other public roads, to the ferries and bridges across the Susquehanna. All the banks removed their money deposits and valuable documents to the cities of Philadelphia and New York. In the yard or garden or adjoining orchard of many of the farms and homes throughout the entire area of York and Adams counties, household treasures were buried in the presence of different members of the family in order that they might afterward be recovered by any one of them.

*Curtin Loyal War Governor*

On the 11th of June, 1863, General D. N. Couch, of the Regular army, was appointed commander of the Department of the Susquehanna. He was a native of New York State, a graduate of West Point, who had served in the Seminole War, in Florida, and on the western frontier, and also commanded a division under General Franklin at the battle of Antietam. Later he commanded the Second Corps in the Army of the Potomac. General Couch took up his headquarters at Harrisburg and in that city assisted in organizing the Pennsylvania Emergency Troops to aid in resisting the advance of the Confederate army under Lee, into the State of Pennsylvania.

Andrew G. Curtin was war governor of Pennsylvania from 1861 to 1863, when he was re-elected for another term of three years. He was one of the ablest men in the country, then holding the high position as the chief executive of a state. It was largely through his intelligent efforts and patriotism that this commonwealth sent to the front nearly 366,000 men, during the four years that the war continued. He sat in the executive mansion at Harrisburg in June, 1863, watching, with the closest interest, the movement of General Robert E. Lee, with nearly 80,000 men, the flower of the Confederacy, beginning to invade Pennsylvania.

President Lincoln and Governor Curtin issued proclamations calling on the citizens to arm in defense of their homes; but the greater number of the able-bodied men among the loyal portion of the people were already at the front. Thousands of men, however, whom various reasons had kept from answering the earlier calls, professional men, businessmen, mechanics, farmers, young and middle-aged, rallied to the standard. As ever before, Hanover was not laggard. A company was hastily organized for the emergency and sent to Harrisburg, where it became Company I of the 26th Regiment Pennsylvania Militia, Captain John S. Forrest in command. Company A of this regiment was composed of students of the college and seminary at Gettysburg.

In ten days after the regiment was formed it was facing an army corps of the enemy, beyond Gettysburg, and on the 26th retreated in good order, with frequent skirmishes with Confederate cavalry, and finally after a most exhausting march and after losing a number of men as prisoners to the enemy, reached Harrisburg on the evening of the 29th.

When the invasion of Lee's army was first anticipated, the Twentieth, Twenty-sixth to Thirty-first inclusive, and Thirty-third Emergency Regiments were organized in different parts of the state, largely at Harrisburg. There were several independent companies, including one containing seventeen veterans of the War of 1812, carrying the tattered flag used by Washington's army in the battle of Trenton, in 1776. These Emergency troops were all under the command of General Couch.

General William F. Smith, of Vermont, who had won a good record as a soldier at South Mountain and Antietam in 1862, and later commanded the Eighteenth Army Corps, under Grant, was placed in charge of a division of troops, which rendezvoused at Carlisle, on June 27. He is familiarly known in the history of the Civil War as General "Baldy" Smith. Major Granville O. Haller, a native of York, graduate of West Point, and a soldier who served in the same regiment with General Grant in the Mexican War, was then an aide on the staff of General Couch. He was detailed from the staff of his commanding officer, and was sent to Gettysburg, arriving there on June 25.

### Students Form Company

The Twenty-sixth Emergency Regiment, commanded by Colonel William H. Jennings, had left the state capital on the evening of the 24th, were halted on the way by a railroad accident and reached Gettysburg, by way of York, on the morning of the 26th. Joseph S. Jenkins, of Hanover, who had been severely wounded while commanding a company of the One Hundred and Thirtieth Regiment at the battle of Antietam, was lieutenant colonel of this regiment. Harvey W. McKnight, afterwards president of Pennsylvania College at Gettysburg, was the adjutant. Company A, commanded by Rev. Frederick A. Klinefelter, of York, was largely composed of students then attending that institution and the theological seminary. Dr. Edmund W. Meisenhelder, for many years a leading physician of York, and the Rev. J. C. Koller, D.D., for thirty years pastor of St. Matthew's Lutheran

Church, at Hanover, both served in this company. Company I was recruited by Captain John S. Forrest, at Hanover.

The only other Federal soldiers on June 26, in Gettysburg and vicinity, were the City Troop of Philadelphia, a company of cavalry which had been organized during the Revolution, and at the time of the Confederate invasion, commanded by Samuel J. Randall, afterward a distinguished lawyer and statesman, and a local company of cavalry recruited by Captain Robert C. Bell, in Adams County.

It was known to Major Haller, as well as to the authorities at Harrisburg, that the advance of the Confederate army under General Lee, had crossed the Potomac River at Williamsport, a short distance above Hagerstown, Maryland, but at this juncture Major Haller did not know that nine thousand infantry and nearly one thousand cavalry had crossed the South Mountains by the Chambersburg turnpike and were approaching Gettysburg. On the morning of the 26th, Major Haller sent Jennings' regiment three miles west of the town, while Captain Bell's cavalry acted as scouts to observe the movement of the approaching enemy and report to the commanding officer. The mountains and the valley west of Gettysburg were veiled in a dense fog, which prevented the Union troops from seeing Early and his men moving down the turnpike. Samuel W. Pennypacker, later governor of Pennsylvania, was then a college student at Gettysburg. He enlisted as a private in Company F of the Twenty-sixth Regiment.

Jennings had moved his regiment three miles west on the turnpike, where he was surprised and driven back by Early's advance. The Thirty-fifth Battalion of Virginia cavalry, commanded by Colonel White, came within firing distance and a few shots were exchanged. When the cavalry dashed upon them, the regiment broke and fell back toward Gettysburg. They lost many officers and men, nearly all of whom were paroled the next day. Company B was almost entirely captured and Company I, of Hanover, lost nearly half its number as prisoners, including Captain Forrest. He was marched at the head of the line with some other officers until Gordon's advance reached York, two days later.

H. M. M. Richards, Reading, a member of the Emergency

*In 1873 the borough improved Center Square in preparation for placing a fountain donated by prominent citizens. The stones were hauled from the Nicholas Fleagle quarry (Bethlehem mines today) by Henry Eck, here on saddle horse. Peter Weaver's photograph gallery and the Welsh home are next to Gitt's store.*

troops, reported that these volunteers marched fifty-four out of sixty consecutive hours. In their retreat toward Harrisburg by the Carlisle road they were overtaken by enemy cavalry at Witmer's House 4½ miles from Gettysburg, and after an engagement, the rebels were repulsed with some loss.

## Emergency Troops Resist

A small detachment of the regiment, after falling back to Gettysburg, had a sharp encounter with a part of White's cavalry in the streets of the town. About the same time, Corporal George W. Sandoe, a member of Company B, Independent Twenty-first Pennsylvania cavalry, was shot and killed a short distance below the National Cemetery at the Nathaniel Lightner property on the Baltimore turnpike. He was the first victim of the battle of Gettysburg, and a monument marks the spot where he fell. Will Lightner who was with him escaped. The Twenty-sixth

Regiment halted at Hunterstown, four miles northeast of Gettysburg, and was drawn up in line of battle. Here this regiment engaged in a sharp conflict with White's cavalry, which was repulsed. The encounter lasted about twenty minutes.

As Early's whole force was approaching Gettysburg, Jennings ordered his regiment to fall back in haste toward Dillsburg. A detachment of the Seventeenth Virginia cavalry, commanded by Colonel French, and two infantry companies, were drawn up in battle line in the vicinity of Dillsburg. At 2 o'clock on Sunday, June 28, the Twenty-sixth reached Fort Washington, opposite Harrisburg, with a loss of 176 men captured and all its equipage and supplies.

The Twenty-sixth Pennsylvania Emergency Regiment offered the first resistance to Lee's forces encountered before the coming of the Army of the Potomac. This regiment fired the opening shots of the battle of Gettysburg. Members of Company I were recruited from Hanover and vicinity.

The following is a muster roll of Company I, Twenty-sixth Emergency Regiment:

Officers—Captain, John S. Forrest; First Lieutenant, John Q. Pfeiffer; Second Lieutenant, Alexander T. Barnes; Sergeants, Joel Henry, William H. McCausland, Howard N. Deitrick, Napoleon B. Carver, Charles Young; Corporals, Josiah Rinehart, Thomas Sneeringer, Henry Schultz, David E. Winebrenner, Henry C. Bucher, Amos F. Klinefelter, Charles T. Kump, Charles W. Thomas.

Privates—William Althoff, Noah Allison, William Bair, William H. Bastress, William F. Baum, William A. Beard, James Blair, John F. Blair, Edward Bollinger, John Bond, David F. Forney, William G. Forney, Jacob Freet, William Gantz, Jacob Gardner Martin Graybill, Lewin Heathcote, Martin Hitzel, Addison M. Herman, John J. Hersh, Josiah D. Hersh, Barthabus Himes, John H. Hinkle, Lewis V. Holter, William H. Holter, Washington J. Johnson, Lewis B. Jones, Isaac Jones, William Leader, Isaac Loucks, Henry C. Metzgar, Jacob H. Michael, Michael D. Myers, William A. Myers, Aaron McLean, Mahlon H. Naill, Hezekiah Ports, Henry H. Pfeiffer, John J. Sanders, George W. Sherman, George E. Sherwood, Henry W. Shriver, William H. Snyder, Eli Snyder, Daniel J. Snyder, Ovid Stahl, George E. Trone, Oliver

Trone, Samuel E. Trone, Fabius N. Wagener, Samuel Weigle, John Willing, Calvin Wirt, William C. Wolf, Cornelius Young, Martin Zimmerman.

---

## WHITE'S RAIDERS PRECEDE TROOPS

On the morning of June 27, when General Early took up the march from Gettysburg toward York, he detached from his command the Thirty-fifth Battalion of Virginia cavalry, commanded by Lieutenant Colonel Elijah V. White. Early moved with his division toward York through East Berlin, while Gordon, with one brigade passed through Abbottstown over the turnpike. Colonel White and his troopers had performed scouting service in the mountains of West Virginia and the Shenandoah Valley during the preceding year. He had received orders to make a dashing raid to Hanover Junction for the purpose of cutting the telegraph wires and burning the railroad bridges at that place and between there and York. This was to be done in order to cut off communication between Harrisburg and Washington. Colonel White left Gettysburg early in the morning and entered McSherrystown about 10 o'clock. Here they halted for a short time in order to find out, if possible, if there were any Federal troops in and around Hanover.

Owing to the conflicting rumors that had been circulated, the citizens of Hanover could not definitely ascertain the movements of the enemy. So they were held in suspense until a farmer rode into town calling out: "The enemy will soon be here. They are now in McSherrystown."

A few minutes later the advance turned into Carlisle Street and began to move toward Center Square. Three or four mounted men preceded the rest and a few hundred yards back came the entire battalion of Confederates riding four abreast. Their object was first to ascertain if there were any Union soldiers in town. So they moved slowly up Carlisle Street, nearly every man with his finger on the trigger of his carbine, ready for any emergency. In the center of the column rode Colonel White, a large man of ruddy complexion. Most of the women and children remained in their homes, and looked at the moving enemy through the blinds and curtains at the windows. There was no organized

*Broadway in 1863 looking from Square towards intersection of York and Abbottstown streets. High structure on right is Albright Building.*

resistance to the advancing Confederates and there was no formal surrender of the town by the borough authorities. After placing guards at the ends of all the streets, the entire battalion assembled in Center Square. Colonel White rode in front of the Central Hotel where he addressed a large crowd of male citizens. He stated that although his soldiers wore faded suits of gray, they were gentlemen fighting for a cause they thought to be right, but would harm no one.

Most of the soldiers then dismounted and went into the different stores to obtain shoes and such clothing as might be of service to them. Some of the stores were robbed of a few articles but the soldiers did not obtain much clothing, because all wearing apparel and valuables had been concealed or taken away. A member of White's staff rode down Baltimore Street to Peter Frank's blacksmith shop, north of Middle Street, and summoning the smith asked that his horse be shod. Frank said he wasn't working because it was a holiday on account of the Johnnies being in town. The officer laid his hand on his pistol holster, whereupon Frank started fanning up a fire with his bellows and went to work. The Confederate paid $2 in greenbacks for two shoes. Another raider entered A. G. Schmidt's drugstore, corner of the square and Broadway, with a request for a bottle of whiskey. Schmidt had none on hand but fetched him a quart from another source. Other cavalrymen took articles which they paid for in Confederate money. After remaining in town about an hour, the troopers dashed out York Street toward Jefferson and reached Hanover Junction about 2 o'clock in the afternoon.

A small squad had been sent in advance along the line of the railroad between Hanover and Hanover Junction to destroy the bridges. Colonel White's battalion on reaching the Northern Central Railroad at Hanover Junction early in the afternoon immediately put the torch to the bridges and cut the telegraph wires. During the two days before, Governor Curtin at Harrisburg had been keeping President Lincoln at Washington posted by telegraph concerning the enemy's movements as nearly as they could be ascertained from couriers who had been sent out from the state capital.

Late in the afternoon of June 27, White's Confederates moved back to Jefferson, then northward to the vicinity of Spring Grove.

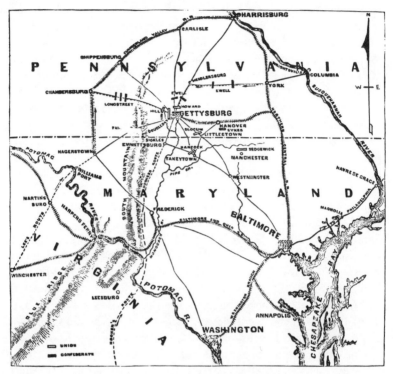

POSITION OF THE ARMY OF THE POTOMAC, JULY 1.

They encamped for the night on the farm of John Wiest, near the village of Nashville. At this point, Colonel White put himself in communication with General Gordon who had bivouacked for the night at Hogstown (Farmers' Post Office), a few miles northwest on the Gettysburg turnpike. The following day, he accompanied Gordon on his march toward Wrightsville, then returned to a position two miles east of York, and encamped during the succeeding two days on the farm of John H. Small, in the meantime destroying the railroad bridges on the line between York and Wrightsville.

General Early meanwhile was entering the borough of Gettysburg. In some cars at the station his troops captured provisions which belonged to the Twenty-sixth Pennsylvania Regiment. This did not satisfy his demands, so he made a requisition upon the borough for money and supplies, which the authorities were unable to furnish. He wrote this requisition while mounted on horseback in front of a store on Baltimore Street, of that borough. Gordon's brigade encamped for the night of June 26, in and around Gettysburg. The other three brigades bivouacked for the night at Mummasburg, a short distance northwest of the borough. After destroying about a dozen freight cars, General Early started with his division toward York. General Gordon with his Georgia brigade of 2,800 men, with Tanner's battery of four guns, moved eastward over the York and Gettysburg Turnpike, passing through New Oxford, Abbottstown and bivouacked for the night in the village surrounding Farmers' Post Office, in Jackson Township. His troops pitched their shelter tents in the adjoining fields. General Gordon lodged at the residence of Jacob S. Altland, and enjoyed the experience of sleeping on a Pennsylvania-Dutch feather bed.

Among the horses brought by raiders to headquarters there was a fine white horse belonging to Samuel L. Roth, a Mennonite preacher living on the Roth church farm in that section. General Gordon rode this steed to York and later the animal was returned to the minister who protested that he needed it in his ministerial labors, but he had to go to Wrightsville to get it.

When Early's troops were passing near their former camping ground on return to Gettysburg on the 30th, they heard cannonading from Hanover. They feared approach of Union forces and planted cannon on the Henry Ramer farm in Jackson Township.

Brigadier General William (Extra Billy) Smith headed troops of Jubal Early's division entering York. He found many citizens on the streets in their Sunday-go-to-meeting clothes. Smith bowed right and left to the astonished people on their way to church, and had an army band strike up "Yankee Doodle" for their benefit, after it had just completed playing "Dixie." The Virginia governor couldn't resist making a speech from horseback.

Church bells were ringing when General Gordon followed with more graybacks. They looked so disreputable, dirty, and unkempt in their tattered clothes that Gordon felt called upon to apologize for their appearance and declared they were a decent sort underneath and were instructed to conduct themselves properly or else. That didn't prevent a bareheaded Johnnie occasionally from picking up a hat off a bystander as the troops marched on.

An incident is related concerning a little girl handing General Gordon some flowers at York. In the bouquet a note was concealed purporting to reveal the disposition of Union troops at the Wrightsville bridge. On arriving at Wrightsville the general found that the information given in the anonymous note was entirely correct.

---

## JEB STUART DISTURBS PEACE

"Our cavalry, under Kilpatrick, had a handsome fight yesterday at Hanover. He reports the capture of one battle-flag, a lieutenant colonel, one captain, forty-five privates, with fifteen or twenty of the enemy killed."

The first official mention of the battle of Hanover appears in these words in the general order issued by General Meade at 7 a.m. July 1, from headquarters at Taneytown, Maryland. The Hanover cavalry engagement was only one of the opening phases of the Gettysburg campaign, but it proved to be a memorable and all-important phase.

There had been slight skirmishes during the invasion of 1863 in York, Adams, Cumberland and Franklin counties, between small detachments, before the encounter at Hanover, where on Tuesday morning, June 30, about ten thousand men on both sides were in hostile array. It was not a battle for which plans had been made by the leaders of the opposing forces. Neither General Stuart, commanding three brigades of Lee's Confederate cavalry corps, moving northward on the right of the Army of the Potomac, nor General Kilpatrick, commanding the Third Division of the Union cavalry corps, knew the exact position of the enemy, twenty-four hours before the engagement opened. In the disposition of the troops by General Meade at Frederick, on the morning of June 29, General Gregg in command of the Second Division of cavalry, four thousand men, was sent through Westminster and Manchester to guard the extreme right of the Potomac army and save Washington from the raids of the enemy. Buford with the First Division, four thousand men, was dispatched across the ridge and took position on the plains around Gettysburg on the morning of June 30. General Kilpatrick was assigned the

GENERAL J. E. B. STUART

*Chief in command of the Cavalry Forces in the Army of Virginia.*

GENERAL JUDSON KILPATRICK

important duty of moving forward through Taneytown to Hanover, for the purpose of reconnoitering the position, and to ascertain the movements of General Early, who with a division of nine thousand men, had occupied York on the morning of June 28.

The position of Stuart's cavalry at this time was not definitely known by Meade, with his headquarters at Frederick. Kilpatrick moved forward to Littlestown, where he bivouacked for the night of June 29. Stuart, having crossed the Potomac at Rowser's Ford, about twenty miles northwest of Washington, with three brigades, had moved northward through Westminster. The head of his column had encamped for the night of June 29, at Union Mills, only seven miles south of Littlestown. The Confederate scouts had learned of Kilpatrick's presence at Littlestown, but the latter, although always on the alert for news and one of the most intrepid cavalry officers of the Civil War, had failed to discover that the Confederate cavalry was at Union Mills, when he took up the march at daybreak on June 30, from Littlestown toward Hanover.

Chambliss' rebel brigade led the advance from Union Mills, nine miles southwest of Hanover, and a detachment of it had scoured the country during the night, reaching a point within five miles of Hanover. Kilpatrick's division moved toward Hanover in the following order: Kilpatrick with his staff and body guard, a detachment from the First Ohio; Custer with the First, Sixth and Seventh Michigan Regiments; Pennington's battery; Farnsworth with the First Vermont, First West Virginia and Fifth New York; Elder's battery; the ambulance wagons, horses

*Rare photograph of Kitzmiller's Mill, the oldest west of the Susquehanna River. Founded in 1738 it was near the location of what is now the Lawrence B. Sheppard residence on the Hanover-Littlestown highway and near the headwaters of the Little Conewago in Conewago Township, Adams County. During the Civil War the mill was owned by John Duttera. Union soldiers under General Kilpatrick's command stopped at the mill for food and water before continuing their march to Hanover.*

GENERAL GEORGE A. CUSTER
*Beau Brummell of the Army of the
Potomac. Intrepid cavalry leader who
ended his days in a massacre staged
by wily Sitting Bull and his Sioux
Indians.*

and pack mules. The Eighteenth Pennsylvania Cavalry, commanded by Lieutenant Colonel William P. Brinton, brought up the rear and was the last to leave Littlestown. This regiment had been in service only a few weeks and had never previously engaged in battle, yet it was assigned the duty of guarding and protecting the wagon train immediately in front of it.

Captain H. C. Potter, with a detachment of forty men, twenty each from Company L and M of the Eighteenth Pennsylvania, was ordered to form the rear guard. He overtook Captain Freeland of the Eighteenth Pennsylvania with a small squad, which had been acting as a scouting party, to scour the country and see if there were any Confederates coming from the south. Freeland and his men, a few miles west of Hanover, moved over to the right, where they came in contact with a small band of Confederates. Shots were exchanged and one Confederate soldier was killed, near Gitt's mill, about three miles southwest of the town. He was the first victim of the engagement. About the same time, Captain Potter and his men came into contact with a Confederate scouting party about three miles west of Hanover on the Littlestown road. A sharp conflict ensued but no one was wounded. Lieutenant T. P. Shield of the Eighteenth Pennsylvania, with twenty-five picked men guarding the flank, was surprised and captured by the Thirteenth Virginia cavalry, formerly commanded by Colonel Chambliss, who at this time had succeeded W. F. H. Lee in command of the brigade which was leading the march toward Hanover. The brigade was composed of the Second North Carolina, Ninth, Tenth and Thirteenth Virginia Regiments, in all about 1,500 men.

## Union Forces Enter Town

At 8 o'clock on the morning of June 30, General Kilpatrick, riding with his staff at the head of his column, entered Hanover. Closely following him, in uniform of velvet and with flowing curls, rode tall and handsome General Custer, who, at the age of twenty-three years, commanded a Michigan brigade of four regiments. These Union soldiers had been on a continuous march of nearly three weeks and were tired and worn out. Kilpatrick in company with Custer entered the residence of Jacob Wirt, on Frederick Street, and while in conversation with the Rev. Dr. W. K. Zieber, pastor of Emmanuel's Reformed Church, said that his men needed food to refresh them on their march. As soon as the announcement was made to the citizens, who then filled the streets and sidewalks, they repaired to their homes and brought coffee, bread and meat to the veteran soldiers who received the provisions on horseback. After resting for a short time, regiment after regiment of Custer's brigade moved out the turnpike toward Abbottstown.

An hour had passed by before the Michigan brigade had left the borough on its way toward York. Then came General Farnsworth, surrounded by his staff, who passed through Center Square. His regiments, too, were bountifully fed. The First Vermont and the First West Virginia regiments had passed through the town by 10 a.m. The Fifth New York, partly dismounted,

RESIDENCE OF JACOB WIRT (1801-1869)
*where Generals Kilpatrick, Custer, and Farnsworth conferred with Dr. Zieber, head of the Citizens Safety Committee. Mr. Wirt gave the officers a large wall map of the region for their guidance.*

were resting in a line extending from Frederick Street, through Center Square, and a short distance down Abbottstown Street. They were then being fed by the patriotic citizens.

Meantime the detachments of the Eighteenth Pennsylvania, under Captains Potter and Freeland, had the experience with the enemy west of Hanover as related.

The brigade of Confederates under Chambliss had by then appeared on elevated ground on both sides of the Westminster road, a short distance southwest of Pennville. At the same time, they planted two cannons on the Samuel Keller farm, near Plum Creek, and two on the Jesse Rice farm, along the Westminster road. The Thirteenth Virginia cavalry began the attack on the Eighteenth Pennsylvania Regiment, then passing through Pennville with its line extending from Plum Creek to the edge of Hanover. They made a stubborn resistance, but owing to the sudden attack, were driven slightly back. General Stuart, who

*The bridge over Plum Creek, Frederick Street, over which General Kilpatrick rode with his staff at the head of his columns, just prior to the battle of Hanover, June 30, 1863. The tree on the left of the photograph is the last of the wild plum trees along this creek. In earlier years these plum trees grew in abundance in this area. It was from these trees the creek derived its name. This bridge has been replaced many times, the present bridge being of modern cement construction.*

himself was within a mile of Hanover, called W. H. Payne, commanding the Second North Carolina Regiment, known as the "Black Horse Cavalry," to charge the rear of Farnsworth's brigade. This regiment contained nearly five hundred men who had participated in many battles in Virginia. Colonel Payne leading part of the regiment, dashed down the Westminster road and came in contact with the Eighteenth Pennsylvania at the eastern edge of Pennville, where the Westminster road joins the Littlestown turnpike.

Meantime one battalion of the North Carolina troopers crossed through the fields south of the Littlestown turnpike and struck the flank of the Federal troops by coming in to Frederick Street through the alleys. The Eighteenth Pennsylvania had been cut in two. Part of it was to the rear in Pennville, and these men retreated across the fields toward McSherrystown. The advance of the regiment dashed pell-mell up Frederick Street, through

GENERAL ELON J. FARNSWORTH, U. S. A.
*He fell at Gettysburg.*

Center Square, and out Abbottstown Street to the railroad, closely followed by the enemy. For a short time the town of Hanover was in possession of the Confederates. When the fight opened, General Farnsworth was at the head of his brigade near the village of New Baltimore, along the road to Abbottstown. He quickly ordered the First West Virginia and the First Vermont to fall back to the left and take position southeast of town in line of battle.

Major Hammond, commanding the Fifth New York, had already reformed his regiment on the Public Common and on Abbottstown Street. With drawn sabers and a terrific yell, this regiment drove the enemy out of town.

### Farnsworth Attacks

General Farnsworth arrived at the scene of action and directed the movements of the Fifth New York. The North Carolina troopers had captured the ambulance wagons and were driving them out the Littlestown pike toward Pennville. There were hand to hand encounters on Abbottstown Street, in various parts of the town and in Center Square, where five horses and two or three men were killed. A spirited contest took place in a field in the rear of the site of the present Methodist Church, and on Frederick Street, a short distance west of the church site, where Adjutant Gall, of the Fifth New York, was killed. This contest was continued out the Littlestown road between Samuel H. Forney's farm and Pennville, and about two hundred yards on the Westminster road. It was along this line, amid much confusion, that a hand to hand encounter took place in which the mounted men on both sides used sabers, carbines or pistols. Captain Cabel, a member of Stuart's staff and in 1906 principal of a military academy at Staunton, Virginia, was cut in the head with a saber in front of the Forney house and remained insensible for about six hours. Twenty-seven horses and about a dozen men lay dead on the road after the contest had ended.

Major White, of the Fifth New York, was seriously wounded near the junction of the Westminster and Littlestown roads.

Captain Barker of the Fifth New York cavalry, commanding a portion of the vanguard, captured a first lieutenant and five privates during the attack on the Union wagon train. Another group of the Fifth, consisting of Captain McGuinn, Lieutenant Boyce and Sergeant McNulty, charged with their command and engaged in a desperate encounter during which McNulty suffered serious wounds of the arm and hand from an enemy color bearer. Private Thomas Burke, Company A, Fifth New York, dashed forward to his aid, shooting the rebel dead and being credited with capture of the battle flag. Upon the retreat, Colonel Payne was slightly wounded and had a horse shot under him in front of the Winebrenner tannery, and then became a prisoner of war.

When the first gun was fired at Hanover about 10:30 a.m., Kilpatrick was riding at the head of his column, and had passed through Abbottstown moving on the turnpike toward York. He had just received a message from General Pleasonton, at Taneytown, through a courier, who had passed north of Hanover, notifying him that he might soon be attacked by Stuart's cavalry. This was the first intimation Kilpatrick had of the approach of the enemy. As the roar of the guns was heard, General Custer reformed his regiments of the Michigan brigade and ordered a countermarch toward the scene of action.

## Wild Ride for Kilpatrick

Kilpatrick rode rapidly along the line over the turnpike till he reached the summit of the Pigeon Hills. Here he left the pike, put his spurs to his horse, and dashed through fields of wheat and corn. The horse that carried the gallant rider to the town of Hanover died a few hours later. The animal which was a captured one bore the brand "CSA," for Confederate States of America. It was buried on Bunker Hill where Union batteries were posted. Kilpatrick arrived in Center Square about the time the contest out the Westminster road had been brought to a conclusion and the enemy had been driven to their guns. He took up his headquarters in room No. 24 in the Central Hotel. There was now a lull in the combat, and the enemy were in position on a ridge extending from the Keller farm south of Pennville clear

GENERAL FITZHUGH LEE
*Brigade commander under Stuart and cousin of Robert E. Lee. He commanded American troops in Cuba during the Spanish-American War.*

across to Mount Olivet Cemetery. They held an impregnable position—one difficult for a cavalry force to attack, because their guns had been planted to their front on the precipitous brow of Rice's hill. The Confederate batteries accompanying Stuart's cavalry were those of Chew, Hart, and McGregor.

During the contest Fitzhugh Lee, who had moved toward Hanover north of the Westminster road, arrived and took position about one mile west of the town in a woods and along a gentle elevation in the fields, and here planted another four guns ready for action. His brigade was composed of the First, Second, Third, Fourth and Fifth Virginia cavalry regiments, numbering in all about 2,200 men. The borough of Hanover was then entirely in possession of the Union forces. General Farnsworth ascended to the roof of Thomas Wirt's residence, later owned by William Boadenhamer, in Center Square, and with a field glass ascertained the position of the enemy. Meantime General Custer with his entire brigade of four regiments had formed in line of battle between the Abbottstown turnpike and the York road with the First Vermont and First Virginia regiments to his front. After the arrival of Lee, Kilpatrick ordered Custer to move his brigade over to the right. The First Michigan cavalry was put in line to support Pennington's battery of horse artillery, six guns, which had been stationed on Bunker Hill west of the Carlisle turnpike. Elder's battery of six guns, also horse artillery, had been planted on Bunker Hill, east of the Carlisle pike and to the rear of the present Eichelberger High School site.

It was nearly 2 o'clock in the afternoon when Wade Hampton arrived with the long train of 125 captured wagons. About two miles southwest of Hanover on the farms of Samuel Keller and Henry Gotwalt this wagon train was parked in the form of a square and heavily guarded. It was this wagon train that had caused the battle. Stuart had determined to protect it. If there was danger of recapture he would order it burned. He moved Hampton over to the extreme right. This brigade composed of the First North Carolina, First and Second South Carolina, Cobb's Georgia Legion, Philip's Georgia Legion and a battery, in all about 2,500 men, was placed in line of battle from Mount Olivet Cemetery across the Baltimore turnpike to a short distance north of the York road. He planted his battery of four guns on the Balti-

*Captured wagon train on move from painting
by Ramon Dubs, Jr., in Hanover Public Library.*

more pike near the cemetery. They were supported by Cobb's
Legion which had previously done gallant service in many battles.

When the Confederates had been driven out of town, Baltimore, York and Frederick streets were barricaded by the soldiers
and citizens. Store boxes, wagons, hay ladders, fence rails, barrels,
bar iron and anything that would prevent the enemy from dashing into town were placed across the streets. When the engagement first opened, Confederate shells and balls had been fired
over the town.

### Shell Hits Winebrenner House

As soon as Pennington's and Elder's Union batteries were
placed in position an artillery duel was opened. This was continued for nearly two hours. Some of the shells fell in town.
Early in the contest a twelve-pound shell struck the residence
of Henry Winebrenner on Frederick Street. It penetrated a door
on the balcony, shattered a bureau inside, went through the

*Henry Winebrenner residence on Frederick Street showing rear balcony where shell from enemy cannon on Rice's Hill entered the house moments after two members of the family had left the balcony.*

floor and ceiling, and struck the brick wall of the northeast corner of the sitting room below where most of the family had gathered. The shell failed to explode. Mr. Winebrenner picked it up and threw it out in the yard.

Just prior to this exciting incident a country woman selling huckleberries had reported that the hills beyong the house were swarming with Rebels, and a Union officer rode up and told them to let the flag continue floating across the street. Mrs. Winebrenner and daughter Martha went out on the rear balcony and saw the flash of cannon in the hills about three hundred yards distant. They had barely entered the upstairs room and closed the door when the ball smashed through the lintle behind them. The Misses Sarah and Martha Winebrenner preserved the shell and a cartridge box dropped by a soldier of the Eighteenth Pennsylvania cavalry as mementoes of the fight. Union sharp-shooters occupied the second story of the woodshed ten yards from the house.

*Chest of drawers in Henry Winebrenner house damaged by Confederate
shell and missile which failed to explode and has been preserved as a
memento of the battle.*

During the lull in the contest Lieutenant Colonel Payne, as a
prisoner, was taken to the headquarters of General Kilpatrick at
the Central Hotel. Both Farnsworth and Custer were present at
this conference. After Colonel Payne had been wounded in front
of the Winebrenner tannery at the edge of Frederick Street and
his horse shot under him, he bounded over a fence into the tan
yard. While trying to escape to a building he fell into a tan vat
which discolored his Confederate uniform. He was helped out of
his position by a sergeant of the Fifth New York. In this sad
plight he appeared before General Kilpatrick and his two brigadiers. Payne knew the tired condition of his fellow soldiers who
had been marching for nearly two weeks without rest and tried
to impress General Kilpatrick that more than twelve thousand
men, Stuart's entire force, were stationed a short distance southwest of Hanover. He did this, as he said at his home in Washington in 1900, to prevent any further attack.

After Custer had moved over to the right of the Union line he
ordered the Sixth Michigan Regiment, armed with seven-shot
Spencer repeating rifles, to dismount. This regiment had nearly

TANNERY SITE

*Photograph taken in the 1890's shows parts of the original Winebrenner tannery on Frederick Street on the left and the cannery of that period.*

six hundred men who formed in line and prepared for a charge. About one hundred men took care of the horses which were arranged in line northward from the front of St. Matthew's Church, upon whose steeple Kilpatrick had gone a short time before to take observation and try to ascertain the disposition of the Confederate troops and their number. About the same time Farnsworth ordered the Fifth New York, which had been supporting Elder's Battery, in line of battle across Center Square and down Baltimore Street. The First West Virginia was drawn up in line out Baltimore Street. The First Vermont was kept as a reserve on the Public Common.

The artillery duel between the twelve guns of Pennington's and Elder's batteries on Bunker Hill, and the twelve guns of the Confederates on the ridge south of town, had ceased. There was another lull in the fight. It was now 2 o'clock in the afternoon. Kilpatrick seated in his room at the hotel wrote a message describing the engagement, and quickly sent it to Pleasonton at Taneytown. What might follow was still a conundrum. The Union commander knew nothing of the long wagon train about

*St. Matthew's Lutheran Church in 1863. The steeple was used as an observatory by Union officers at time of Hanover battle.*

two miles southwest of Hanover, parked for the purpose of being destroyed by fire, in case Kilpatrick had gained the advantage in the fight. The gallant Farnsworth had already won the victory, and Custer with a battle line one mile in length, was behind the guns on Bunker Hill. He was ready for the fray.

About this time, mounted regiments of the Confederates had repeatedly moved down the slope of the hill, feigning an attack and then returned to their positions. The Sixth Michigan, already dismounted, marched toward the Littlestown turnpike in a battle line extending from the edge of town to Pennville, crossed the

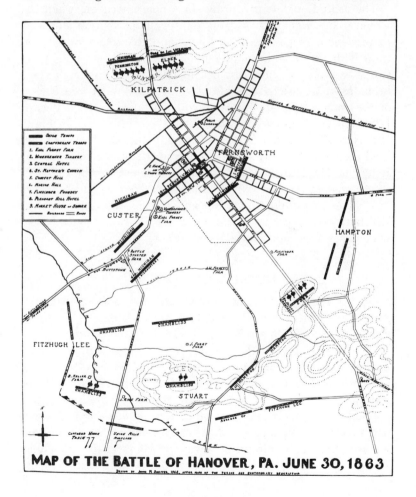

MAP OF THE BATTLE OF HANOVER, PA. JUNE 30, 1863

pike and crept on their hands and knees up the slope in the Forney field, and fired with their repeating rifles upon the enemy, three hundred yards away. The right of the line had been flanked and fifteen men of this regiment became prisoners of war. It then fell back and repeated the same movement to be ready for any attack of the Confederates. By this movement of Custer to the north of Hanover, Kilpatrick had opened communication with the Twelfth Army Corps resting at Littlestown and a short distance westward. His courier could now convey his dispatch to Taneytown.

The attitude of Stuart during the whole afternoon, when the Union troops were maneuvering for advantageous positions, was to prevent a reopening of the fight and to protect the wagon train with its valuable munitions of war. As the Twelfth Army Corps was only a short distance to the rear of Fitzhugh Lee's brigade, Stuart ordered the latter to move southward, take charge of the wagon train and proceed with all possible speed toward Jefferson. The fight had now ended but the brigades of Chambliss and Hampton remained in position until the sun had sunk behind the western horizon. They followed the wagon train toward Jefferson. The local incidents of this movement will be found in the Confederate reports which follow. Stuart's men had captured 385 horses in Codorus township and by the time they reached Dillsburg they were in possession of 1,000 York County horses which they rode into battle at Gettysburg.

## DETAILS OF ACTION

On Saturday, June 27, news of the retreat of the 26th Emergency Regiment was received at Hanover and caused dread and dismay to those having relatives or friends in the command. The excitement and fear of the people were intensified by the dashing into town of Colonel White's ragged Rebel raiders—"guerillas," as they were termed. They held the town at their mercy, seizing considerable booty and making dire threats. Citizens who did not halt promptly when commanded were fired at and some narrow escapes were reported. After an hour's most unwelcome sojourn, they rode piratically away to Hanover Junction and thence to York to join Early, burning the railroad bridges along the Northern Central on their way, and exchanging their worn-out mounts for farm horses where they found them.

All the news that could be relied upon was favorable to the Confederates. From all directions came reports of raiders. Early was at York and Wrightsville, Ewell's corps near Harrisburg, the Cumberland Valley was filled with Confederates, and on the mountains above Gettysburg could be seen their campfires. This entire section was in the grip of the enemy. "Where is the Army of the Potomac?" was the anxious cry from every Union heart.

At this time of the darkest gloom came the joyful tidings of the approach of the Union army; scouting parties of our cavalry-men were reported from the southeast. But on the morning of June 30, bad news was again received, the enemy being reported to be advancing from Littlestown.

About 8 o'clock the troops were seen slowly riding in Frederick Street, but they wore the Union blue and carried the stars and stripes. Men and horses were dusty and tired, all reduced by hard marching and short rations, the cavalrymen having been in the saddle for three weeks, almost day and night.

### Welcome Boys in Blue

Dirty, bedraggled and unshaven as they were, most cordial and enthusiastic was the welcome they received. Cheers from men, patriotic songs from the girls, greeted them on all sides. The cheers and songs for the flag and boys in blue were the more hearty because of the gray-clad visitors of a few days before, and because of the great fear and anxiety of the people for the cause of the Union they loved so well and for the safety of themselves and their property. To their inexperienced eyes, these five thousand cavalrymen seemed a force able to cope with Lee's whole army, and happy were they, for secure once more they thought was all they held most dear.

It was soon learned that the young commander, who rode at the head, was General Judson Kilpatrick. Battery M, Second U. S. artillery, Lieutenant Pennington, was with Custer's Michigan brigade, and Battery E, Fourth U. S. artillery, Lieutenant Elder, accompanied Farnsworth's brigade.

Generals Kilpatrick and Custer and some of their staff officers halted at the home of Jacob Wirt and at the Central Hotel, while the regiments slowly filed out Abbottstown Street. General Kilpatrick mentioning the fact that his men had had no breakfast, the Rev. Dr. W. K. Zieber, who was present as chairman of the local committee of safety, made this announcement to the crowd assembled outside, and every one at once hastened to collect coffee, sandwiches, pies, cold meat, and anything eatable that could be quickly prepared. Food and drink, tobacco and cigars were soon being handed freely to the passing soldiers. The Square and sidewalks were crowded with women and girls with baskets of good things to eat. These were speedily emptied and then the bearers hastened to their homes where their mothers or sisters were busy baking more bread and cakes and pies, to feed the boys in blue, still riding into town. As the regiments halted briefly many of the men dismounted and mingled with the people; others ate their food as they sat on their horses.

The halts were brief and by 10 o'clock the last regiment, the Eighteenth Pennsylvania, was entering the town. Part of the Fifth New York, preceding them, were halting in the streets.

## Taken by Surprise

While the Square was crowded with people, firing was heard out Frederick Street, and soon a cannon boomed and a shell flew over the town. Major Hammond, of the Fifth New York, shouted out to the people to run into their houses, as a fight was on, and in a few minutes up Frederick Street came the retreating Union cavalrymen followed by their gray-clad enemies at full gallop. The many dismounted soldiers ran for their horses, or if cut off, fled into alleys and houses, or jumped fences into yards and gardens, in their eagerness to escape capture.

The fierce yells, the clashing of sabers, the discharges of revolvers and carbines, the clatter of iron-clad hoofs on the roadway, all told that a cavalry fight was on. Dead and wounded men and horses fell here and there. The Federals were driven out Abbottstown Street to the railroad. Many prisoners were taken by the enemy and with captured ambulances were started out Frederick Street to the rear. While the principal fighting was on Frederick and Abbottstown streets, and the Square, small parties scattered over the town and hand to hand fights were to be seen everywhere. Cavalrymen riding through the open market house on the Square thought it was a covered bridge because of the hollow sound from the beating hooves upon the flooring due to the excavation underneath which served as the town gaol.

## Rebel Triumph Short-Lived

Loud shouts of triumph came from Confederate throats as the Union horsemen disappeared out Abbottstown Street. But the triumph was of short duration. The Fifth New York was quickly turned back and on the Common formed in battle array, and with the reformed squadrons of the Eighteenth Pennsylvania made a counter charge, driving the Confederates headlong through the town, recapturing the ambulances and taking many prisoners. Adjutant Gall, of the Fifth New York, was shot dead on Frederick Street, and Major White, of the same regiment, was severely wounded. Along the Westminster road a hot fight followed, the result being the Confederates were driven back to the cover of their artillery, posted on a hill at the farm of Jesse Rice. In the first assault, Lieutenant Thomas P. Shields, of Company G, Eighteenth Pennsylvania cavalry, and about twenty-five men were taken prisoners by the enemy.

The First Vermont and the First West Virginia were pushed forward by Farnsworth on the left flank, south of Frederick Street, and by a gallant charge assisted in driving back the enemy. General Farnsworth showed great ability in handling his brigade, reversing the column quickly and bringing back the advanced regiments to assist the rear .

Sharpshooters of the enemy swarmed in the fields south and east of the town and even boldly advanced into the borough limits, while the Union skirmishers and sharpshooters occupied every place of vantage in the suburbs. The town limits were not as extended then as now, there being no streets and few houses between Baltimore and Frederick streets, and between Carlisle and Frederick streets. Through the fields the cavalrymen rode freely, openings having been made in the fences.

When Stuart's advance neared Hanover, the Westminster road on which they were traveling joined the Littlestown road at a

This early scene looking northwest from the former Abner W. Forney farm near the present location of Boundary Avenue is the main part of the area where the battle took place. In the distance can be seen Winebrenner's Tannery and part of the Karl Forney farm where the battle raged at its height.

sharp angle. The rear guard of the Eighteenth Pennsylvania and the advance guard of Confederates each saw that an enemy was confronting them. A mutual attack was made.

Stuart's report says that "the enemy soon discovered our approach and made a demonstration toward attacking us, which we promptly met by a gallant charge by Colonel Chambliss' regiment, which not only repulsed the enemy but drove him pell-mell through town in great confusion." Colonel Hammond (Fifth New York) says the attack was made on the Union ambulances and stragglers at the rear. Major Carlington, of the Eighteenth Pennsylvania, in his report says the attack was sudden, but that several squadrons of his regiment had formed, when ambulances created so much confusion in the narrow street that they were compelled to retreat. Captain Potter of the Eighteenth, had command of the rear guard, and says his men opened fire and dashed through the Confederates that blocked their path at the junction of the roads, and then rode into town, closely followed by the enemy.

## Hand to Hand Encounters

There were numerous thrilling events and hand to hand encounters in single combat on the streets and in the suburbs of the town during the battle. Sergeant Isaac Peale, of the Second North Carolina, was wounded in Center Square and his horse shot under him. When he fell to the pavement his skull was injured. While in a dazed condition he was tenderly cared for by the Rev. Dr. W. K. Zieber. Later he was removed to a hospital where the last rites of the Catholic Church were administered by the parish priest. His remains were buried in the churchyard adjoining Conewago Chapel. The soldier who had been killed early in the morning near Gitt's mill was buried nearby. Some years later his brother came from the South, took up the body and conveyed it to Virginia.

Henry Holman, of the First West Virginia, had been seriously wounded when his regiment moved on the enemy west of Baltimore Street. He was brought to the house of Mrs. Agnes Spangler and his wounds were dressed by Dr. Culbertson on the porch. Holman had been a clown in a circus before the war, and a

*The Market House dating from 1815 stood until 1872 when it was pulled over by Cyrus Diller with mule power. It was 60 feet long and cost $800. Diller paid $42 for it. Troopers riding through took it for a covered bridge.*

friend and neighbor of Sergeant Collins of the same regiment, who was mortally wounded and had his horse killed on Baltimore Street near Center Square. Collins was taken to the home of George W. Welsh and afterwards removed to the hospital on York Street where he died. His leg had nearly been severed from his body by a globular shell fired from one of Hampton's guns on the turnpike near Mount Olivet Cemetery. About this time a conical shell passed over the Square and severed a limb from the tree which stood in front of the residence of Henry Wirt, on Carlisle Street. Another shell struck the residence of Conrad Moul, on Abbottstown Street. The fighting was widespread as shown by the fact that a wounded soldier was brought to the Wertz home on Ridge Avenue in the east end. Miss Lydia Wertz was alone at the time. It was a terrifying experience for the girl. Her father had taken the horses away to prevent their falling in the hands of the invaders. Miss Wertz later became the wife of Jonas Serff. A descendant, Mrs. Lydia Anthony, Highland Avenue, is the fifth in the family to bear the given name of Lydia.

In a clash at close quarters on Abbottstown Street near Broadway a Union soldier, refusing to surrender, was shot by his antagonist and died on the spot. A thrilling encounter took place between two men a short distance farther up Abbottstown Street, and at the same instant three men met in mortal combat in the alley adjoining the public school building.

## John Hoffacker Slain

One of the saddest incidents of the day was the untimely death of Corporal John Hoffacker of the Eighteenth Pennsylvania Regiment. He was shot and instantly killed while riding through town when his regiment met the first charge of the enemy. He was a manly fellow and universally popular with his compaions. He died while defending his country and flag almost within sight of his birthplace. Only two months before he had left his home in West Manheim Township near the Maryland line, to enlist in the army. His body rests in Mount Olivet Cemetery beside the grave of his brother, also a Civil War casualty.

During the lull in the contest of the afternoon, patriotic citizens carried the wounded into their houses, where they were tenderly cared for. Corporal James McGinley, of the Fifth New York, was seriously wounded and taken to the home of Henry Long on Frederick Street, where he remained for ten days or more. He then returned to his home. Forty-two years passed by, when Corporay McGinley returned again to Hanover, where he met the family of Mr. Long, who was living at the age of 86 years. Henry Long was the father of John Luther Long, author of the story "Madame Butterfly," which furnished the Italian composer Puccini the libretto for his famous opera. The corporal presented him with a gold-headed cane, in gratitude for the service rendered to him by Mrs. Long and daughters, in caring for him as a wounded soldier boy. Mr. Long was a silversmith and his workshop was the storeroom in the homestead. In the rear was a bellows, and several other Union soldiers came to the workshop

**HOFFACKER GRAVE MARKER**

*In Mt. Olivet Cemetery on Lot No. 19 in Area G are buried Corp. John Hoffacker, killed in the battle of Hanover, June 30, 1863, and his brother William Hoffacker, mortally wounded at Spotsylvania, Va., Court House, near Fredericksburg, May 12, 1864. On this same lot, purchased by H. M.*

*Hoffacker, year 1858 or 1886, are buried Jackson Craumer, who died October 20, 1897, and Eliza A. Craumer, who died August 25, 1918. She was 79 years old at the time of her death. John Hoffacker, an enlisted man, was in the army only two months when he was made a corporal. He served with the Eighteenth Pennsylvania Cavalry. John and William were the sons of H. M. and Elizabeth Hoffacker, West Manheim Township, York County. The section at Hobart, south of Pleasant Hill and near Sherman's Church and the Maryland line, is known as Hoffacker Valley. The family may have originally resided at Alesia, near Manchester, Md. The brother William's stone is similar in appearance to John's and attracts attention because of its unusual inscription: "William Hoffacker lost his life in defence of his Country at the Battle of Spottsylvania Court House May 12, 1864. Born Jan. 12, 1841. Died Feb. 3, 1865. Aged 24 years and 22 days."*

---

and hid themselves under the bellows, until the Confederates had left town. Mr. Long was not at home at the time of the battle, having left early in the morning with his horse and one of his neighbor, the Rev. Samuel Yingling, of St. Matthew's Lutheran Church, for his former home in Longstown, below York, to save these horses from capture by the enemy.

## Girls Sing National Airs

When the Union cavalry rode through Hanover a group of girls gathered in front of the Lutheran parsonage on Frederick Street and sang in loud and clear tones all the national airs as the soldiers passed. Confusion followed when the rear guards were attacked. Horsemen at full speed dashed along the streets. Wagons were sighted, each surrounded by a score or more of Union and Rebel soldiers fighting for possession. Not only the streets from curb to curb but the sidewalks as well were filled with a surging mass of pursued and pursuers. There was a brief pause and then the Rebels became the pursued and Union troops out of every alley and lane leading into Abbottstown Street charged in orderly fashion over the then vacant fields now comprising the populous streets of High, Franklin, Chestnut extended, and Poplar. Wounded were being taken into homes. The combatants in the streets slashed at each other as they galloped at full speed. A Confederate trooper rode up and shot Adjutant Gall in front of the residence of Mrs. Samuel Bechtel, then owned and occupied by Colonel Willliam Wolf. A woman handing out food looked the man right in the face as he rode through the crowd thinking he wanted some of the cake and pie she was handing around and did not know he shot until he wheeled around and his victim toppled from his saddle, but it was over so quickly that those nearest scarcely realized what had happened.

Mrs. Jeremiah Kohler lived on Carlisle Street where later the home of Mrs. George N. Forney stood. Her husband and son Albert were in the army and another son George had gone with some of Davis Garver's horses being taken across the Susquehanna. She was engaged in baking when her daughter Kate came rushing in and said there was going to be a fight. With her daughter and son Millard she watched from a front window. They saw a Union soldier fall from his horse when struck by a bullet. He was assisted into the house by Kate Kohler. A Union horseman advised them to go to their basements. Jacob H. Caufman who happened to be passing at the time joined them. Later when he looked out toward the square a bullet whizzed by him and struck a board two feet above his head. He decided to return to the cellar. They witnessed a death struggle between a Union soldier who had taken refuge in their stable and a Rebel who discovered him there, and they saw a horse killed on Chestnut Street across from their home and the rider a Union soldier escape unhurt.

### Raiders Seek Telegraph Wires

Mrs. Daniel F. Stair told of her experiences during the battle and visit of White's raiders preceding on the occasion of the forty-second anniversary. She remembered that there was a branch telegraph office in George Grove's store on Frederick Street. The wires had been removed the evening before White's arrival, rolled up and thrown into the loft above the old market house. The raiders took notice of the pole planted in front of the store, entered and searched the building for evidence. They left without damaging the property. Hanover was cut off from the outside world after the wires had been cut and rails torn up at Hanover Junction. Hanover heard from farmers that all day Saturday Rebel troops were passing along the turnpike from Gettysburg to York. Citizens who had fled to York with horses and property found Yorkers were leaving for Wrightsville. Just after dark on Sunday night the whole horizon in the northeast

*View of Abner Forney farm along the Becker Mill road south of town. A son David Forney occupied the place. The residence still stands. Cemetery Ridge is seen in the background.*

was lit up by a lurid glow. It was feared York was being destroyed, but later it was learned that Colonel Frick had found it necessary to set fire to the bridge over the Susquehanna, and part of Wrightsville burned from spreading flames.

The farm of David F. Forney in Penn Township, with the residence and farm buildings along the Beck Mill road just beyond the town's southern limits, was within the battle zone. The Hanover Herald of June 28, 1902, reports that when cutting down a cherry tree on the property the axe severed a ball from a cavalryman's carbine in the block. Other souvenirs of battle found on the Forney farm included a twelve-pound cannon ball, shell fragments, cap box, cartridge box, canister case, carbine, and buckshot and ball cartridge with Maynard primer attached, used in 1859 Harpers Ferry musket. On Soldiers' Hill along the Westminster road various assorted shells were found by members of the Keller family.

---

## STUART'S ADJUTANT SPEAKS FRANKLY

Major H. B. McClellan, adjutant general and chief of staff to General J. E. B. Stuart, wrote a volume entitled "Campaign of Stuart's Cavalry," which was published in the year 1885. One of the chapters of this interesting volume gives an extended account of the cavalry engagement at Hanover. The author also describes the march of Stuart's cavalry corps after it crossed the Potomac until it reached Hanover and finally Gettysburg, with so much care and exactness that his account is given herewith in full, because of its historic value. Major McClellan gives a graphic description of the manner in which Stuart's cavalry crossed the Potomac at Rowser's Ford, about twenty miles northwest of Washington, and captured Meade's wagon train, which incident gave rise to the engagement at Hanover. He says:

"Stuart's men carried the contents of the caissons and limber chests across the Potomac at Rowser's Ford and put them back after the caissons and limber chests had been taken over, Stuart, with three brigades, commanded respectively by Wade Hampton, Fitzhugh Lee and Chambliss, completed the crossing of the river at 3 A. M. of June 28. No more difficult achievement was accomplished by our cavalry during the war. The night was calm and without a moon. No prominent object marked the entrance to the ford on either side, but horse followed horse through the water, which often covered the saddles of the riders. When the current was strong the line would unconsciously be borne down the river, sometimes so far as to cause danger of missing the ford, when some bold rider would advance from the opposite shore and correct the alignment. Energy, endurance, and skill were taxed to the utmost; but the crossing was effected, and so silently that the nearest neighbors were not aware of it until daylight.

## Wagon Train Proves Burden

"It was past noon when Stuart entered Rockville. While halting for the purpose of destroying the telegraph line, and to procure supplies, information was brought of the approach from Washington of a large train of wagons on the way to Meade's army. Lieutenant Thomas Lee, Second South Carolina Cavalry, with four men from his regiment, dashed along the train and routed its small guard. Although some of the wagons in the rear had turned about and were moving rapidly toward Washington, Lee reached the one foremost in the retreat, and halted and turned it about within sight of the defenses of the city. Chambliss' brigade followed, and the whole train was secured. One hundred and twenty-five of the wagons, and all of the animals belonging to the train were turned over to the chief quartermaster of the Army at Gettysburg.

"It must be acknowledged that the capture of this train of wagons was a misfortune. The time occupied in securing it was insignificant, but the delay caused to the subsequent march was serious at a time when minutes counted almost as hours. Had Stuart been entirely unimpeded, he would have probably passed Hanover on the 30th before the arrival of Kilpatrick's division, and would have been in communication with General Lee before nightfall on that day. That this would have altered the result of the campaign is a matter of grave doubt, but it would certainly have relieved the movement of the cavalry around the rear of Meade's army of the disapprobation to which some have given expression.

"Much time was necessarily consumed in tearing up the track at Hood's mill, in burning the bridge at Sykesville, and in destroying the telegraph line; but this work was effectually accomplished and the last means of communication between General Meade's army and Washington was destroyed. Stuart now pressed on to Westminster which he reached about 5 o'clock P. M. Here the advance encountered a brief but stubborn resistance from two companies of the First Delaware Cavalry, commanded by Major N. B. Knight. This fight was more gallant than judicious on the part of Major Knight, for he reports a loss of sixty-seven men out of ninety-five. Two officers of the Fourth Virginia Cavalry who were well known as among the best in the regiment— Lieutenant Pierre Gibson and John W. Murray, were killed in this affair.

"For the first time since the 24th an abundance of provisions for men and horses was obtained at Westminster; and moving the head of his column to Union Mills, on the Gettysburg road, Stuart rested for the remainder of the night. Here he ascertained that Kilpatrick's cavalry had reached Littlestown, seven miles distant, on the same evening, and had gone into camp. At this day we can see that it would have been better had Stuart here destroyed the captured wagons. Up to this time they had caused no embarrassment, for the necessary delay in destroying the railroad and telegraph on the previous day had given ample time for the movement of the train. But now the close proximity of the enemy suggested the probability of a collision on the morrow, and the separation of the brigades by the wide interval which the train occupied was a disadvantage which might well have caused its immediate destruction. But it was not in Stuart's nature to abandon an attempt until it had been proven to be beyond his powers; and he determined to hold on to his prize until the last moment. This was unfortunate. Kilpatrick's division, at Littlestown, was only seven miles from Hanover. His march would of course be directed upon that point early the next morning.

### Misses Big Opportunity

"To reach the same place Stuart must traverse more than ten miles; but an early start and an unimpeded march would have placed him in advance of his adversary. As it was he struck the rear of Farnsworth's brigade at about 10 o'clock on the morning of the 30th, in the town of Hanover, and scattered one regiment, the Eighteenth Pennsylvania Cavalry, inflicting upon it a loss of eighty-six officers and men. The Second North Carolina Cavalry, temporarily commanded by Lieutenant Colonel W. H. Payne, of the Fourth Virginia Cavalry, made this attack, which, if it could have been properly supported, would have resulted in the rout of Kilpatrick's command. But Hampton was separated from the leading brigade by the whole train of captured wagons, and Fitz Lee was marching on the left flank to protect the column from an attack by way of Littlestown. There was nothing at the front but Chambliss' small brigade; and before anything could be brought to the assistance of the Second North Carolina, General Farnsworth rallied his regiments, and drove the North Carolinians from the town. In this charge Lieutenant Colonel Payne was captured.

"The road upon which the fight occurred debouches from the town of Hanover toward the south, and at a distance of perhaps three hundred yards from the town makes a turn almost at right angles as it ascends the hill beyond, enclosing a piece of meadow land, through which flows a small stream, whose steep banks form a ditch from ten to fifteen feet wide. . . . Stuart, with his staff and couriers, occupied this field, on the side next to the enemy. When the Second North Carolina broke and retreated under Farnsworth's charge, this party maintained its positions for some moments, firing with pistols at the flank of the enemy, who pursued the North Carolina regiment on the road.

### Horse's Leap Saves Stuart

"The position soon became one of extreme personal peril to Stuart, whose retreat by the road was cut off. Nothing remained but to leap the ditch. Splendidly mounted on his favorite mare, Virginia, Stuart took the ditch at a running leap, and landed safely on the other side with several feet to spare. Some of his party made the leap with equal success, but not a few horses failed, and landed their riders in the shallow water, whence by energetic scrambling they reached the safe side of the stream.

The ludicrousness of the situation, notwithstanding the peril, was the source of much merriment at the expense of these unfortunate ones.

"Upon the repulse of the Second North Carolina, Stuart retired to the hills south and east of Hanover, which gave him such commanding position that the enemy declined further advance. Hampton, on his arrival, was moved to the right, and by means of his sharpshooters dislodged the enemy from that part of the town. Fitz Lee, in moving up on the left, had encountered a part of Custer's brigade, and captured a member of Kilpatrick's staff and a number of other prisoners. In the meantime the wagons had been placed in close park, and preparation had been made to burn them should the necessity arise. But Custer's brigade, which had at first been placed on Kilpatrick's left, was subsequently moved to his right, and Hampton's success relieved Stuart's right, he now determined to send Fitz Lee forward with the train, through Jefferson toward York, hoping thus to gain information which would guide his future movements.

"It was, however, late in the afternoon before this could be effected, and not until night had fallen did Stuart deem it prudent to withdraw from Kilpatrick, who still maintained his threatening position in front of Hanover. Kilpatrick showed no disposition to hinder Stuart's withdrawal, or to pursue him on the following day. He had been roughly handled during the short engagement at Hanover, and himself acknowledged an aggregate loss of 197. He moved as far northward on the next day as Abbottstown, and sent a detachment, under Lieutenant Colonel A. J. Alexander, which followed Stuart's trail as far as Rossville, but neither of these movements came within Stuart's observation.

"During the night march to Jefferson, the wagons and prisoners were a serious hindrance. Nearly four hundred prisoners had accumulated since the parole at Cooksville. Many of these were loaded in the wagons; some of them acted as drivers. The mules were starving for food and water, and often became unmanageable. Not infrequently a large part of the train would halt in the road because a driver toward the front had fallen asleep and allowed his team to stop. The train guard became careless through excessive fatigue, and it required the utmost exertions of every officer on Stuart's staff to keep the train in motion. The march was continued through the entire night, turning north-ward near Jefferson. When Fitz Lee reached the turnpike lead-ing from York to Gettysburg he learned that Early had retraced his steps, and had marched westward. The best information which Stuart could obtain seemed to indicate that the Confeder-ate army was concentrating in the vicinity of Shippensburg."

## Blackford's Version of Leap

In his description of the battle of Hanover Stuart's adjutant, Lieutenant Colonel Blackford, relates how the Confederate leader was nearly cut off from his troops by the charging column of Union forces. He writes: "The road was lined on each side by an ill-kept hedge grown up high, but at some places, fortunately for us, there were gaps of lower growth. Stuart pulled up and waving his sabre with a merry laugh, shouted to me and then lifted his mare, Virginia, over the hedge into the field. . . . I followed him. I had only that morning, fortunately, mounted Magic, having had her led previously, and Stuart had done the same with Virginia, so they were fresh. As we alighted in the field, we found ourselves, within ten paces of the front of a flanking party of twenty-five or thirty men which was accom-panying the charging regiment, and they called us to halt; but as we let our two thoroughbreds out, they followed in hot pur-suit, firing as fast as they could cock their pistols. The field was in tall timothy grass and we did not see, nor did our horses until close to it, a huge gully fifteen feet wide and as many deep stretched across our path. There were only a couple of strides of distance for our horses to regulate their step, and Magic had to rise at least six feet from the brink. Stuart and myself were riding side by side and as soon as Magic rose I turned my head to see how Virginia had done it, and I shall never forget the glimpse I then saw of this beautiful animal away up in mid-air over the chasm and Stuart's fine figure sitting erect and firm in the saddle."*

When the scouts reported to Kilpatrick that Stuart was moving eastward, he did not prepare to follow, because of his orders

* "War Years With Jeb Stuart," Charles Scribner's Sons, New York.

from Meade to keep in touch with the army headquarters at Taneytown. When Kilpatrick left Frederick he was instructed to keep Stuart, if he met him, to the right, while Gregg was moving eastward toward Hanover Junction. At this time Gregg, with the Second Division of cavalry, was near Manchester, twelve miles south of Hanover. Sedgwick, with the Sixth Army Corps, numbering sixteen to eighteen thousand men, was near West-minster moving eastward. Sykes, with the Fifth Army Corps, numbering 15,400 men, was on the way toward Union Mills, with Hanover as his destination. Kilpatrick was in communication with the Twelfth Corps, under Slocum, then at Littlestown, while the Eleventh Corps, under Howard, was a short distance to the west. Stuart had no other direction to take than to move eastward, for his scouts had conveyed to him the news that Gregg's cavalry was a few miles away to the southwest.

## OFFICERS WRITE OWN STORIES

At the time the engagement opened, Meade in command of the Army of the Potomac, had his headquarters at Taneytown, Maryland, where he was laying plans for the impending battle with Lee. General Alfred Pleasonton in command of all the cavalry of the Potomac army, remained with Meade at Taney-town, during the afternoon of June 30 and on July 1. Lieutenant Colonel A. J. Alexander, assistant adjutant general of Pleasonton's cavalry, had been moved forward to Littlestown, seven miles west of Hanover. From this point, he sent out couriers to notify the head of the army and General Pleasonton, of all the move-ments of the contending forces in the vicinity of Hanover and York. Early in the afternoon of June 30, General Kilpatrick, at his headquarters, wrote the following report of his engagement with Stuart and sent it by courier to Pleasonton:

### Kilpatrick Reports From Hanover

"General—Five minutes after your dispatch saying that General Stuart was making for Littlestown, my rear guard was at-tacked in Hanover, driven in, and a vigorous charge was made upon the rear and flanks of my commands. At the same time the enemy opened with artillery from the hills at the right of town.

*Headquarters of General Kilpatrick located in the Central Hotel rooms just below the word "CENTRAL" in the photograph*

Brigadier General Farnsworth quickly threw his brigade into position and by quick and vigorous charges, checked the attack and drove the enemy out of town. The enemy soon showed himself in force on the left of Hanover, and foolishly put himself in my rear. After a fight of about two hours, in which my whole command at different times engaged, I made a vigorous attack upon their center, forced them back upon the road to Littlestown, and finally succeeded in breaking their center. Stuart then retreated toward York. As the enemy was reported to be advancing toward me from East Berlin, I made no further attempt to intercept Stuart's command. I have captured one battle flag, Lieutenant Colonel Payne, one captain and forty-five privates. Upwards of fifteen of the enemy have been killed. My loss was eleven killed and several wounded. I have gone into camp at Hanover. We have plenty of forage, men are in good spirits, and we don't fear Stuart's whole cavalry composed of three brigades."

Soon after sending the above dispatch, General Kilpatrick rode out the turnpike toward Abbottstown. His force was then going into camp for the night on both sides of the turnpike between Hanover and the Pigeon Hills. He was continually sending out scouts to ascertain the movements of the enemy and in this work was remarkably successful. On the morning of June 30, General Early, with his division of 9000 men, had left York and reached East Berlin in the evening, on his way toward Gettysburg. He had moved toward Heidlersburg to join the other two divisions of Ewell's corps, which had been moved from Carlisle toward Gettysburg. About 7 o'clock in the evening having obtained this information and with his headquarters in his saddle, on the highest point of the turnpike, over the Pigeon Hills, Kilpatrick wrote a second dispatch and sent it to Alexander at Littlestown, who conveyed it to Pleasonton, at Taneytown:

"General—I have the honor to report that after an encounter with General Stuart's force, I have succeeded in cutting his column in two. One portion, estimated at about 4000, with from five to seven pieces of artillery, is now encamped in the woods on the left (east side of the turnpike from Hanover to Baltimore; the other is also in the woods on the right (west) side of the road from Hanover to Littlestown. I am not informed as to its strength. I have sent out scouts to ascertain the exact position of the first division and intend, if possible, to attack their camp at daybreak. A strong column of the enemy's force, under General Early, left York this morning to march westward. I conclude that they are concentrating at Gettysburg. I will attack if I can by any means find proper roads. Stuart is now moving toward York, cutting his way through the fields southeast of Hanover. There is a considerable force at East Berlin. I am now midway between Abbottstown and Hanover. I cannot advance farther and keep communication open with Littlestown. Scouting parties have been sent out toward York, Dover and Carlisle."

## Report of Major Hammond

General Farnsworth, whom Kilpatrick credits with having saved the day at Hanover, was killed on the extreme left of the Union line at Gettysburg, on July 3. No official report of his brigade appears in the government records. Major Hammond, who commanded the Fifth New York at Hanover, in August, 1863, made the following report:

"My regiment was fourth in column on the march from Littlestown, the First Vermont, First West Virginia, and Elder's battery being in advance and the Eighteenth Pennsylvania Cavalry in the rear. After we entered Hanover, we halted on the main street. While resting, an attack was made on the Eighteenth Pennsylvania, which moved forward in confusion upon the rear of my regiment, which had faced about and was trying to clear the streets of the fugitives preparatory to making a charge upon the advancing column of the enemy. They finally succeeded; and, without waiting for orders, immediately charged upon the enemy, driving them to the outside of the town, where we found a large force drawn up in the road as a reserve, and received from them a severe fire, causing the men to halt for a moment. General Farnsworth, arriving from the front at this time, the men were re-formed, and made anotther charge, driving the enemy in confusion along the road and through the fields. Private Thomas Burke, of Company A, captured a battle flag from the enemy in this charge, and subsequently turned it over to General Kilpatrick. The enemy finding himself repulsed, opened upon the town with artillery. Skirmishers were immediately sent forward, and a reserve force placed at the outer edge of the town. On returning to the other side, where the rest of the brigade was drawn up in line, I was ordered to act as a support to Elder's battery. Finding that our position endangered the town, we moved around to the eastern side, when the Second Brigade, having returned, I was ordered by General Kilpatrick to flank the enemy's position and capture the battery, if possible, and to order an advance of the skirmishers on the right which was done."

## Kilpatrick's Official Report

On August 10, 1863, forty days after the engagement at Hanover, General Kilpatrick, then in camp in Virginia, sent his official report of the Gettysburg campaign to the government. In this report he makes the following statements:

"On June 29, in compliance with orders from headquarters cavalry corps, I assumed command of the Third Division, till then known as Stahl's division. The actual strength of the division was 3500 although it numbered on paper upward of 4000 men for duty. On the morning of June 29, the First Brigade (General Farnsworth), consisting of the Fifth New York, Eighteenth Pennsylvania, First Vermont, First West Virginia Cavalry, and Elder's Battery, United States Horse Artillery, left Frederick City, and marched to Littlestown, Pennsylvania.

"The Second Brigade (General Custer), consisting of the First, Fifth and Seventh Michigan Cavalry, and Pennington's Battery, United States Horse Artillery, reached the same place at 10 P. M. the same day.

"At daylight on the morning of the 30th, the division marched to find the enemy. We reached Hanover at 10 A. M. and while passing through the town (the Second Brigade in advance), the First Brigade (General Farnsworth) was attacked in flank and rear by the Confederate cavalry under Stuart. Some confusion ensued. The attack was determined and fierce. The main and side streets swarmed with the enemy's cavalry. The Eighteenth Pennsylvania was routed, but the gallant Farnsworth had passed from front to rear ere the shout of the Confederate charge had ceased to ring through the street, faced the Fifth New York about, countermarched the other regiments, and with a rush and blow struck the enemy's hosts in full charge. For a moment, and a moment only, victory hung uncertain. For the first time in the conflict our troops had met the foe in close contact; but we were on our own free soil; fair hands, regardless of the dangerous strife, waved our men on, and anxious eyes looked pleadingly out from every window. The brave Farnsworth made one great effort, and the day was won. The foe turned and fled.

"General Custer's brigade had now returned, and to save the town, I moved first to its left and afterward to its right. The main streets were barricaded and held by our troops and the citizens, who gallantly volunteered to defend their homes. After an artillery duel of an hour, in which Pennington and Elder both participated, the enemy gave way and we formed a junction with the main army, from which we had been separated for several hours.

"In this engagement we lost: Officers, 2 killed, 6 wounded, and five missing; enlisted men, 17 killed, 35 wounded, and 118 missing, making an aggregate of 197 killed, wounded and missing. Owing to the nature of the attack, our loss was greater than that of the enemy. We killed upward of twenty, took fifty prisoners, and captured one battle flag. The First Brigade (General Farnsworth), and especially the Fifth New York Cavalry, was greatly distinguished in this engagement. July 1, the division marched to Berlin, via Abbottstown, to intercept Stuart, but failed. A detachment under Lieutenant Colonel A. J. Alexander pursued Stuart to Rossville."

## Custer's Report Brief

General George A. Custer, in his official report, made out September 9, 1863, says:

"First Michigan of my command was ordered to support Battery M, Second U. S. Artillery, at the Hanover engagement. No loss was sustained, as this regiment was not actually engaged.

Fifth Michigan was also in the fight but suffered no loss. Sixth Michigan Cavalry drove the enemy to their guns, which we found supported by a heavy force of cavalry. A sharp engagement followed, in which we were outnumbered by the enemy six to one. This regiment lost 15 captured. Battery M, Second

U. S. Artillery, under my command, while between Hanover and Abbottstown, had a chest of one caisson explode, mortally wounding one man and killing 2 horses."

## Stuart Reveals Strategy

In September, 1863, General J. E. B. Stuart reported to his government at Richmond the part he took during the Confederate invasion of 1863 into Pennsylvania. His account of the engagement at Hanover will be read with interest:

"I engaged a squad of the First Delaware Cavalry at Westminster, Maryland, June 29th. They soon retreated towards Baltimore. We encamped, that night, a few miles above Westminster, General Fitzhugh Lee's brigade in advance, halting the head of the column at Union Mills, midway between Westminster and Littlestown. At Union Mills we heard that the Federal cavalry had reached Littlestown and was encamped there June 29th. Early next morning we resumed our march by a cross route for Hanover. General W. F. H. Lee's brigade, then commanded by Chambliss, was now in the advance. General Wade Hampton was in the rear with the wagon train and Fitz Lee's brigade was moving on our left flank between Littlestown and our road.

"About 10 A. M. the head of our column reached Hanover and there we found a large body of the enemy's cavalry going through the town, moving toward a gap in the mountains (Pigeon Hills) which I intended using on account of the elevation. The enemy soon discovered our approach, and made a demonstration toward attacking us, which we promptly met by a gallant charge by Colonel Chambliss' brigade, which not only repulsed the enemy, but drove him pell-mell through the town in great confusion. We captured ambulances and a large number of prisoners, all of which were brought safely through to our lines, but were closely followed by the enemy's fresh troops. If my command had been well closed now, this cavalry column which we struck near the rear, would have been at our mercy, but owing to the great elongation of the column by reason of the one hundred and twenty-five captured wagons and the hilly roads, General Hampton was a long distance behind us on his way to Hanover, and Fitz Lee was not yet heard from. In retiring with the prisoners and ambulances, Lieutenant Colonel W. H. Payne, of the Fourth Virginia Cavalry, temporarily in command of the Second North Carolina Cavalry, was taken prisoner in a gallant attempt to cut off a body of the enemy by a flank movement on the town. The delay in getting up reinforcements enabled the Federal cavalry to gain possession of the town.

"Hanover is situated in a valley surrounded by heights which were in our possession. These heights were crowned with artillery. Our position was impregnable to cavalry even with so small a force. We cut the enemy's column in twain, General Fitz Lee in the meantime fell upon the rear portion, driving it handsomely and capturing one of Kilpatrick's staff. Our wagon train was now a subject of serious embarrassment, but I thought by a detour on the right, by Jefferson, I could save it. I therefore determined to try it, particularly as I was satisfied from any accessible source of information, as well as from the lapse of time, that the Army of Northern Virginia must be near the Susquehanna. My supply of ammunition was nearly exhausted. I had an immense train of wagons and four hundred prisoners which I had captured in Hanover and on the way northward. General Hampton arrived at Hanover in the meantime, and engaged the enemy farther to the right, and finally with his sharpshooters, dislodged the Federal force from the town of Hanover. The enemy then moved to our left, apparently to re-unite his broken columns, but pressing us with dismounted men on our left flank.

"General Fitz Lee's brigade was now just at the head of the column, and he was instructed to push on with the train through Jefferson to York, and communicate as soon as possible with the army. Hampton brought up the rear. We were not molested on our march, which was over a very dark road on the night of the 30th of June. Our soldiers were much fatigued. Whole regiments slept in the saddle on the march, their faithful horses keeping the road unguided. In some instances they fell from their horses, being overcome with sleepiness. We passed on through Jefferson to Dover, reaching there on the next morning. There we paroled our prisoners. (Editor's note—Many of these were farmers picked up en route in order to prevent their revealing to the enemy knowledge of the captured wagon train and course taken.)

"I heard that General Early had marched westward from York. We then pushed on to Carlisle, going through Dillsburg. I believed while on this march that most of the Army of Northern Virginia was then around Harrisburg."

## HOME TOWN PAPERS COVER BATTLE

Two English weekly papers were published in Hanover during the Civil War. The Hanover Spectator founded by Senary Leader and continued after his death in 1858 by his widow, Mrs. Maria Leader, was strongly Republican. During the '60's Mrs.

MARY SHAW LEADER
*Pioneer newspaperwoman.*

Leader was assisted by her daughter, Mary Shaw Leader, and two sons, W. H. and E. J. Leader, in issuing this publication which had a wide circulation in York and Adams counties. The frame office building adjoined the Leader home at 54 Frederick Street. The Spectator's account follows:

Our town on Tuesday for the first time saw and felt all the incidents, scenes and horrors of actual war. We have been unable to obtain full particulars of the battle, but we give below

*The Leader home on Frederick Street and office of the Hanover Spectator adjoining on left.*

such facts as we have been able to obtain from various sources, which we consider reliable:

At about 8 o'clock A. M., on Tuesday, June 30th, the head of a column of Union cavalry and artillery reached the town from the south, which proved to be a Division of Cavalry and two batteries of artillery, all under command of Acting Major General Kilpatrick—of the number of the force we do not deem it prudent to speak for obvious reasons. The following were some of the regiments comprising this force, which was on its march to give battle to and drive the Rebels from the State when or where they might be found in force: The 18th Pennsylvania, 1st West Va., 1st, 5th, 6th and 7th Michigan, 1st Vermont, 5th New York, and others. The head of the column halted in Frederick street and was enthusiastically received by our citizens, who furnished refreshments liberally to the troops. Regiment by regiment thus passed through until about 10 o'clock, when suddenly cannonading was heard in the rear of the column. At first this was supposed to be an impromptu salute for our troops, but a sudden dash upon the troops crowded in the street by three regiments of Rebel cavalry, soon told us that a large body of Rebel cavalry,

under Gen. Stewart, supported by artillery, had placed themselves on the hills and wooded heights south of the town about
daylight, awaiting the approach of the Union troops—that this
could be done and our citizens not know it, is a matter of
wonder. The 5th New York, Major Hammond in command, was
in the street and received at this point the first shock of the
Rebel attack, which was made by a furious charge by a Rebel
brigade consisting of the 1st and 13th Virginia and 2nd North
Carolina regiments. Major Hammond at once placed his regiment in column for a charge, and the movement was executed
promptly and gallantly, scattering the rebels in every direction in
confusion and disorder, and now commenced a scene of thrilling
hand to hand fighting in the streets and alleys, along the Frederick road and in the fields South and West of the town. This
running fight was kept up for several hours, resulting in the
slaughter of some 40 Rebels, 75 prisoners and the capture of
several battle-flags, numerous horses and equipment, and a large
number of carbines, revolvers and sabres. The Rebels were completely routed and fled to the shelter of their cannon on the hill-
sides, and our streets were soon freed of their presence. The
entire force of our troops was then massed in line of battle, supported by artillery, to repulse any further attack that might be
made by the Rebels, but they made no further demonstration,
and about 5 o'clock began a hurried retreat from the scene of
their defeat.

The 18th Pennsylvania was the first regiment to form in the
rear and charge upon the Rebels, and they displayed their usual
coolnes and valor under a heavy fire from the enemy.

There were many and curious and exciting conflicts, some of
which will probably never be known. Two or three fell under
our observation, and are indelibly impressed upon our memory.
Captain Farley, of the 5th New York, led a charge of Carbineers
on the enemy, executing the orders gallantly in the front and
right of the Union lines; a private named Bogue, of the 5th New
York, was captured by a squad of Rebels and his horse shot in
front of this office—in less than ten minutes this same Rebel squad,
15 in number, were captured by the 5th New York, and Bogue
released. The 5th New York captured the flag of the 13th Virginia

after a desperate conflict in a lane a short distance from town. Many other similar cases occurred during the engagement.

Adjutant Gall, a gallant officer of the 5th New York, who fell at the head of his men while leading a charge at the end of Frederick street, was interred at St. Matthew's Lutheran burial ground, on Chestnut street.

Our citizens turned out and assisted the troops in burying the Rebel dead, among whom was a Captain Davis—said to be a noted officer of the famous Louisiana Tigers. Quite a number of horses were killed on both sides, and the carcasses were collected and burned.

Wounded soldiers were kindly taken care of by our citizens at their private residences, where the brave fellows received the kindest and most tender treatment, and everything possible is being done for their comfort and relief.

The Government has taken Eckert's Concert Hall, on Market Square, Marion Hall, on Foundry alley, Albright's Hall, on Broadway, and Pleasant Hill Hotel, on Baltimore street, for Hospitals, to accommodate the large number of wounded soldiers.

A vast number of trophies have been picked up by our people from the battlefield in and around our town. These trophies consist in part of broken carbines, pistols, sabres, cartridge boxes, pieces of shell, brass letters and ornaments, etc. These articles all bear witness to the severity of the fight, and are interesting relics of the first battle which has occurred in and near our town since the commencement of the present war.

## The Hanover Citizen

The Hanover Citizen was published every Thursday by G. W. Welsh and Joseph Dellone from an office in the brick Newman property described as the second house on Frederick Street, west of the Public Square. It stood between the Central Hotel and the Jacob Wirt residence. In politics The Citizen was decidedly anti-Lincoln and anti-Curtin.

On the same inside page presenting the story of the Hanover encounter The Citizen carried a three-column account of the battle of Gettysburg under a four-tier headline with two lines in 18-point type:

## BATTLE OF GETTYSBURG
## A DECISIVE VICTORY

At the bottom of the page was a paragraph to the effect that "as we were going to press we received the intelligence that Vicksburg is ours."

### Understatement of Century

Our readers will observe that the outside of today's paper is dated July 2nd and the inside July 9, which was caused by the suspension of business through the rebel invasion. The outside was pressed off prior to the raid, and we deemed it proper to defer its publication until things assumed a more tranquil phase. Our readers will please pardon us for all deficiencies which may occur in this week's edition as *we have been unable to get but little news* within the past week on account of having no mail.

On Tuesday, June 30th, our formerly peaceable and quiet town was thrown into a most desperate confusion by the collision of the cavalry forces of General Kilpatrick and Stewart's rebel horde. The two brigades of the latter made an attack upon the 1st brigade of Kilpatrick's Division, comprising the 1st Virginia, 1st Vermont, 5th New York, and the 18th Pennsylvania cavalry. The rebels were supported by artillery stationed on a hill to the south of and commanding the town, from which position they threw shell and confusion through our town, an act wholly unworthy of a civilized people and contrary to the usage of civilized warfare. Many of the dwellings of our citizens were penetrated by their death-dealing missils which played with desperate fury throughout various parts of the town. Soldiers fell, either killed or wounded, and the novelty of seeing dead men upon our streets was soon overcome by the too frequent occurrence of this sad fate to many a brave and worthy man.

The 1st Virginia, led by Col. N. P. Richmond and the 5th New York by Major Hammond led the charge and behaved with great gallantry; also the 1st Vermont. The 18th Pennsylvania betrayed their usual trait of character, although some of the companies in this regiment fought with bravery.

In the rear of the forces engaged in this action was a portion of the 5th and 6th Michigan cavalry who did nobly and also sustained some losses in wounded and prisoners; they also captured many prisoners. The number of the enemy killed was about the same as on our side. A number of their wounded have fallen into our hands, and are receiving the same attention in the hospital as our own men.

The enemy being repulsed and the tumult subsided, Marion Hall was opened as a hospital, and through the efforts of the citizens soon each aching head and shattered limbs reposed upon a comfortable couch. The ladies had been untiring in the administration to the wants and necessities of the wounded, and continue to furnish every needed good. God bless the ladies of our town, and forbid that their nerves ever again be shocked by the roar of cannon, the clashing of steel, or the ghastly visage of murdered men.

On Wednesday after this collision at an early hour in the day, Surgeon Gardner, in charge of all the wounded cavalry, reported as the surgeon of the hospital at this post, bringing with him an official corps of stewards and nurses, and soon brought order out of confusion. Soon the wounded were mounted upon snug bunks furnished by the carpenters of this place, and the hitherto crowded room presented the appearance of ease and comfort. The majority of the wounds received in this action were of a most serious character, requiring many capital operations, which were performed at an early hour in a most excellent manner by Surgeon Gardner.

The rebel horde that prowled through this county, about a week ago stole about two thousand horses, and we would not doubt if the number would be considerable more. The loss sustained in York county by this thieving horde is very heavy.

### Excerpts From York Gazette June 30, 1863

The York Gazette of date Tuesday, June 30, reported that a York safety committee composed of Chief Burgess Small, Arthur Farquhar, George Hay, Thomas White and W. Latimer Small on the previous Saturday conferred with General Gordon of the advance rebel forces of Major General Jubal A. Early's division estimated by a Union scout as numbering some ten thousand.

The citizen's committee asked for terms for sparing York from destruction. Gordon's brigade passed through the town and encamped on the turnpike two miles east of town.

General Early with another brigade took possession of the Fair Ground and government hospital. Demands were made upon the citizens for $100,000, 165 barrels of flour, 28,000 pounds of bread, 32,000 pounds of beef, 21,000 pounds of pork, and considerable quantities of sugar, salt, shoes, socks, and hats. Part of the requisitions was met and $28,000 raised. Early signified his satisfaction and agreed to accept the offer.

Gordon's brigade reached Wrightsville Sunday afternoon and after a slight skirmish in which two of Bell's Adams county cavalry were supposed to have been captured, our forces consisting of several regiments of New York and Pennsylvania militia fell back across the Susquehanna, destroying the bridge in their rear by fire. Monday evening Gordon's brigade encamped several miles from York along the Carlisle road. Tuesday morning the 30th the other brigades followed westward with their artillery and munitions, including the brigades of Hoke, Hayes, and Smith ("Extra Bill," recently elected governor of Virginia.)

## Letter to Editor

A communication to the Hanover Spectator, W. H. Leader editor, July 17, 1863, exposes the bitterness felt by citizens of Hanover over White's raid:

The approach of the rebels from the South Mts., through Cashtown and Gettysburg to our place, had been heralded for several days by hundreds of fugitive citizens, bringing with them their horses and cattle, and whatever they could take along in their precipitate flight. The exaggerated accounts given by these refugees of the many depredations committed by the advancing foe, spread terror and confusion through all classes of society. Courageous men seemed for the time being to lose their usual fortitude of mind, and thought only of hasty retreat. To add to the general confusion and hurry-scurry of the scene, the scouts and Philadelphia Cavalry, who had been on duty along the base of the mountains and valley around Gettysburg, came dashing into our usually quiet borough in such a tremendous hurry, upon their foaming chargers and begrimed with mud as if all bedlam were at their heels. After these came the commanding officer of this district, in a more composed manner, and in greater military bearing. Upon the trail of these individuals came a swift messenger bringing the very unwelcome news that our regiment of infantry had been cut to pieces and scattered as chaff before the driving blast.

One company of this regiment had promptly been raised in Hanover, at the first information of the threatened danger to our State, and was one of the first to arrive at the Capital to offer their services to the Governor. This company was composed of the first and most heroic young men of the place. The sad tidings of their overthrow, taken in connection with the conflicting rumors already afloat, added distress and anguish to the already agonizing scene of confusion which ushered in the night, in which the ragged chivalry of the South were to make their appearance in our midst. During the vigils of this ever-to-be-remembered night, balmy sleep never came to the relief of the eyes of our Gotham. Every undefinable object, seen through the mists of the night, was magnified into a spectral army of invaders, and gave fresh motives for an early skedaddle.

Carriages and wagons, equestrians and footmen, civilians and soldiers, white and black, hurried forth in one stream of inextricable confusion from the avenues of the town to seek a safe refuge from the minions of Jeff Davis. 'Till morning all who had horses to save, or who feared the loss of other property had taken their departure and left the place an easy conquest to the enemy and well nigh deserted of all but women and children.

At an early hour the approach of the cavalcade was duly announced, and those who had tarried to see the entrance of the Rebels, were ready, mounted upon swift horses looking wistfully out Carlisle Street to catch a first glimpse of the cavalry which was cautiously feeling its way into the street. Their longing eyes were soon greeted with the sight of one, and then another horse-man, with cocked pistols in their hands, moving slowly and steadily up the avenue and commanding all who attempted to flee to halt.

Thus two and three in a squad at a time, moved up to the Square, until some thirty had rallied around their leader. No doubt these bold warriors were as much surprised at their cold indifferent reception as we were at their tatterdemalion appearance, for they looked more like Falstaff's regamuffins, so graphically described in Shakespeare, than the boasted veterans of Lee's army.

A few of their sympathizing friends then introduced themselves, and informally surrendered the town to them. They assured us, upon their honor, that no private property should be touched and no citizen would be molested. After this assurance our ladies and children ventured to see and converse with our common enemy.

Their pickets were now sent out the different streets, and then began a series of John Gilpin rides, that can be far better imagined than described. Those who remained to note their arrival now commenced to ride away, and in many instances were commanded to stop, but through fear and determination they put spurs to their horses and dashed off at lightning speed, with a pack of yelling Rebels at their heels firing their carbines at them as they dashed through the mud which flew in plentiful showers over the fleeing, reckless riders. Fortunately the fugitives escaped and nobody was hurt in these promiscuous charges. One carriage with a lot of jewelry, we understand, was overhauled and its contents soon graced the fingers and persons of those who but a few minutes before had pledged their honor to respect and protect our property. [The jewelry valued at $200 was the property of William Boadenhamer.]

The next dash was made on hat, shoe, dry goods, and clothing stores, for an inspection of their contents, and all those that happened to be closed were ordered to be opened, when the men selected whatever suited their wants or fancies. For a few articles they paid good currency, but in most cases our shopmen had to be contented with their bogus paper, and in many instances they deliberately took goods and offered nothing. A certain merchant received an order or draft on the Southern Confederacy for a large bill of goods. The merchant inquired of the man, who gave the draft, if, in case he should visit the South this document would be good in that country; the fellow promptly replied "it would not be worth a darn."

Happily for Hanover, their visit was a short one—as their object was to destroy bridges and otherwise damage our railroads and Junction. They hastened on their mission, fearing that our forces might overtake them before they had accomplished their ends.

The actions of men, as well as the expressions of their countenances, are said to be an unmistakable index of their souls. If there be truth in this, there was many a secession heart lifted up that day, and spoke out its sentiments through a bright and jubilant countenance, if it did not dare to do so with its lips. As the carrion crows will collect around their stinking feast, so our sympathizers flocked around these vagrant thieves, to make themselves generally agreeable and ingratiate themselves into their good graces. But alas, they had their labor for their pains, and the contempt of the Southern banditti, for their traitorism to their country. Whilst, they were yet congratulating one another upon their great moral courage to stay at home and face the foe, and whilst they ridiculed their Republican friends for running away with their property, and abandoned, as they sneeringly said, their families to the tender mercies of the Rebels, Stuart with his cavalry came along and swept away their horses and other property, in spite of all their grips and signs, and desperate efforts to prove that they were his friends and co-adjutors.

Many farmers, after their horses and grain had been taken, were compelled to go with the army to pilot the way, and after their services were no longer required, they were sent, rejoicing, on foot, to their pilfered homes, with the pleasing unction at their hearts that they had enjoyed the society and benefit of a visit from their "magnanimous" friends whose cause and principles they had so warmly espoused and advocated.

To all who have been thus deluded by lying politicians and editors, we would say: "Denounce, forever, such false leaders; Place them upon their wooden horses and ride them out of your minds and community, and suffer them no longer to exercise any influence among honest men."

Ajax.

## HANOVER BATTLE GETS RECOGNITION

The battle of Hanover is celebrated in bronze and granite on the battlefield of Gettysburg in the almost unvisited part of the field dedicated to the cavalry beyond the Devil's Den, and southwest of Round Top. There stands the fine granite monument, with a mounted cavalryman cut in relief, erected by the Fifth New York Cavalry. The monument bears an inscription on a bronze tablet, detailing the part taken by the regiment in the battle of Gettysburg, and revealing further:

"This regiment, June 30th, 1863, met and repulsed a portion of Lee's cavalry, under the personal command of Gen. J. E. B. Stuart, in the streets of Hanover, in a hand to hand fight, capturing Lieut. Col. Payne and 75 men with a loss of 26 men, killed and wounded."

Survivors of the Fifth New York Cavalry which fought both at Gettysburg and Hanover dedicated the monument on the former battlefield July 3, 1888. Charles B. Thomas was the principal speaker. W. T. Ziegler, Gettysburg, furnished a copy of that part of the address pertaining to the battle of Hanover to the Hanover Herald. It appeared in that paper July 7, 1900, as follows:

### Gives Close-up of Battle

When the Confederate troops made their first charge up Frederick street towards the markethouse square, Major John Hammond of the 5th New York turned the head of his column to the left down a side street toward the railroad depot and formed into line on the vacant field which was part of the Commons. Breaking by fours he ordered and led a charge with drawn sabers against the enemy. We met them at the markethouse and were instantly engaged in a hand to hand conflict. Our onslaught was so sudden and strong that notwithstanding they made a gallant resistance they were compelled to withdraw although fresh regiments were brought up to their support again and again, and fell back over the hill under cover of their guns.

In less than fifteen minutes from the time they charged they were driven from the town. Many were found hiding in a wheat field through which they had charged and in other out of the way places, leaving the streets strewn with many of their dead, dying, and wounded, with many dead and wounded horses, and the debris that always follows such a conflict. The loss of the enemy amounted to 25 dead and 80 prisoners. Thirty or forty of their wounded escaped.

### How Colonel Payne Was Captured

Among the prisoners taken was Colonel Payne who commanded a brigade. He was made prisoner by Abram Folger, Company H. The facts as told by Folger were as follows:

"While charging at the edge of town and getting separated from our regiment I was made prisoner by Col. Payne and was being taken to the rear on the main road. Just outside the town was situated a tannery, the vats of which were not covered and very close to the street. I was walking along beside the colonel's orderly, and as we came near these tannery vats, I saw a carbine lying on the ground. When I came up to it, I quickly took it, and seeing it was loaded I fired and killed Payne's horse, which in its death struggle fell over towards the vats, throwing Payne head first into one of them completely under the tanning liquid. Seeing the colonel was safe enough for the moment I turned my attention to the orderly, who finding his pistol had fouled and was useless, was about to jump his horse over the fence to the right and escape that way if he could, but not being able to do so, concluded he had better surrender. The reason I did not fire upon him was that the last shot in the captured carbine was fired at the colonel's horse. As the orderly did not know this it was my play to make him think that instant death awaited him if he attempted to escape.

"So I took him in and disarmed him, and made him help to get the colonel out of the tanning liquid. His gray uniform with its velvet facing and white gauntlet gloves, his face and hair had all been completely stained, so that he presented a most laughable sight.

"I then mounted the orderly's horse and marched them before me to the marketplace, where I turned them over to the authorities who laughed heartily at the comical predicament of the colonel. I had been captured by Col. Payne's command the winter before, and you can just believe I was glad to return to the compliment with interest."

The loss to the 5th at Hanover was nine killed, 31 wounded, and 15 missing. Adjutant Alexander Gall was among the killed. A Minie ball entered his left eye causing instant death.

The inscription on the monument bears witness to the Fifth New York having participated in the battle at Hanover. It reads as follows:

> "5th New York Cavalry, 1st Brigade, 3rd Division Cavalry Corps, Major John Hammond. This regiment June 30 met and repulsed a portion of Lee's cavalry under personal command of General J. E. B. Stuart in the streets of Hanover in a hand to hand fight, capturing Lieut. Col. Payne and 75 men with a loss of 26 men killed and wounded. July 2, attacked Stuart at Hunterstown, and made flank movement here on hill southwest of Round Top."

## STUART'S "PILGRIM'S PROGRESS"

The cavalry battle at Hanover, in accordance with the views of some military critics, including Major General Pleasonton, was the turning point of Lee's invasion of Pennsylvania in 1863. If it had not been for his captured wagon train, Stuart would have passed Hanover and joined Early near York on the morning of June 30. The conflict of arms at Hanover prevented Stuart from passing in front of the Army of the Potomac and uniting with Ewell's corps in the Cumberland Valley or with Early near York, which he had planned to do when he crossed the Potomac on June 27. After the battle had ended at Hanover he could not move westward toward Gettysburg or northward toward East Berlin without meeting a large force of Union infantry or cavalry. He was compelled to make a detour through York County and thus was prevented from communicating with General Lee, who was then concentrating his forces around Gettysburg, preparing for the impending battle. Even though he was successful in delivering the captured wagon train to Lee's quartermaster general, at Gettysburg, on the evening of the second day of the battle, he had not arrived in time for Lee properly to utilize his cavalry force to ascertain Meade's intentions and the disposition of the Federal army corps. Lee, Longstreet and Hill all lamented the absence of Stuart's three brigades of cavalry during the first two days of the great contest. The engagement at Hanover will eventually pass into history as the first serious encounter between the contending forces in the battle of Gettysburg. Its success to the Union arms had an important influence in Meade defeating Lee and driving him back to Virginia.

One can appreciate the supreme importance of the battle of Hanover if one makes it the center of a circle, or the hub of a wheel, and puts General Kilpatrick's victorious forces in the center, and General Stuart's on the rim, and keeping him in that position, traveling three-fourths of a circle of nearly a hundred miles and preventing all communication with his main army, while two whole days of the greater battle of Gettysburg was being fought, and these two days the most critical. It was in these two days that the Confederates victoriously drove our forces over Seminary Ridge east and south through the streets of the town, turning the right back and down Rock Creek inward to Spangler's Spring, and tight upon Culp's Hill. It was at this juncture that General Lee, with anxiety depicted in every line of his face, addressing General Longstreet, asked: "General, where is our cavalry?" He felt their supreme need these two days. The shape of the Federal line at the end of these two days was that of a fish hook, with the line end driven through the Sherfy peach farm over the Valley of Death to Round Top. The prolongation of the battle may have been in great part due to the fact that General Stuart's six thousand cavalry were detained at Hanover and in York County.

Lieutenant Colonel W. W. Blackford, Stuart's adjutant, says in his "War Years With Jeb Stuart": "At Hanover we met Kilpatrick's division of cavalry and had a hot affair with them. We were just opposite Gettysburg and if we could have made our way direct, the fifteen miles of distance to that place would have passed that day, and we could have effected a junction with General Lee the day before the battle began. It was here the wagon train began to interfere with our movements, and if General Stuart could only have known what we do now it would have been burned."

The great point made by General Kilpatrick was to force

General Stuart from his northward course, preventing communication or intercourse with the main Confederate army then in the vicinity of Fairfield and Cashtown, twenty-five miles westward. By the battle of Hanover, General Stuart's command was forced to abandon the highway of travel, into the hill country, of poor roads and indirect communication, going through the borough of Jefferson and as far as New Salem, near the Codorus Creek, twenty-eight miles east of Gettysburg.

At 10 o'clock on the evening of June 30 Stuart called for a conference with his brigade commanders, Wade Hampton, Fitzhugh Lee, and John R. Chambliss. The meeting took place at the residence of John E. Ziegler, a farmer near Hanover Junction. Stuart was completely lost as to where the Confederate army was as well as to where the Union forces were. The council decided to head for Carlisle where he expected other Rebel cavalry would be found.

Hearing of the approach of General Gregg's forces to his right General Stuart turned abruptly north, and after an all-night ride reached Dover, twenty-five miles northeast from Gettysburg, on the morning of July 1.

At Dover about two hundred cavalry captured at Hanover and elsewhere were paroled and allowed to proceed to York. Stuart ordered preparation of a bountiful breakfast at one of the hotels for his staff and other officers. The proprietor was pleasantly surprised when the hotel clerk, George Dick, was paid in U. S. greenbacks instead of in Confederate currency. The citizens of the Hanover area who had been acting as guides were dismissed and other guides pressed into service to show the way to Carlisle. Lee's scouts had not yet contacted Stuart. The captured wagon train was routed from Dover toward Dillsburg and York Springs. Many Dover Township farm horses, estimated at 387, which were taken by General Early's soldiers June 30 were killed on the battlefield at Gettysburg. On that day Early was on his way back to Gettysburg. Early and his officers had dinner at the William Julius Hotel in Davidsburg. Unlike Stuart at Dover Early paid for his meal with four $5 Confederate bills instead of greenbacks. The Confederates when at Davidsburg could hear cannonading to the south, unaware that Stuart and Kilpatrick were battling at Hanover.

Stuart's forces crossed the Baltimore pike at the Brockley farm three and a half miles south of Hanover. Some of his horsemen stopped at the Parr house near the Black Rock road. A spur left by a trooper was retained as a souvenir of the visit.

Mrs. George Dubs, near Dubs' Church, was at home alone when advised that Rebels on a foraging expedition were in the neighborhood. She led a black stallion into the vaulted cellar of the house and carefully closed door and windows. When they arrived, they found two work horses in the barn, but Mrs. Dubs raised so strong a protest that the officer in charge ordered the soldiers to put them back in the stable. Horses captured by Stuart's men in York County numbered about one thousand.

Stuart's visit was the second time the Confederates stopped at Jefferson. White burned a carload of bark there owned by Henry Rebert. Stuart set up cannon at both ends of the town to guard against Union cavalry he feared would follow him. His men robbed market wagons and ransacked the stores of William Christ, Albert Kroft and Jacob Rebert. The last of his troops left the place at 3 a.m. Wednesday. A thousand of Gregg's Union cavalry arrived there Wednesday night. His troopers sang "Dear Father, Will You Meet Us" and "We Will Meet You in the Promised Land" as they marched through.

When between Jefferson and York New Salem some of Stuart's troopers passed Ziegler's stone church amid wooded hills while graveside funeral services were being held in the church cemetery, and they heard the mourners singing "When the Roll Is Called Up Yonder." The entire line of Stuart's corps at dawn of July 1 extended from York New Salem to the borough of Dover.

A brief halt, and Stuart continued his hurried march north through Wellsville, Dillsburg, and rounding the east spur of South Mountain, entered the Cumberland Valley, passing through Boiling Springs to Carlisle, twenty-eight miles north from Gettysburg, and putting the mountain between himself and the main army under General Lee. He called upon the Union troops at Carlisle to surrender. Brigadier General W. F. (Baldy) Smith defied his demands. After burning the U. S. barracks and shelling the town, and hearing that Lee's army had left the Cumberland Valley, General Stuart began to retrace his steps by turning due south, passing through "the Gap" at Mt. Holly, crossing the

*The Karl Forney residence, Frederick Street, central point around which the battle of Hanover was waged June 30, 1863.*

mountain on the Hanover 'pike and traveling towards Hanover almost to New Oxford, where on the evening of July 2, he was intercepted by General Kilpatrick's forces who had all this time remained in the vicinity, encamping June 30 on Bechtel's farm, three miles north of Hanover, and July 1 on Smith's farm, four miles south of Hampton.

In this encounter Stuart's forces were again driven north and west, terminating in a severe skirmish in and about Hunterstown. In the darkness of the night he escaped by the State road into Gettysburg, ten miles away, where he arrived the evening of July 2, with men and horses in exhausted condition.

The first Union troops to enter York after the evacuation of the Rebels consisted of twenty cavalrymen from Kilpatrick's forces Thursday, July 2. The flag on Center Square which had been removed by the Confederates was replaced by one from a soldiers' hospital.

## FORNEY BOYS VIEW FIGHTING

Samuel H. Forney was residing with his parents, Mr. and Mrs. Karl Forney, at their ancestral home on the Littlestown

turnpike in the suburbs of Hanover in 1863. It was here that
Adam Forney located in 1730 as one of the early settlers west
of the Susquehanna. On Tuesday, June 30, 1863, Samuel Forney
and his brother John, later prominent citizen of Steubenville,
Ohio, went to the field on the Forney farm, immediately north
of the Littlestown turnpike and adjoining the village of Pennville. They worked for two hours in the field without anything
specially to attract their attention. About eight o'clock, as they
cast their gaze toward Littlestown, they noticed that the public
road was full of soldiers on horseback. The color of their uniform
convinced them that these mounted men were Union cavalry.
As the advance guard passed through Pennville and was approaching Hanover, Mr. Forney and his brother tied their horses
and sat upon the fence along the road over which the soldiers
were moving four abreast. Near the head along the turnpike rode
the youthful Kilpatrick, who had been promoted a Major General
of cavalry a few days before the age of twenty-six. On both sides
of him were the members of his staff. Half an hour later came
the gallant Custer with his flowing curls, riding a beautiful bay
horse and with two mounted aides on either side of him. Thus
the soldiers passed by, sometimes halting and engaging in conversation with the farmer boys sitting on the fence.

"But you have a soldier in gray coming yonder," said Samuel
Forney to a Federal officer bearing the rank of a lieutenant.

"Yes, he is a scout, we captured him up the road and he is
our prisoner now."

A minute later the man in Confederate uniform stopped his
horse and engaged in conversation with the Forney boys on
the fence.

"So you are plowing corn," he said. "I often plowed corn
myself down in North Carolina, before I entered the army. I am
a soldier now but I wish I were back in my native State, working
in the fields quietly like yourselves, for this is a cruel war and
I hope it will soon be over."

Then the column moved onward into town and still another
captured scout in Confederate uniform came riding along with
other soldiers.

And so the Federal troops moved on two long hours without
incident. Just before ten o'clock in the forenoon, the heroic

Farnsworth, riding with his staff at the head of his brigade passed through Pennville and entered Hanover. He was a dashing young soldier of twenty-seven, who had just been made a Brigadier General at Frederick, Maryland. Meantime the Forney boys had gone back to the plow. The horses were moving slowly along between the rows of corn.

A few minutes after ten o'clock, loud yells and shrieks were heard out the Westminster road, one hundred yards from Pennville. The Thirteenth Virginia Cavalry came dashing down the road, and just as these mounted men were approaching the rear of Farnsworth's brigade, they fired a volley from their carbines. This was a signal for the opening of the engagement. It was the Eighteenth Pennsylvania Cavalry, commanded by Major Darlington that received the first attack of the enemy.

"In a few minutes," said Mr. Forney, "the fields immediately north of the Littlestown road and west of Hanover were filled with mounted soldiers. The Union troops had quickly fallen back through town to the assistance of the rear regiment which had been attacked."

While the air was filled with yells and shrieks, and the opposing forces were in deadly combat along the Littlestown and Westminster roads, the Forney boys unhitched their horses and hastened with them across the fields toward McSherrystown, while the enemy's balls were whistling over their heads. They escaped to the Geiselman farm where they remained until late in the afternoon. Some twenty dead horses lay along the road between the Forney farm and the Keller home on the Westminster road that evening. Mr. Forney helped to drag these dead horses away the following day. When he returned to his home in the evening, three wounded Union soldiers and one Confederate were lying in the front room on the northwest side of his home.

The Confederate soldier was near the end of his career; he had fought his last battle. He had been shot through the breast, and was now struggling with death. Even the wounded Union soldiers lying by his side asked that he should be comforted. The Forney family tenderly cared for him until the next day when he died. Before he breathed his last he pulled from his inside pocket a copy of the New Testament and opening the lid, help up to the sister of Mr. Forney the open book. On a flyleaf was the name of his only sister, a young woman residing in North Carolina.

"Take this book," he said, "and send it to my home. That address will reach my sister. She gave me this book when I left home two years ago, and she asked me to keep it and bring it back again when the cruel war shall have ended. It has ended now for me."

The name of this soldier was Samuel Reddick. He was a sergeant in the Second North Carolina Regiment, and had served nearly two years in the army. Miss Forney opened a correspondence with the soldier's sister, when it was learned that his father was a clergyman. In reply to her letter the father requested that the soldier's grave be marked. Meantime he communicated with another Confederate soldier who had been wounded and taken to the hospital in Hanover. He told Mr. Reddick that his son had been buried along a fence under locust trees by the roadside. The position of the grave was near a red barn covered with slate within a hundred yards southwest of Hanover. A year later some friends or relatives came to Hanover, took up the body and sent it to North Carolina, where it was buried in the village graveyard. Samuel Reddick had been wounded in front of the Karl Forney home.

During the fight he moved into the yard, and climbed up the steps to the porch, where he lay for several hours.

The Federal soldiers who were in the Forney home were removed to the hospital on Baltimore Street, then known as the Pleasant Hill Hotel, and later the property of Mr. Strubinger.

---

## "CONFEDERATE GRAVE UNDER THE ROSES"

### From "Bullet and Shell" by George F. Williams

"Late in the afternoon of the first day of July we reached the picturesque town of Hanover. Near the cross-roads were lying the bloated carcasses of half a dozen cavalry horses, evidently slain in an engagement between Kilpatrick's and Stuart's troops, a few hours before our arrival.

"Close to the road, near the scene of the cavalry fight, stood a farmhouse, at the gate of which was an old-fashioned pump and horse-trough. The pumphandle was in constant motion, as the weary, foot-sore soldiers flocked around it to quench their thirst with the delicious water that flowed into the mossy trough.

"Coming up and waiting for my turn to drink, I noticed a sunburnt, gray-haired man leaning over his rude gate, watching the troops. He was dressed in a faded, well-worn suit of homespun, having, no doubt, spent the day in the hayfield; and I could see that he was pleased that his pump was doing such good service.

"'Good evening, sir,' said I to him, removing my cap, and mopping the perspiration from my face. 'It's rather hot weather, this, for marching?'

"'I 'spose 'tis, though I never did any marching,' was his brief response.

"As the old farmer uttered the words he moved a little, and my eye was attracted by a new-made grave among a clump of rose bushes, just inside the fence. Wondering at the sight, I ventured to ask the reason for its being there.

"'Whose grave is that?' said I, pointing to the mound of fresh earth.

"'A Johnnie,' he replied laconically. 'One that got killed in a fight the horsemen had here yesterday.'

"'Indeed! and so you buried him!'

"'Yes; buried him myself. They left him lyin' in the road out thar, just as he fell.. I could do no less, you know.'

"'Of course! But why did you make your rose-garden a graveyard?'

"'Wa-al, it was the wimmen that wanted it so. Yer see, stranger,' and the old man's voice trembled and grew husky— 'yer see, I had a boy once. He went out with the Pennsylvanay Resarves, and fou't along with McClellan, down thar among them Chioka-oming swamps. And one day a letter come. It was writ by a woman; and she told us as how a battle had been fou't near her house, whilt she and another woman lay hid all day in the cellar. When the battle was o'er, them wimmen came out, and found our Johnny thar, his hair all bloody and tangled in the grass. So they digged a grave in the soft earth of their garden, and buried my boy right amongst their flowers, for the sake of the mother who would never see him again. So when I saw that poor Johnnie a-layin' out thar, all dead and bloody in the dust of the road, I sed I'd bury him. And the gals, they sed, "Yes, father, bury him among the rose-trees," That's why I did it, stranger.'

"Then the poor old father's voice was choked by a smothered sob, while a faint cry behind him betrayed the presence of a sister to the dead hero lying in his garden grave near Richmond.

" 'Indeed, sir,' said I, feeling my own throat tighten over the sweet pathos of the little story, 'I can appreciate the love you bear your dead son. It must be some consolation to remember what you have done for the man whose body lies there under the bushes.'

" 'Yes, stranger; that 'ere grave ain't much,'—and the old man turned to look at the rude mound his hands had made—'it ain't much, but it will be something to remember our Johnny by.'

"Bidding the farmer good-by, I hastened after the regiment, my eyes dimmed with tears, but my spirits strangely strengthened by his touching instance of human love and forgiveness."

---

## PASTOR ZIEBER RECOLLECTS

This account is not intended to be a description of the entire engagement, but such part of it as was witnessed by an honored citizen, Dr. W. K. Zieber, who in 1905 was in his eightieth year.

The Rev. William K. Zieber, D.D., came to Hanover in 1859 as pastor of Emmanuel Reformed Church. He soon became prominent and influential in the affairs of the borough, and in 1863, when Pennsylvania was threatened with invasion by the Confederate Army under General Robert E. Lee, he was chosen president of the Committee of Safety for the borough of Hanover. His recollections of events at Hanover during the war and battle of June 30th 1863, are given in the following words:

The town of Hanover was in a condition of suppressed excitement from the time of the opening of the Civil War until the arrival of the first Confederate troops on June 27th, 1863. Even before the hostilities began, many refugees from Virginia largely from the Shenandoah Valley, passed through Hanover, coming by way of Harper's Ferry and Frederick. They were fleeing from

(Hanover Herald, July 15, 1905. Prowell)

Dr. William K. Zieber
1825-1916
*Pastor of Emmanuel Reformed Church.*

their State which threatened to be the seat of war in the east. These people traveled in wagons, loaded with bedding, furniture and household utensils, often stopping over night in Center Square and telling marvelous tales of the progress of secession in the South. Some of them brought their horses and cattle with them. Most of these refugees from Virginia were loyal people who did not want to join the secession party, while others, frightened by what they feared would occur, traveled aimlessly northward with no definite place of destination.

The excitement was intense when our citizens received the news of the attack on the 6th Massachusetts regiment while passing through Baltimore April 19, 1861, on its way to Washington. The whole town and community round about were thrown into confusion soon after a false rumor to the effect that a band of ruffians from Baltimore were marching into Pennsylvania toward Hanover. The cause of this strange story seems to have been owing to the fact that a number of Baltimore citizens who sided with the Secessionists marched through Maryland into the valley of Virginia to join the Confederate army.

One Sunday morning in April, 1861, while I was preaching a sermon to my congregation in the Reformed Church at Hanover, a messenger came to the door of the church, passed up the aisle and told one of my congregation that if there were any members of the local military companies in the audience, they were to report immediately for duty. The gentleman who received the news from the messenger walked up to the pulpit and asked me to make this announcement to the audience. I stopped in the midst of my sermon and spoke as follows:

"If there are any members of the Marion Rifles or the Hanover Infantry present in this audience, they are expected to report at once at their places of rendezvous."

It was on that day that these two companies in answer to a telegram marched to the railroad station and went on a special train to York where they immediately enlisted in the three months' service in answer to the first call of President Lincoln for 75,000 men. It was difficult for me to continue services in the church, owing to the confusion, and I dismissed the congregation. Soon afterward, drums were beating and fifes playing the march for the soldiers on their way to the train. The excitement that day was at a high pitch but the prompt action of our local military companies showed a patriotic ardor and loyalty to the United States government that was of the highest commendation.

It was not until 1862, just before the battle of Antietam, that the first real indications were shown of the danger of an invasion by the southern army, but the feeling was not intense at that time in Hanover.

Soon as the news came in 1863 that Gen. Lee with his army had crossed the Potomac, there were constant rumors of the approach of the enemy toward Gettysburg and Hanover. Farmers in the vicinity fled with their horses across the Susquehanna. Bank deposits and valuable articles owned by private citizens were sent away. Some people concealed their treasures in their houses or buried them in their yards or gardens. Large supplies of goods and merchandise were also hidden away.

It was on Saturday morning, June 27, 1863, that a countryman rode into town calling out to the citizens:

"The Confederates are coming. They are now in McSherrystown. . . ."

This being the first approach of the enemy, women and children went into their houses, closed the windows and looked out through the half open shutters as the Southern troopers entered the town. This was a detachment of cavalry, 240 men, under Lieut. Col. White, which Gen. Early had sent from Gettysburg to burn the railroad bridges at Hanover Junction when he and his division of 9000 men were to take possession of York on the following day. I was standing in the Square with a number of male citizens, watching to catch the first glimpse of the approaching enemy. Looking out Carlisle Street, I saw two cavalrymen coming into the street from the McSherrystown road.

"There they come," shouted the Rev. J. C. Kurtz, who was standing by my side.

These two mounted soldiers rode up to the Square. A hundred yards behind them, accompanied by a citizen from the vicinity of McSherrystown, rode Col. White, commander of this body of men, the 35th Virginia Battalion. They seemed to be in a state of trepidation. Every man had his carbine in his right hand with his finger on the trigger ready for any emergency. We remained standing by the market shed watching their movements when a soldier in the lead rode up to us and said:

"Where do all these people come from?"

"From the town of Hanover and its immediate vicinity," I replied.

"Are there any Yankee soldiers in town?" he continued. But no one gave a definite answer. He seemed surprised that there were so many able-bodied men in Pennsylvania who had not yet enlisted in the Union Army, for at that time nearly all the Southern men were under arms.

"So you Yankees are not all in the army, I see," continued the soldier.

"No," I replied, "we are not but we are beginning to find out what real war is, and I suppose we will soon all join the Union Army."

"The devil you say!" responded the Confederate soldier. The

rest of the soldiers came slowly riding up Carlisle Street. The commander immediately sent guards to the ends of every street. This was done to prevent citizens with their wagons and horses from leaving town. Stores were visited where some soldiers obtained boots or shoes and articles of clothing. They did not ask for anything to eat during the half hour or more that they remained in Hanover, but they took a few horses belonging to country people who had come to Hanover in order to find out the news. At a given signal, the entire squad of Confederates started on their way out the York road toward Hanover Junction, where they burned the railroad bridges and then moved northward joining Early's forces at York.

For two days thereafter, our town was entirely cut off from communication with the oustide world. We received no newspapers; the telegraph wires were cut, and all we could learn of the movement of the Union or Confederate forces toward Gettysburg was gathered from rumors. The day after White's Cavalry left Hanover, a few stragglers were found in town. As there were no Union soldiers here, these Confederates were impudent and boastful in their manner. There were no police authorities present to arrest them and as chairman of the Committee of Safety, I walked up to them and said: "What are you doing here?" And with the assistance of others, arrested them and took them to the Central Hotel, where they were placed on a wagon and conveyed to Westminster, Md.

On the following day, June 29th, rumors were rife concerning the approach of the enemy, for we had heard that Gen. Early was then in possession of York. The excitement was very high in Hanover because we were unable to get authentic news of the movement of the armies.

On the morning of June 30th, several persons came into town stating that the enemy was coming from Littlestown. When the advance guard of these troops entered Frederick Street from the southwest, loud cheers of welcome were heard from both men and women because we saw they wore uniforms of blue and carried the American flag. It was the arrival of Major Kilpatrick's division of cavalry, numbering 4000 men. They came up Frederick Street marching six abreast, moving slowly across Centre Square, out Abbottstown Street, and halted for a while in the town, most of the men remaining on their horses. I was standing at the head of York Street and, like other citizens, greeting our men and giving them words of cheer. Some one told me that Gen. Kilpatrick and other officers had gone into the residence of Mr. Jacob Wirt, on Frederick Street (now the site of the State Theater), and gave me the message that I should go there and meet them. A large number of citizens had gathered at the house when I entered. I met this youthful commander of twenty-six years, who two days before had been promoted a Major General of Cavalry, in the parlor of Mr. Wirt's house. I engaged in conversation with him as he stood looking out of the window. Gen. Custer, with his long, flowing curls, and dressed in a suit of velvet, stood by his side. They were both tired and worn out from the continuous marching of several days.

Gen. Kilpatrick turned around to Mr. Wirt and myself after he had looked up and down the street viewing his warriors on horseback, and said:

"I pity my men, for they have had no breakfast and they are very hungry. We have been marching hard ever since we crossed the Potomac and have been short of rations for three days. I do not have all my commissary wagons with me."

I answered him immediately by saying: "Our people are thoroughly loyal and we are glad to have you come. We have been expecting the approach of the enemy for the past two days. All you have to do is to give the word and we will see that your soldiers are fed."

He thanked us heartily for our generous offer and then I walked out to the front steps of Mr. Wirt's residence, where a large number of citizens, both male and female, were still assembled, and spoke to them as follows:

"These soldiers are our friends and protectors. They are tired and hungry. The best thing we can do is to feed them."

Immediately after hearing this, the crowd of citizens dispersed to their homes. In a remarkably short time men, women, girls and boys from every street in town were busily engaged in carrying food to the soldiers. They brought bread, meat, coffee, milk and anything good they had in their houses. The soldiers were very thankful and frequently turned around to their generous friends remarking: "This is God's country."

As soon as one regiment or brigade had been given their lunches, which they ate on horseback, they moved onward toward Abbottstown to give place to another brigade, which was fed in the same way. The whole division of 4000 men had nearly all passed through the town by 10 o'clock. At that time, when our citizens were feeding the rear of Gen. Farnsworth's brigade including the Eighteenth Pennsylvania Cavalry, we heard shooting out the Westminster road within a short distance of town. At this instant a Union officer, Major Hammond, of the 5th New York Cavalry, mounted on a black horse, rode hastily up Frederick Street to the Square and in loud tones spoke as follows:

"Citizens will please go to their homes and into their cellars. In a few minutes there will be fighting on your streets."

This remark was passed along the line all through the town. Many went to their homes but still others remained on the streets when the Confederate advance came up Frederick Street in close pursuit of the rear of our troops and through every alley, dashing into Centre Square, where a hand-to-hand, encounter occurred. They drove our troops out Abbottstown Street to the railroad.

I then returned to my home on York Street, in the residence later owned by Cornelius Young. I placed my family in one room. They closed all the shutters and locked the front door of the house. I then gave every member of my family directions that when I returned I would give a certain knock on the door so they would know me. Walking up York Street toward Center Square I met Dr. Hinkle and said to him:

"Doctor, our services are needed; there are wounded soldiers up there. Will you go with me and render them assistance?"

"Yes, sir I will go," responded the doctor promptly. We walked up to the head of York Street. At this instant a band of Confederates was coming down Abbottstown Street toward the Square with a number of Union prisoners and ambulance wagons. After they had passed out Frederick Street the doctor and I picked up three or four dead soldiers, lying on the street between Centre Square and the Reformed Church, and carried them to the side-walks. We also looked after the wounded lying in the place and the doctor began to render surgical aid. There were a number of dead horses lying on the streets.

*Civil War Abbottstown Street looking towards Center Square. Top of Albright Building on Broadway noticeable. Melsheimer home and Emmanuel Reformed Church on right.*

During the return charge of the Federal troops driving the enemy out of town, I saw a body of men led by Gen. Custer come dashing down Abbottstown Street. They met a squad of the enemy right in front of us, and a sharp encounter took place.

The doctor and myself like other citizens who remained on the streets during the fight, had lost all consciousness of danger and whenever we saw our troops gaining any advantage over the enemy, we applauded them.

Soon after this there was a lull for an hour or more. I walked down to the Square and at the northwest corner of Broadway and Centre Square, I saw a man lying on the street, blood issuing profusely from his head. He was a Confederate soldier, but as he was a fellowman supposed to be dying, I went to his assistance. As I lifted his head from the ground he partially recovered consciousness and with a dazed expression looked into my face saying, "Where am I?"

"You are a wounded man and in need of assistance. I come to help you," I replied.

"Have the Yankees got me?" he said.

"No matter where you are, you are in the hands of friends," was my response.

At this instant he seemed entirely to recover consciousness and continued: "God bless you. I was forced into this war and compelled to enter the army. Are you a surgeon? If you are, do what you can for me."

"I am a preacher," I answered as I was washing the blood from his face. Then he said, "Pray for me. My wound is serious. I am suffering extreme pain."

The lull in the battle still continued. The dead and wounded had been taken from the Square and in response to his request, I knelt and offered up a fervent prayer for him. Then he told me that his name was Sergeant Peale and that he belonged to the 2d North Carolina Cavalry. He had been shot in the breast and his wound was serious. In falling from his horse his skull had been fractured. I was washing the blood from his face with a sponge and water handed me by Dr. William Bange, when a Confederate officer dashed across the Square followed by a squad of about ten men, toward us. Dismounting from his horse and raising his sword, I heard him say "Halt."

Then he approached me, saying: "What are you doing to that man?"

I replied. "We are trying to aid a wounded man and we will take care of him." "Thank you, sir," said the officer. He then mounted his horse and with his troopers rode away. These were the last Confederate soldiers that I saw in town that day for the fighting on the streets had ended.

Then the question came up what we should do with the wounded. After talking with some citizens, we decided to use Marion Hall, near the public school house as a temporary hospital. The cavalry fighting had ended but the opposing forces were still watching each other expecting another attack. While this was going on, citizens carried the wounded soldiers to the hospital where they were taken care of by the local physicans, Drs. Smith, Culbertson, Eckert and Hinkle and the army surgeons.

Meantime a cannonading took place across the town between

the Confederate batteries, located on the Cemetery grounds, and west of them the Union batteries on Bunker Hill. The screaming and bursting of shells continued for an hour or more. Several balls and shells fell on the streets of Hanover.

---

## SAMUEL ALTHOFF'S NARRATIVE

Samuel Althoff at the age of 83, related with enthusiasm in July, 1905, his observations in Hanover, June 30, 1863, when the cavalry fight took place between Kilpatrick's division of Union cavalry and three brigades of Lee's Confederate cavalry corps under General "Jeb" Stuart. He said: "I was at my home where I now reside on Baltimore Street when Kilpatrick's men entered Hanover. Like the rest of our citizens interested in seeing them move through town, I went up to Centre Square and watched them passing by and helped to pass out food to them as they moved along on horseback. Shortly before 10 a.m. I was standing in front of Shirk's hardware store when someone in the store handed me a box of cigars. I took them out to the soldiers who eagerly grabbed for them and the box was soon empty. When I heard the shooting out the Westminster road, I returned to my home on Baltimore Street where my family had gone to the cellar. Eager to watch the contest, I went to the garret of my house and climbed out the trap door to the roof. I saw the mounted soldiers dashing back and forward along the roads and in the fields west of town. In a grain field southwest, I saw Confederate sharpshooters rising from the tall grain and firing at the Union troops in and around the town. The Confederate cannon on Cemetery Hill and near the Westminster road began to fire shot and shell over the town at the Federal soldiers on Bunker Hill.

"About this time, an officer of the New York Regiment rode down Baltimore Street and commanded me to get off the roof of the house, for I was in danger of being shot, so I went down stairs. Sometime later a squad of soldiers, probably two companies formed in line on horseback on Baltimore Street facing toward the Confederates west of Mt. Olivet Cemetery. I noticed a captain riding along the line, who in loud and impetuous manner, commanded each soldier to watch his men and take aim, if

the enemy again dashed into town. But there was no charge by
the Confederates into town after this incident.

"Late in the afternoon, I went to the Square, where I saw half
a dozen dead horses lying. The wounded soldiers had been
carried to Marion Hall near the No. 1 Public School building,
where they received careful surgical attention from Dr. Gardner,
the army surgeon, and Doctors Smith, Culbertson and Hinkle,
of Hanover.

"During the fighting in the Square, Sergeant Peale, of North
Carolina, was seriously wounded at the northeast angle of the
Square. In falling from his horse, his head struck a stone which
fractured his skull. This was chiefly the cause of his death. He
too, with other Confederates wounded, was taken to the im-
provised hospital at Marion Hall and in the Flickinger foundry
on York Street. After the Federal soldiers were taken care of, the
surgeons and Hanover citizens looked after the wounded Confederates for they were fellow Americans in distress who needed
attention. Surgeon Gardner and Dr. Smith presently stood by
the cot upon which Sergeant Peale, the Confederate, was lying.
He was in a dazed condition. The doctors tried to treat the
fractured skull, when he arose from his stupor and asked for a
clergyman. It was discovered that he belonged to the Catholic
Church. Father Kittannig, of Conewago Chapel, was sent for.
When the parish priest arrived, he administered the last rites
of the church to the dying soldier, who breathed his last in the
hospital on the following day. Sergeant Peale was a man of
large stature and possibly 40 years old. When asked if he had
any relatives living, he answered that he had a sister in North
Carolina. Late in the evening of the following day his death
occurred. This North Carolina soldier was buried in the Catholic
Cemetery adjoining the Conewago Church."

## TELEGRAPHERS IN DEMAND

Stories of the Civil War, when they describe local incidents,
will always have romantic interest. For a period of three weeks
in June and July, 1863, the seat of the war in the East had been
transferred — Virginia to Maryland to Southern Pennsylvania.
Flushed with his victory at Chancellorsville, General Lee with

an army of eighty thousand men composed of infantry, cavalry and artillery began his march northward during the early part of June. This was "The Flower of the Confederate Army," and every man of rank and file was persuaded to believe that Lee would march in triumph through the Keystone State, down the Cumberland Valley through Harrisburg and York, to Philadelphia and capture that city and dictate the terms of peace in the city of New York.

The advance of Lee's army reached Chambersburg where the commander and two army corps rendezvoused for three days while General Ewell, with the Second Corps moved to Carlisle and halted there before threatening Harrisburg. General Early with one division of Ewell's corps moved eastward over the mountains by way of Chambersburg Turnpike and reached Gettysburg in the afternoon of June 26. The same day Early dispatched a band of four hundred cavalry under Colonel White of the Fifteenth Virginia Regiment, to gallop in haste through New Oxford and Hanover to Hanover Junction, where he was ordered to burn the railroad bridges there across the Codorus, and to cut off railway communication between Harrisburg and Washington. Orders were also given to destroy telegraph lines, or at least to capture operators, seize their instruments, and compel them to use their knowledge of telegraphy for the Confederates.

Hugh D. Scott, then a dapper young man with black hair, mustache and goatee, was the operator at Gettysburg. He remained at his post sending out such information to Washington, Baltimore, and Philadelphia as came to him, in reference to the movements of the Confederate forces. In the afternoon of June 26, the people of Gettysburg heard of the advance under Early moving down the turnpike. A dense fog hung over the mountains and this prevented couriers from seeing the enemy until they were approaching Gettysburg.

### Escapes by Spring Wagon

Early's advance had a skirmish at Marsh Creek with the Twenty-sixth Pennsylvania Regiment of Emergency men, who on account of the fog could not see the enemy until he had reached within range of rifles. This small body of Union men were driven into Gettysburg in haste and marched northward toward Harrisburg.

When operator Scott, sitting by his instrument, in his telegraph office at Gettysburg, heard that a band of Confederate cavalry was within two hundred yards of town, he had a splendid horse hitched to an open spring wagon, and then with a companion, drove rapidly down the turnpike towards York. Half a dozen Confederates pursued him on their spavined plugs. Operator Scott had a fleet horse and escaped unhurt, although he was fired upon with carbines by the mounted men. He reached York in safety, and often related with enthusiasm his escape from being captured. Before he left his office he sent a telegram to Daniel E. Trone, the operator at Hanover, to prepare to flee. His last message was "The Johnnies are now entering Gettysburg." Then he cut loose his instrument, threw it in his wagon, and disappeared with all possible haste.

### Rolling Stock Sent Away

Two days before, Captain A. W. Eichelberger, president of the Gettysburg and Hanover Railroad, had sent the locomotives and other rolling stock to Hanover Junction and from thence through York to Columbia to a place of safety. He did not want to have the Confederates take the equipment, and so sent it out of their reach. On June 28, or the day after the arrival of the Confederates at Hanover, the bridge over the Susquehanna at Wrightsville was burned by the Union troops at Columbia for the purpose of preventing the Confederates from crossing, without fording the river. They were kept at Columbia until after the battle at Gettysburg and then brought back to Hanover by way of Harrisburg and York.

The town of Hanover was in a state of excitement in the morning of June 27 when Colonel White and his men entered the town. Daniel E. Trone threw his new instrument in a loft above his office, and left two defective ones on the table. As soon as the Confederates entered Carlisle Street three of them were sent to capture the telegraph operator, but he had fled "to parts unknown." They took the old instruments and dashed them to pieces. Fortunately they did not find the good one in

*Captain A. W. Eichelberger (1819-1901), president of the Hanover Branch Railroad, donated the Eichelberger Academy building to Hanover borough for use as a High School in 1900. He was a great-grandson of Philip Frederick Eichelberger who migrated to Lancaster County from Sinsheim, Germany, in 1761, and later bought 220 acres of land southeast of Hanover. Captain Eichelberger was a carpenter by trade. He spent from 1843-1851 in Georgia and Alabama, dealing in carriages and coverlets sent to him from the north and operating a gristmill and sawmill with his brother Jacob.*

the loft, and it remained there untouched for future use, when the operator returned, three days later.

Colonel White and his men galloped toward Hanover, and they were heard passing through McSherrystown. A clergyman from Hanover rode out the McSherrystown turnpike, and when he caught sight of the enemy, returned to Hanover and notified the people. At this time Joseph S. Leib, the freight and passenger agent for the Hanover Junction, Hanover and Gettysburg Railroad, was at the station on Railroad Street. Daniel E. Trone had been the operator for the Railroad Company since 1860, when the first telegraph line was extended from the Junction to Hanover. William H. Shock, living in West Virginia, at the age of 84, told Historian Prowell that Mr. Trone learned the art of telegraphy under him at Hanover in six weeks. In 1863 he was rated as a first-class operator. His last dispatch was sent to the Junction and to Baltimore. In this message he said to the operators at the other end of the line: "The Confederates are coming, and I guess I will leave."

## Danny Trone Writes Letter

The following letter to Captain A. W. Eichelberger, president of the Hanover, Hanover Junction and Gettysburg Railroad, from Daniel Trone, telegrapher, telling of his experiences during Lee's invasion of Pennsylvania, was presented to the Hanover Public Library's historical collection by Mrs. William D. Himes, New Oxford, and is included in this volume by permission of Mrs. Mabel C. Wolcott, librarian.

Balto. June 30. 1863

A. W. Eichelberger
    Phila. Dr. Sir,

I left home at 11:15 a.m. on Saturday (June 27). The rebels arrived at 10 o'clock. The first notice I had of their Approach was hearing firing and yelling, when I looked out of the window of my office and saw about a dozen rebels after Abdiel Gitt and another man who I did not recognize coming as hard as they could ride up the alley between Youngs warehouse and Wintrodes Hotel. The Rebels were about 40 yards behind and they shot at least a dozen times after them while going across the commons in the rear of the warehouse and up towards the Abbottstown pike. The rebels ran up against the cut of Grove & Schmucks switch which brought them to a halt and before they could get around Mr Gitt was up at the pike and escaped. As soon as I saw them coming I pulled up my instruments and ran up in the garret of the warehouse and hid them under the floor. Wm. Stall was with me and he was looking out of the gable-end window after the rebels who went after Mr. Gitt. After they gave up the chase they returned by the same way and 3 or 4 of them stopped on the back platform of the house and commenced to force the door in seeing which Stall & I

DANIEL E. TRONE
*Hanover Telegrapher.*

thought it best to leave as soon as possible so we went down and out the front door which was standing open. I locked the door quietly and we then went up the track intending to go towards the Junction but when we got to Abbottstown pike we saw that they had left a picket there and we could not get out. Stall then went over towards the foundry which is the last I saw of him while I went down to the warehouse again and found that the rebels had not yet forced the door in so I went down to Wintrodes Hotel and stayed there until the (*sic*) had broken in when I heard them breaking open things and forcing the safe; I then went up town and stopped at McCauslands while about 50 rebel Cavalry were on the square. McCausland told me he heard Jos Dellone tell the rebels that you were Capt. of the cavalry Company. I then tried to escape as I feared the Copperhead would inform on me, as I passed Heimans Clothing Store the rebels were in and helping themselves. They also had opened other stores I got out by the Westminster road walked about 3 miles then got a horse and rode to Westminster and from there here by railroad. If you see Mr Metzger tell him that Reuben Young had driven him (What horse?) down to his warehouse and was feeding him with oats when the rebels came in. I had a half hour previously sent his book in to his wife with a boy so the book is all safe. I dont know anything about what became of the horse and buggy. he was still standing at the door of the warehouse when I passed and Wm. Young has a letter here from Reuben who says that they did not take the horse. The instruments I had all packed in a box and stowed away and don't know whether they found them or not. I had not time to take them away. The reason why I did not learn sooner is because I placed considerable reliance in that despatch I sent you from Mr. Busby stating Rebels would not be there that day and probably not that night. It is well you refused to send it as not more than a half hour later the rebels came in. I tried to get home last night by way of Westminster but the rebels had possession of the place and the train returned to Balto. I just saw a letter from Hanover saying that the rebels were after me and were hunting for me in town. I don't think I will venture home now until I can be assured of being safe. I will give you particulars when I see you. The train from the Junction came down safely Saturday night. I came down in it from Relay House. Telegraph communication is all right to Junction and no bridges burned between here and Junction. They burned all the cars at Junction and also our turntable and Nor Central bridge there. Have not heard of any other damage to our road.

From

D. E. Trone

## Leib Leaves by Handcar

On hearing of the approach of the enemy raiders Joseph Leib, agent for the railroad, put to use the last remnant of rolling stock left at Hanover. This was a handcar which was operated by two revolving wheels. It required considerable muscular effort to move it with speed. Fortunately a trackman with two brawny arms trained to hard physical labor was available. He turned the one wheel and Mr. Leib the other. In that way they moved rapidly out from the freight yard on the way toward Hanover Junction. Two Rebels followed them on horseback firing their carbines and shouting: "Halt, you sons of Yanks," but they were beyond the range of the balls from the carbines. It took them several hours to reach Hanover Junction, but they arrived there in safety. Many farmers came there to hear the news. "Well, it's lively enough," said Joseph Leib. "The Confederates are in Hanover, and I believe they are coming down here to burn the railroad bridges. This fact had been given to the people of Hanover, and I guess we will get our handcar over to the Northern Central and move toward Baltimore."

### Search Town for "Yanks"

Meantime Colonel White and his mounted men had halted in Hanover for an hour. They passed up Carlisle Street to the Square, each man with his forefinger of the right hand on the trigger of his carbine, for they thought there might be some Union troops in town and fire upon them from where they were concealed in buildings or in the alleys. They were frequently heard to say "Are there any Yanks in town?" The answer was given in the negative. They stopped in Hanover briefly to buy hats and shoes and paid for them in Confederate money.

They then remounted and rode away through Jefferson and in that vicinity captured nearly three hundred farm horses which they exchanged for their own worn-out mounts; then went on to the Junction, burned three bridges there, ransacked the store of Henry Bott at Seven Valleys and rode to York. There they joined Early's Division of ten thousand men who had taken possession of the town.

Two hours before the troops reached Hanover Junction, Leib had left for Baltimore. In that city, he found Trone. Confederate sympathizers poked fun at them for running away.

"This is what you get supporting the Lincoln administration, which will soon be done gone. We hear that Lee with a big army is moving on Harrisburg. The jig will be up, and the war ended."

"Not quite so bad as that," said Danny Trone. "Before I left Hanover I heard that the Potomac Army is after Lee under a new commander and there will soon be a heavy battle somewhere in southern Pennsylvania, but no one can tell where." The people of Baltimore who supported the Union received this news with deep interest for the same information had come to Baltimore by wire from Frederick where Meade and his army were concentrating.

## Last Train for Junction

An account of the railroad and telegraph activities was given by Joseph Leib, of the Western Maryland, whose long service in the railroad business at Hanover began in 1855. The telegraph line was completed from Hanover to the Junction in 1860, and then for the first time the intelligent burghers could talk by electricity with the outside world. The railroad had been in operation for several years before this event, and as soon as Captain Eichelberger, its president, heard of the approach of the Confederate army in its advance northward in 1863, he made preparations to ship all the engines and rolling stock of the railroad company from Hanover to the Junction, as a temporary place of safety.

Conductor John Eckert and an engineer took the last Hanover Branch train to the Junction. The rolling stock did not remain there long, being moved on to York and then to Columbia; but Superintendent Blair of the Northern Central Railroad, had telegraphed to Hanover for the officials of the local railroad to keep one engine at Hanover Junction to await orders for any special purpose that might be needed. This order was obeyed until 4 o'clock on Saturday afternoon, when someone shouted "The Johnnies are coming." It was the same body of men that had disturbed Dan Trone in his telegraphic communication with them a few hours before at Hanover.

"Put on steam," said Conductor John Eckert to the engineer, "and we will hurry away as fast as we can. We need no more pressing orders to leave than the approach of the enemy. They shall not have the train if we can help it."

Just then the Confederates caught sight of the train and they galloped ahead with all possible speed, expecting to catch it before it rounded the curve below the Junction, but they did not succeed.

The engine was called "The Heidelberg," and was long ago cast into discard, but the coach, which, with the engine, completed the train that escaped being captured at the Junction was still in existence in 1904.

### Return to Hanover

Leib and Trone remained in Baltimore until the evening of June 30, and then prepared to return to Hanover after getting permits required. The United States Government had taken possession of the Northern Central, also the Hanover and Gettysburg Railroad. The two men had heard by then of the cavalry fight at Hanover which ended in Kilpatrick's driving a force of five thousand men under Stuart out of town.

After leaving Baltimore, Trone and Leib got as far as Parkton, and there slept in a car one night and the next day drove to Shrewsbury. At the station they mounted a four-wheeled lime car, which on account of the down grade, moved by gravity nearly to Hanover Junction. They frequently had to draw brakes to answer questions, for everybody wanted to hear the latest news. There were no trains running then on account of the bridges' being burned over the Codorus Creek at Seven Valleys.

From Hanover Junction, they started on foot to Hanover, inspecting the telegraph lines along the way. They were badly damaged by the Confederates when they passed through Jefferson a few days before. At Valley Junction, a government engine overtook them and they were asked to ride on it to Hanover. The engine went as far as New Oxford and then returned to Baltimore with dispatches from the battle of Gettysburg, which was then taking place. By the next day at noon, government telegraphic operators had the telegraph line repaired to Baltimore, and Dan Trone climbed up to the loft above his office and there found his battery and sounder, which were fortunately still in good condition.

## First News to Lincoln

About two hours after his arrival he was called upon by newspapermen representing the New York Tribune. They asked Danny Trone for the exclusive right of his instrument to send news to New York and Washington the next two days. They had the description of the first two days of the battle written and ready to be sent. During the next forty-eight hours operator Trone sat at his desk and sent over the wire the report of the battle as given by the newspapermen. The news sent from Hanover was the first definite knowledge that President Abraham Lincoln received concerning the progress of the battle.

Trone was then given a chance to take a nap, for a government operator had arrived. After sleeping for several hours, he returned again to his instrument, relieved the government operator, and continued to send the results of the third day's battle. Late in the night of July 3, he telegraphed word to Washington and New York that the Potomac army had won a great victory at Gettysburg. Trone was sent to the scene of the battle several times to convey special messages to the military authorities there.

Daniel Trone continued in the service of the railroad company for several years as operator, and then turned his attention to the banking business. Joseph Leib became a clerk at the railroad office in Hanover in 1855, three years after the road was built from the Junction to Hanover and Gettysburg. Later he was the passenger and freight agent for nearly half a century and continued to hold that office in Hanover until the time of his death, November 29, 1906.

Telegrapher Danny Trone was a gentle and likable soul who kept a diary of his activities starting in September, 1857. He was then serving as weighmaster on the Hanover Branch at its meeting with the Northern Central Railway at the Junction some twelve miles from Hanover, making two or three trips daily in fair weather and foul. He shared this job with John C. Hunt. Sometimes he continued on to Baltimore to replenish his supply of segars. He also clerked at auctions held at Metzger's store. When not working he read such books as "The Artist's Bride" or played on the fiddle and flute. He also took lessons on the melodeon and often went to Joseph Leib's home to hear him play on that instrument. Talks in the Lecture Room of Immanuel Reformed Church by Pastors Alleman and Sechler also occupied his attention. Danny died in 1882.

### Rush After Battle

Conductor John Eckert's experiences during the week following the battle of Gettysburg were remarkable. The military railway service, then under the management of Colonel Thomas A. Scott, of the Pennsylvania Railroad, took charge of the Northern Central and the Hanover Branch road, leading to the battlefield. Thousands and tens of thousands of people arrived at the Junction to be conveyed to Gettysburg. The engines and cars of the local railroad were all beyond the Susquehanna and could not be obtained. In this emergency the government got any kind of cars that could be procured from the Pennsylvania Railroad. Box cars, stock cars, old worn-out passenger coaches, were sent to Hanover Junction to make up trains, and on these the eager people rode to Gettysburg. John Eckert was the conductor and it was quite difficult for him to pass from one car to the other to collect the fares, for no tickets were sold in those exciting days. Mr. Eckert had charge of one train of twenty-three cars, on the last of which was the Governor of Maryland. For three days and three nights after the battle, Mr. Eckert did not sleep a minute, for he was managing the trains conveying the people to Gettysburg all that time without cessation, and he was faithful to his trust.

The government controlled these roads for one month after the battle and during that time, thousands of wounded soldiers were taken away to the hospitals or to the homes of their friends.

---

## ARMIES CONVERGE ON GETTYSBURG

At four o'clock Wednesday afternoon, General Barnes, commanding the First Division of the Fifth Army Corps, arrived at Hanover from Union Mills, over the same road that Stuart had passed the day before. He was closely followed by the Second Division, under General Ayres. The Third Division, under General Crawford, commanding the Pennsylvania Reserves, brought up the rear. The entire corps made preparations to bivouac for the night in the fields and meadows southwest of Hanover. Nineteen beeves had been slain on the Sell and Keller farms in preparation of a bountiful supper for the hungry men. Kettles, pots and skillets had been placed over open fires, with coffee and meat, which was cooking for the evening meal, when a dispatch bearer from Meade, at Taneytown, ordered General Sykes to move at once toward Gettysburg. The Fifth Corps had previously been commanded by General Meade, who was now the head of the Potomac army, preparing to move his headquarters from Taneytown to Gettysburg, where the battle had been opened by the First and Eleventh Corps, on July 1. When the courier arrived, he found General Sykes, and six of their aides seated at the supper table, at the home of Henry Sell, one mile west of Hanover on the Littlestown road.

### Sykes Ordered to Front

General Sykes received the dispatch, read it aloud to his officers, who immediately went to their divisions, and ordered the bugles to be sounded for the night march toward Gettysburg. The provisions were still cooking when the men were formed in line and moved toward Gettysburg. The following two days this corps took a prominent part in the great battle.

General Gregg, who commanded the Second Division of Union Cavalry in the Gettysburg campaign, resided in Reading, Pennsylvania, in 1906, when he gave the following report of his movements on June 30 to July 3, 1863:

"My division arrived at Westminster only a few hours after General Stuart's Confederate cavalry had passed through on the way to Hanover. I arrived with my division at Manchester on the 30th and was there while General Stuart and General Kilpatrick were engaged in a sharp conflict at Hanover, but at that time I knew nothing about this fight, although I was expecting that I might come in contact with Stuart myself at any hour that day.

"At Manchester I received orders to move eastward to Hanover Junction and protect Baltimore. If Baltimore was not threatened by the enemy I was to proceed with my division to York. I arrived at the Junction on the morning of July 1, the day the battle of Gettysburg opened. I had three brigades, then commanded by General McIntosh, General Irwin Gregg, who was my cousin, and Colonel Huey. I ordered Coloney Huey back to Manchester to guard my baggage train. I passed from Manchester across York County to Hanover Junction on a forced march, and arrived there shortly after General Stuart and his brigade commanders, Hampton, Lee and Chambliss, had held a conference in the farm house of John A. Zeigler, not far away. The station house at the Junction and the railroad bridges nearby had all been burned by Colonel White's Virginia cavalry, sent there by General Early on June 27, on his way to York.

"While at Hanover Junction I was unable to communicate with York or Baltimore, for the telegraph line had been cut by the enemy, but received two messages by couriers from General Meade, whose headquarters were then at Taneytown, Maryland. One of these messages ordered me to move toward Baltimore, which movement I began to make when the second message directed me to proceed with all possible haste toward Gettysburg where the opposing armies were concentrating and where fighting had already begun.

## Gregg Moves Via Hanover

"I expected to reach York on the afternoon of July 1, but I moved northwestward from the Junction through Jefferson to Hanover. It was midnight when we passed down through York Street. It was full moon and the moving shadows of our horses could be seen on the streets. We halted from 12 o'clock midnight to 3 A.M., in Center Square at Hanover, and on the leading streets. Many of my soldiers slept on the pavement, for they were tired after two days of hard marching. The citizens of Hanover brought provisions in abundance to my hungry men. We received a hearty welcome from every citizen of that town. While I stopped in Hanover with my two brigades, numbering about 3,000 men, I learned definitely of the cavalry engagement at Hanover and that General Early had occupied York with a division of Confederate cavalry for two days. After three hours' rest at Hanover, I received another message from the commander-in-chief. This was early in the morning of July 2nd, and soon afterward we heard the booming of cannon and the rattle of musketry from the battle of Gettysburg."

General Gregg then took up the line of march, and in the afternoon of July 3, engaged Stuart on the Rummel farm, where he defeated his antagonist in the effort to turn the right of the Union line.

General Sedgwick, with the Sixth Corps, resting two miles west of Manchester, at 6 o'clock in the evening of July 1, began his rapid march over the Baltimore turnpike, reaching Gettysburg at 4 p.m. the following day, after performing one of the most rapid movements of an army corps during the whole period of the Civil War.

## SAGA OF A GRAND MARCH

If Meade counted on natural fortifications for his Pipe Creek defense line, he couldn't have pitched on a better place for his extreme right pivot point than the Manchester section of Carroll County with its Dug Hill and range of ridges to the north of Bachman's Valley.

Major General John Sedgwick, Connecticut-born, huge-framed and self-assured, with his fifteen thousand to eighteen thousand strong Sixth Corps, arrived at this point from Virginia by way of Poolesville and Westminster the evening of June 30. He was to stand guard for any attack upon Baltimore from the north. He made his headquarters at old Fort Hill school originally built in 1805. Reconstructed into a brick building in 1896 it still stands along Old Fort Schoolhouse Road, west of Manchester, on the farm of W. E. Hossler, in use as a farm shed. On nearby timberland the men of the Sixth Corps bivouacked under sheltering oak trees and drank cool water from bubbling springs after a forced march under a torrid sun.

There were no further orders for July 1. The militia had a whole day ahead of them to relax, play games, write letters, and eat. The corps of three divisions was made up of thirty-six infantry regiments and eight batteries of artillery. No sooner had this immense army arrived, built fires for the evening meal and set up shelter tents when residents of the region flocked to the scene.

Through the whole of the next day the camp was turned into a fair, a picnic, a carnival. The people of this part of Maryland were mostly of German descent like those of York County and Union sympathizers. This was the first time they had a chance to see and talk to their defenders at close hand, and they made the most of it. They came in buggies and wagons, by horseback, and on foot from miles around, men folk, women folk, and children, red-cheeked girls in ginghams and calicoes, and sun-burnt boys wishing they were old enough to join up right away. Their elders brought fresh-baked loaves of bread, juicy fruit pies, and gingerbread, apple butter, smierkase, and smallbeer such as farmers took along to their harvest fields. It was harvest time to the boys in blue, and a day to be long remembered and brought back to memory by Carroll countians for many a year to come.

The visiting crowds were reluctant to leave, but peace finally settled on the camp, and all was serene, with men and officers looking forward to another such day, when a dispatch-bearer on foam-sweated horse galloped up to headquarters with orders from Meade. Sedgwick's close friend Reynolds had fallen the first day at Gettysburg, and the gallant Sixth was instructed to take the road at once and reach Gettysburg by 4 p.m. July 2— less than twenty hours and thirty-five miles to go!

First orders were to head for Taneytown, but a second message by courier changed the course to the Baltimore-Gettysburg turnpike. It is not clear at what hour the start was made but there was some confusion and delay when the van which started for Taneytown had to cut back across fields to get on the pike, but finally Sedgwick on his horse Cornwall and staff managed to straighten things out and the Grand March under the summer full moon began to cover distance at a quick step.

The greatest obstacle to the moving ranks on the pike was the train of white-covered supply wagons miles long ordered back to Westminster by Meade, and then ambulances mile after mile with wounded from the battlefield. Nothing was allowed to hinder the Sixth Corps. Food supplies and wounded had to pull aside to let the army pass on. In the sultry heat some dropped in their tracks and were left off the road to be picked up by ambulances. Many lightened their loads to keep up with the pace by dropping haversacks, shelter tent halves, and other accoutrements by the wayside. Moonlight, dry throats, dust and sweat were with them every step—through Union Mills, Silver Run, the state line, and return of daylight with a sizzling sun. Then Littlestown and the railroad tracks, where wounded gathered to be taken by train to Hanover, and ten miles yet to go.

"Uncle John" Sedgwick reported to Meade at 2 p.m. and at 4 o'clock his men started reaching Rock Creek where they plunged their feet in the water back of Little Round Top. A cheer went up along the Union ranks. The hurrahs must have reached Lee's ears. The balance in numbers now was in favor of the Army of the Potomac. There was plenty of support along the Cemetery Ridge Fish Hook from right to extreme left, for any maneuver Lee might make against it.

Connecticut John Sedgwick was to join Reynolds in a heroes' Valhalla the following year when struck by a Confederate rifleman's bullet in the Wilderness.

Comparable with the march of the Sixth Corps from Manchester was that of the Second Corps from beyond Frederick to Uniontown June 28. Led by Brigadier General John Gibbon of the Wisconsin Iron Brigade the corps covered the distance of thirty-two miles from 8 a.m. to 9 p.m.

---

## GETTYSBURG

"Spin, spin, Clotho spin,
    Lachesis twist, Atropos sever,
In the shadow year out, year in
    The silent Headsman waits forever."

When R. F. McIlheny, Gettysburg merchant, ran an ad in The Compiler in June, 1863, to the effect that he was in a position to supply the public with men's fine calf boots, Balmorals, Wellington boots, Congress gaiters, and brogans, he never had the slightest intimation that a whole army might respond. It is altogether possible that Confederate General Harry Heth of Hill's Corps in the vicinity of Cashtown may have noted the advertisement. Shoes were of all things what his men needed most, and he had accordingly sent Pettigrew's brigade to look into the matter. The brigade reconsidered when they saw blue troopers in the distance and decided to put off their quest for shoes till the next day which happened to be July 1.

John Buford with two brigades of cavalry and a six-gun battery of regular artillery had been sent to Gettysburg by Pleasonton in advance of the First and Eleventh Corps of the Army of the Potomac. Both these Union generals had ideas about Gettysburg terrain. It had amazing potentialities for the army that got there first. Armed with the new seven-shot Spencers Buford determined to hold off the Rebels till Reynolds, commander of the left division, arrived. Reynolds at once sent word to Meade, it is reported, that here was the place for battle. He had scarcely had time for disposal of his troops when he fell victim of a sharpshooter's bullet. A rapid change of leaders ensued. Doubleday took over in the field till Howard appeared, and then at about 4 p.m. Hancock, who on taking one look at Cemetery Ridge, declared "Here we'll take our stand," and rode off to Taneytown to give his appraisal of the situation to Meade, leaving Slocum in charge. Lee arrived on the scene at the same time Hancock did. His first words were: "We want to avoid a general engagement here if possible." It was not the kind of terrain he would have chosen for strategic maneuvering in open country. It was his idea to take on and destroy the several Union corps one at a time.

In his testimony before the joint committee on the conduct of the war in 1864 Major General Pleasonton said that when General Meade sent for him soon after Meade's assignment, he mentioned that from his knowledge of the country obtained the year before, in the Antietam campaign, he considered the result of the present one depended entirely upon which of the two armies first obtained possession of Gettysburg, as that was so strong a position that either army, by holding it, could defeat the other. He therefore directed General Buford, who commanded the first cavalry division, and who was ordered to Gettysburg, to hold that place at all hazards until the Union infantry could come up.

Buford arrived at Gettysburg on the night of the 30th of June, in advance of the enemy, and moved out the next day very early, about four miles on the Cashtown road, when he met

GENERAL JOHN BUFORD
*He started something he couldn't end.*

A. P. Hill's corps of the enemy, thirty thousand strong, moving
down to occupy Gettysburg. Thus it befell that Buford with
his four thousand cavalry attacked Hill, and for four hours
splendidly resisted his advance until Reynolds and Howard were
able to hurry to the field and give their assistance. To the in-
trepidity, courage, and fidelity of General Buford and his brave
division the country and the army owe the battlefield of Gettysburg. His unequal fight of four thousand men against eight times
their numbers, and his saving the field, made Buford the true
hero of that battle, Pleasonton later declared.

With this advice to Meade in mind which Pleasonton testified
to a year later the usual comment that the meeting of the em-
battled forces at Gettysburg was purely accidental will hardly
hold water. Fate was in the making. Where else could a Gettysburg have been fought? Meade had sent Hancock the Superb
forward to appraise the situation. He trusted Hancock and accepted his appraisal, abandoning his previous plan for a Pipe
Creek battle line. With full reliance upon Hancock's wisdom

Meade hastened to the scene of conflict arriving there at 2 a.m. July 2.

In the conduct of the Gettysburg campaign Jeb Stuart for the Confederate and Dan Sickles for the Union cause may be considered in the same category. Stuart is held to a large degree responsible for defeat of the South and Sickles for nearly scuttling success for the North. Stuart failed in his commitment of Lee's orders express or understood and Sickles for disobeying Meade's orders to take proper position on the left of the Cemetery Ridge line July 2. In 1863 cavalry formed the antennae of the army. Its main purpose was to scout and obtain information of the enemy's whereabouts and intentions. It may have had a secondary design of harassing the foe but its principal objective was to keep command headquarters enlightened to the very utmost of its possibilities. In this Stuart lamentably failed. All accounts point to Lee being greatly perturbed over Stuart's absence. With Jackson missing, Lee needed Stuart sorely for counsel and support. "Old Pete" Longstreet was hard and stubborn; "Baldy" Ewell weak and indecisive; and Stuart in the hour of crisis was not at hand.

After capturing the town and chasing the remnants of the First and Eleventh Corps to the hills on the east, Lee's army had four hours of daylight left the evening of July 1 to advance its gains. Ewell and Early failed to occupy Culp's Hill at minimum price and Longstreet muffed a chance to get a foothold on Little Round Top on his right. Longstreet's dilatory attitude on July 2 and the ineffectual efforts of collaboration on the part of Lee's generals in timing their assaults at both ends of the Union line that day brought their leader little comfort.

Meade's famous council of war the night of July 2 is usually considered by historians of as great significance as any strategic aspect of the battle. The lamented Lieutenant Franklin A. Haskell gives it full treatment in his brief and vivid story of Gettysburg. It was to be a fight to the finish on the established front.

The monstrous duet of hundreds of blazing cannon and Pickett's immortal charge were not the end. Two anti-climactic cavalry encounters were to take place at the fag end of the last day. On the far right between the York and Hanover roads the belated Stuart and his ablest lieutenants, Wade Hampton and

GENERAL WINFIELD SCOTT HANCOCK
*"The Superb."*

Fitzhugh Lee, were about to throw between six thousand and seven thousand cavalrymen into the fray.

Guarding against any attempt to get in the rear of the Union lines was David McM. Gregg with some five thousand troopers who included Custer's Michigan brigade. Jenkins' Rebel troopers were to fight afoot among the Rummel farm buildings, but these skirmishers were provided with a mere ten rounds of ammunition apiece and were soon put to flight.

Issuing into the open prematurely from a wood where they lay concealed the first Confederate riders were cut down by rifle and artillery fire. Other gray-clad ranks came charging out at breakneck speed, sabers pointing breast-high, as Custer's Wolverines dashed forward to the assault, their fair-haired boy at the head. The screaming columns met in full momentum, man and horse, crashing, smashing, and mixing in a grand melee. The casualties were light, five hundred at the most, considering the numbers involved and the fury of impact. Wade Hampton was among the wounded. Jeb Stuart withdrew his exhausted men

GENERAL DAVID McM. GREGG
*U. S. Cavalry Division Commander.*

and jaded horses. He had his fill, and so far as he was concerned
Meade's right wasn't going to be turned.

Under orders of Pleasonton Jud Kilpatrick at the other end
of the line, south of the Round Tops, held in leash parts of two
brigades commanded by Farnsworth and Merritt. When word
came along of Pickett's repulse, Kilpatrick, out of turn, called
for a charge against well-protected Texan troopers behind a reinforced rail fence. Merritt had been sent on a reconnaissance
toward Fairfield. The courageous Farnsworth, who had won
glory at Hanover, led two desperate charges and laid down his
young life in vain, proving again that soldiers on horseback
were no match for soldiers behind ramparts. Lee's line still
held firm.

Before the dawn of July 4 nature took over as the heavens
spouted down and the reverberations of their thunder provided
but a pale simulation of the man-made thunder of the previous
day. More storms brought torrential floods to the corpse-littered
field. In the compassionate rain and sheltering darkness Lee

gathered his tattered legions together and quietly faded away.

In his general orders issued July 4, General Meade declared: "The privations and fatigue the Army has endured and the heroic courage and gallantry it has displayed will be matters of history to be remembered. . . . It is right and proper that we should on all suitable occasions return our grateful thanks to the Almighty Disposer of events, that in the goodness of His providence He has thought to give victory to the cause of the just."

Addressing Pickett after his futile charge General Lee remarked: "This was all my fault. This has been my fight and the blame is mine. Your men did all men can do. The fault is entirely my own."

And in Washington Lincoln said, "I went to my room and got down on my knees in prayer. I felt that I must put all my trust in Almighty God. . . . I prayed that He would not let the nation perish."

# PART II

## REQUIESCANT IN PACE

Under the sod and the dew
Waiting the judgment day—
Under the one the Blue;
Under the other the Gray.
*—F. M. Finch*

## GENERAL GEORGE G. MEADE

George Gordon Meade was born December 31, 1815, in Cadiz, Spain, son of Richard Worsam and Margaret Coates Butler Meade. He was aged forty-seven at the time of the battle of Gettysburg. His paternal ancestors were engaged in trade in the British West Indies and later in Philadelphia. His mother was the daughter of a wealthy New Jersey merchant. Richard Meade made a home for his wife and family of eleven children in Spain, where he carried on an export business.

Mrs. Meade returned to Philadelphia with her son George in 1816. He attended a military school in Germantown. The family later made their home in Georgetown, D. C. George was appointed a cadet at West Point by President Andrew Jackson and graduated nineteenth in his class of 1835. A slender six-footer, wearing glasses and with large Roman nose, the brevet second lieutenant was assigned to Company C, Third Artillery. At the end of the year's service required of him, he secured jobs as surveyor on Long Island and in Florida. Then with the Topographical Bureau he had assignments from Texas to Maine, including the Mississippi River Delta and the Great Lakes area, as well as work for the Lighthouse Board.

As second lieutenant of Topographical Engineers he was married December 31, 1840, on his twenty-fifth birthday, to Margaret Sergeant, daughter of Congressman John Sergeant. For a brief time he was back in the army with General Zach Taylor in the invasion of Mexico until the capture of Monterrey. His association with Taylor whom he greatly admired as a soldier and man was of great value to the future general.

After the First Battle at Manassas he felt it his duty to defend

*Union soldiers in garb of the day. This photo was made just prior to the Battle of the Wilderness in May, 1864. Pine and cedar trees can be seen in the background which is typical of this area in Virginia. The soldier in the center is Pvt. John L. Krebs of Company B, 138th Regiment of Pennsylvania Infantry Volunteers. He was the grandfather of Lachlan W. Krebs of Hanover.*

the Union. He was appointed volunteer brigadier general through the efforts of Senator David Wilmot and assigned to the Second Brigade of the Pennsylvania Reserves, which were being organized by General George A. McCall. General John F. Reynolds and General O. C. Ord of Maryland were other brigadiers with a total of 10,465 volunteers. On entering the army Meade bought two horses, Old Baldy, which had been wounded in the first Bull Run battle, and Blackie to use for show. Baldy was twice wounded at Gettysburg.

Meade took prominent part at the second battle of Manassas, Antietam, Fredericksburg, Chancellorsville, and The Wilderness. When Grant displaced Halleck as General in Chief, he retained Meade as commander of the Army of the Potomac, with the difference that he also took to the field in the East. General Philip H. Sheridan replaced Pleasonton as cavalry head.

Although hailed as victor at Gettysburg honors came slowly to Meade. He did not trust volunteers who lacked the toughness of fiber that could only come from experience, and he had no faith in "political" generals like Sickles. The latter never forgave him for the reprimand at Gettysburg and twisted facts to put Meade in a wrong light before the inquiry into the conduct of the war. It was not Meade's nature to curry favor with the public and he was short of temper. He could never be enshrined in the hearts of his soldiers as was Lee. When Edward Cropsey of the Philadelphia Inquirer put a false slant on his story concerning Meade, the general had him drummed out of camp. As a result the correspondents gave him the silent treatment. William Swinton of the Times and William Kent of the Tribune were expelled from the front for slanderous reports on complaint of Grant and Hancock, but Meade got the blame and forfeited any chance of fair treatment in the news.

At the Grand Review May 23, 1865, in Washington Meade led the Army of the Potomac on his show horse Blackie. When the country was divided into military sections Meade was appointed to the Division of the Atlantic with headquarters at Philadelphia. Meade was promoted to Major General in the fall of 1864. He expected to be named Lieutenant General after Sheridan had been so honored but this honor was denied him. However, Meade received important recognition when invited to Harvard commencement at Cambridge where the honorary degree of Doctor of Laws was bestowed upon him.

The general had been twice wounded in action for possession of the New Market road at Beaver Dam Creek toward the end of the war. He had suffered from attacks of pneumonia before, but a final attack proved fatal November 6, 1872. Burial took place in Laurel Hill Cemetery, East Fairmount Park. He left his wife, two sons and four daughters. His eldest son Sergeant died during the war. His son, Colonel George Meade, a West Point graduate, served on his father's staff. Two horses were shot under him at Gettysburg. Like Lincoln, General Meade had relatives who favored the South.

Not a great strategist maybe but in action on the field he was a marvel. He had an amazing gift of seeing the battle as a whole. Take that second day at Gettysburg. He fitted the pieces together like a jigsaw puzzle, dashing up and down the line from Culp's Hill to Round Top, pulling out a section here where the requirement was less and putting it in there where urgently needed, and calling out orders on the spot to brigadier or lieutenant whoever was at hand. He may not in ordinary life have created the image of a popular hero, but the lowliest private could not have but been inspired by their captain's enthusiastic example.

## GENERAL ALFRED PLEASONTON

A son of Stephen and Mary Hopkins Pleasonton, Alfred Pleasonton was born at Washington, D. C., June 7, 1824. He attended the public schools in the capital city and received an appointment to West Point Military Academy in 1840. He stood seventh in a class of twenty-five when he was graduated in 1844. He was a classmate of Jeb Stuart and his opposite in command of the Union cavalry during the Gettysburg campaign. There was a prospect of rivalry that gave a special fillip to the actions of the two opposing cavalry forces.

Commissioned second lieutenant, Second Dragoons, in 1845, he served throughout the Mexican War. He was brevetted first lieutenant for his gallant services at Palo Alto and Resaca de la Palma. He became captain during campaigns against Indians in Florida and Western states and territories, and was placed in command of the Second Cavalry during its transfer from Utah to Washington, D. C., for protection of the city in 1861.

Advanced to the rank of major in 1862, he served in the Peninsular campaign and won promotion to brigadier general

GENERAL ALFRED PLEASONTON
*Stuart's opposite in U. S. A.*

of volunteers July 16, 1862. He fought at South Mountain, Antietam, and Fredericksburg, and for his outstanding services at Chancellorsville and Brandy Station was appointed major general of volunteers June 22, 1863, just prior to the cavalry battle at Hanover.

He was transferred to the Department of Missouri March 13, 1865, when Grant brought Phil Sheridan East to command the Army of the Potomac cavalry. For remarkable services on the Western front he was brevetted brigadier general and in recognition of his impressive career during the war major general March 13, 1865.

He resigned his commission January 1, 1868, when displeased with assignments to serve under officers who had previously served under him. He was a district collector of internal revenue for several years and president of a western railroad also for a few years. Congress gave him belated recognition when commissioning him major on the retired list in 1888. The final twenty years of his life he made his home in Washington. He was unmarried and last survivor of his immediate family. His death occurred February 17, 1897.

He undoubtedly brought the cavalry of the Army of the Potomac to a higher state of efficiency than it had previously possessed. His brilliance was not to be denied. He was not a show-off like Stuart or Sheridan but he had an air of bravura and cockiness in his behavior that was distasteful to his associates. He was too sure of his own opinion and too free with advice to his superiors. His attack on Meade before the committee on the conduct of the war was less than kind.

## GENERAL JUDSON KILPATRICK

General Hugh Judson Kilpatrick, commander of the Third Division of Union cavalry at the battle of Hanover, was born of Scotch-Irish parentage near Deckertown, New Jersey, January 14, 1836. He was graduated from the United States Military Academy at West Point in 1861, in the same class with General Custer. On May 9 of the same year he was appointed captain of volunteers and commanded his company at the battle of Big Bethel, the first engagement of the Civil War, where he was wounded and disabled from service for several months. In August, 1861, he assisted in recruiting a New York cavalry regiment of which he became lieutenant colonel. In 1862 he engaged in skirmishes near Falmouth, the movement to Thoroughfare Gap, and raids on the Virginia Central Railroad. He was conspicuous for his gallantry in the second battle of Bull Run, and commanded a brigade of cavalry on an expedition against Leesburg in September, 1862. With the rank of colonel, he commanded a brigade of cavalry on Stoneman's famous raid toward Richmond, extending from April 13 to May 2, 1863. In this movement he displayed remarkable courage and dash which afterwards distinguished him as one of the greatest cavalry leaders in the Civil War.

After Chancellorsville he commanded a brigade at the battle of Aldie when the Potomac army was preparing for its movement in pursuit of Lee, who was moving toward Pennsylvania. When the army arrived at Frederick, he was raised to the rank of brigadier general and placed in command of the Third Division of Meade's cavalry corps.

Following the Gettysburg battle he was engaged in constant fighting at Smithsburg, Hagerstown, Boonsborough, and Falling Waters. In the operations in Central Virginia, from August to November, 1863, he commanded his cavalry division, and took part in an expedition to destroy the enemy's gunboats "Satellite" and "Reliance" in Rappahannock River, the action at Culpeper on September 13, and the subsequent skirmish at Somerville Ford, the fights at James City and Brandy Station, and in the movement to Centreville and the action of October 19 at Gainsville.

In March, 1864, he was engaged in a raid toward Richmond and through the Peninsula, in which he destroyed much property and had many encounters with the enemy, beginning with the action at Ashland on March 1. In May, 1864, General Kilpatrick took part in the invasion of Georgia as commander of a cavalry division of the Army of the Cumberland, and was engaged in the action at Ringgold and in the operations around Balton until, on May 13, he was severely wounded at the battle of Resaca. His injuries kept him out of the field till the latter part of July, when he returned to Georgia, and was engaged in guarding the communications of General Sherman's army and in making raids, which were attended with much severe fighting. He displayed such zeal and confidence in destroying the railroad at Fairburn that Sherman suspended a general movement of the army to enable him to break up the Macon road, in the hope of thus forcing Hood to evacuate Atlanta. Kilpatrick set out on the night of August 18, 1864, and returned on the 22d with prisoners and a captured gun and battle flags, having made the circuit of Atlanta, torn up three miles of railroad at Jonesborough, and encountered a division of infantry and a brigade of cavalry.

In the march to the sea he participated in skirmishes at Walnut Creek, Sylvan Grove, Rocky Creek, and Waynesboro. In the invasion of the Carolinas his division was engaged at Salkehatchie, South Carolina, on February 3, 1865; near Aiken on February 11; at Monroe's Cross Roads, North Carolina, on March 10; near Raleigh on April 12; at Morristown on April 13, and in other actions and skirmishes. He was brevetted colonel in the regular army for bravery at Resaca, and on March 13,

1865, received the brevet of brigadier general for the capture of Fayetteville, North Carolina, and that of major general for services throughout the Carolina campaign. He commanded a division of the cavalry corps in the military division of Mississippi from April to June, 1865, was promoted major general of volunteers on June 18, 1865, and resigned his volunteer commission on January 1, 1866. He was a popular general, inspiring confidence in the soldiers under his command, and gained a high reputation as a daring, brilliant and successful cavalry leader. He resigned his commission in the regular army in 1867.

In 1865 he had been appointed minister to Chile by President Johnson, and he was recalled in 1868. He then devoted himself chiefly to lecturing, and took an active interest in politics as an effective platform speaker on the Republican side. In 1872 he supported Horace Greeley, but returned to his former party in 1876, and in 1880 was an unsuccessful candidate for Congress in New Jersey. In March, 1881, President Garfield appointed him again to the post of minister to Chile. He died at Valparaiso, Chile, December 4, 1881. In October, 1887, his remains were brought to the United States and buried near the tomb of General Custer at West Point. While on his lecture tours, he twice visited Hanover and York. Many of the facts found in the preceding narrative of the battle of Hanover were obtained from a personal interview with him by Historian Prowell.

## GENERAL GEORGE A. CUSTER

General George A. Custer, who at the age of twenty-three commanded the Michigan brigade at the battle of Hanover, was born at New Rumley, Harrison County, Ohio, December, 1839, and had a brilliant military history. He was graduated from the United States Military Academy at West Point in June, 1861, was assigned to duty as lieutenant in the Fifth Cavalry, and took part in the first battle of Bull Run. For a time he served on the staff of General Kearney and later of W. F. Smith. While on this duty he was given charge of the balloon ascensions, to make reconnaissances. In May, 1862, General George B. McClellan was so impressed with the energy and perseverance that he showed in wading the Chickahominy alone, to ascertain what would be a safe ford for the army to cross, and with his courage in reconnoitering the enemy's position while on the other side, that he was appointed aide-de-camp, with the rank of captain. Captain Custer applied at once for permission to attack the picket post he had just discovered, and at daybreak the next morning surprised the enemy, drove them back, capturing some prisoners and the first colors that were taken by the Army of the Potomac.

After General McClellan's retirement from command of the army, Captain Custer was discharged from his volunteer appointment and returned to his regiment as lieutenant. He had served there but a short time when General Alfred Pleasonton, on May 15, 1863, made him aide-de-camp on his staff. For daring gallantry in a skirmish at Aldie and in the action at Brandy Station, as well as in the closing operations of the Rappahannock campaign, he was appointed brigadier general of volunteers, dating June 29, 1863, and assigned to duty at Frederick, Maryland, as commander of the Michigan brigade, which he led as the Union troops entered Hanover on the morning of June 30, 1863. After leaving Hanover, General Custer's brigade was temporarily assigned to Gregg's cavalry division and took a leading part in the great cavalry fight on the Rummel farm near Gettysburg, where he won distinction for gallantry. In this he assisted Gregg in defeating General Stuart's effort to turn the right flank of the Union army. General Custer was wounded at Culpeper Court House. In 1864, in command of his Michigan brigade, he led Sheridan's cavalry forces in the dash towards Richmond and received recognition from the war department at Washington for gallant and meritorious services at the battle of Yellow Tavern, May 11, 1864, where Stuart, the Confederate cavalry leader, was killed. At the battle of Trevillion on the second movement toward Richmond, General Custer saved the colors of his regiment by tearing them from the standard, held in the hands of a dying color sergeant, and concealed the flag in his bosom. On October 19, he was promoted to the rank of major general of volunteers in the Union army for gallantry in action in the battles of Winchester and Fisher's Hill. In command of the Third Division of cavalry he defeated his former West Point classmate, General Rosser, at Woodstock, October 9, and drove the enemy twenty-six miles, capturing everything but one gun. In the spring of 1865 the Third Division under Custer fought the battle of Waynesboro. He defeated the enemy, capturing eleven guns, two hundred wagons, one thousand six hundred prisoners and seventeen battle flags, thus demoralizing the opposing army. He served under Sheridan in the movement southwest of Richmond, and for meritorious services in the battles of Five Forks and Dinwiddie Court House was brevetted brigadier general in the regular army. Custer was present with his Michigan division at the surrender of Lee April 9, 1865. In addressing his own troops the day Lee surrendered, General Custer said: "During the past six months, though in most instances confronted by superior numbers, you have captured from the enemy in open battle one hundred eleven pieces of field artillery, sixty-five battle flags and ten thousand prisoners, including seven general officers."

After the close of the Civil War General Custer took command of the Seventh Cavalry and served on the western frontier. In 1871 he defeated the Indians at the battle of Washita, Indian Territory. In May, 1876, General Custer in command of the Seventh Cavalry was sent on an expedition against the Sioux Indians in Dakota. He arrived at their village along the Little Big Horn River. His entire force numbered only 1,100 men, while the Indians, most of whom were armed, exceeded nine thousand. While approaching the Indian village, with 275 men, General Custer and his entire command were slain. This was the sad end of one of the ablest and most brilliant cavalry officers of American history. The officers and men were buried on the spot where they were slain. In 1877 the remains of General Custer were removed to the cemetery at West Point on the Hudson.

Elizabeth Bacon, whom he married in 1864, accompanied him during the last year of the Civil War, and was with him during his nine years of service in the western frontier. In 1885 she wrote and published a book of rare literary merit, entitled "Boots and Saddles, or Life with General Custer in Dakota."

## GENERAL ELON J. FARNSWORTH

General Elon J. Farnsworth, who commanded the Second Brigade of Kilpatrick's division at the battle of Hanover, was born at Green Oak, Livingston County, Michigan. He was educated in the public schools and spent one year at the University of Michigan, after which he served in the quartermaster's department of the army during the Utah expedition of that year.

In 1861 he became assistant quartermaster of the Eighth Illinois Cavalry, which his uncle was then organizing. He was soon promoted to captain, and in 1862 took part in various battles in the Peninsular campaign on McClellan's march toward Richmond. He was also conspicuous for his gallantry at the second battle of Bull Run, and for meritorious services was promoted in May, 1863, to the rank of colonel, and placed on the staff of General Pleasonton, commanding the entire cavalry force in the Army of the Potomac. He won distinction for gallantry at the battle of Chancellorsville. General Meade took charge of the Army of the Potomac at Frederick, Maryland, on June 28, 1863. Colonel Farnsworth was promoted to the rank of brigadier general and put in command of the Second Brigade, Third Division, Pleasonton's cavalry corps.

He took a leading part in the engagement at Hanover, was in the thickest of the fight with Kilpatrick at Hunterstown July 2, was instantly killed near Little Round Top in the Battle of Gettysburg. General Farnsworth was universally popular, and his untimely death at the age of 27 years was deeply lamented by the entire army.

## GENERAL ROBERT E. LEE

A biography of General Robert E. Lee would not only involve a complete history of the Civil War but even go back to colonial times and the Revolutionary War period. He belonged to a patrician family and married into the first family of Virginia. His ultimate fate was decided for him when that state joined the Southern states in secession from the Union.

A son of Henry "Light-Horse Harry" Lee, famed cavalry general in Washington's army, Robert Edward Lee was born January 19, 1807, of a second marriage, at "Stratford," Westmoreland County, Virginia, and was aged fifty-six years at the time of the Gettysburg battle. His mother was Anne Hill Carter, daughter of a wealthy planter. He was reared in Alexandria, Virginia. His father died in 1818 when the youth was eleven, one of eight children. He received an appointment to West Point in 1825. He was graduated second in standing in the class of 1829 which numbered forty-six cadets. Classmates included Jefferson Davis, Albert S. and Joseph E. Johnston, John P. Buford, and Leonidas Polk.

While stationed at Fortress Monroe as second lieutenant of engineers, he was married June 30, 1831, at Arlington to Mary Ann Randolph Custis, daughter of George Washington Parke Custis and granddaughter of Martha Washington.

He was made first lieutenant of engineers in 1836 and captain in 1838. He was engaged in various engineering projects for the government until 1846 when he was sent to San Antonio, Texas, as assistant army engineer. He served during the war with Mexico, under Generals John Wool and Winfield Scott. He was slightly wounded in front of Chapultepec. He attained the rank of brevet colonel for gallantry under fire in 1848.

He was in charge of the construction of Fort Carroll in Baltimore Harbor when he was called to the superintendency of the Military Academy at West Point in 1852. In this post he came into intimate contact with many cadets who served under him or against him later during the Civil War. They included Jeb Stuart, Phil Sheridan, Fitzhugh Lee, O. O. Howard and many others. At his own request he was placed on active duty in March, 1855, as lieutenant colonel of Second Cavalry. He

served in command of the Department of Texas. He happened
to be in Washington temporarily in 1859, when he was assigned
the duty of quelling the John Brown insurrection at Harpers
Ferry. He was recalled from Texas to Washington by General
Scott in February, 1861. On March 16 he accepted a commission
as colonel of the First Cavalry.

From this time on the career of Robert E. Lee poses many
questions. He was opposed to slavery, he was opposed to
secession, he was not interested in politics. As an officer of the
U. S. Army he was in duty bound to serve and protect the
Union. Yet he declined an offer to command the U. S. Army
in the field and resigned his army post April 20 to accept the
offer to command the forces of his native state April 23. It was
not until June 1, 1862, that he really was in command of the
Army of Northern Virginia. His opponent in the field was
Major General George B. McClellan at the start, but he had
to contend with President Davis at Richmond who considered
himself a military genius. On his home grounds Lee always
proved the master strategist but he was not as fortunate in his
campaigns in Maryland and Pennsylvania.

It is generally conceded that Lee was one of the great
soldiers of all time. He was an admirer of Washington and
patterned his military career after his fellow Virginian. Like
Washington he had to make the most of the little at hand. He
was idolized by his men and has been criticized for not de-
manding more from his generals. He had only one Jackson
whom he could depend upon to carry out his plans.

Lee had one consolation when he surrendered to Grant at
Appomattox. He was not yielding to a second-rater. He accepted his defeat with the equanimity of a Christian gentleman
and urged his followers to do likewise. As a paroled prisoner
of war he remained at Richmond and applied for a pardon. In
the fall he accepted the presidency of Washington College at
Lexington where he afterwards resided. He died October 12,
1870, from a heart condition. The college was renamed Washington and Lee University in his honor. Burial was at Lexington.
Seven children were born to the Lees. Only two of them, William H. and Robert, married and had children.

## GENERAL J. E. B. STUART

General J. E. B. Stuart, who commanded the cavalry corps of
the Army of Northern Virginia, was born in Patrick County,
Virginia, February 6, 1833. He was educated at Emory and
Henry College, and graduated from West Point in 1854. He
served in the western territories against the Indians and was
wounded in an action against the Cheyenne tribe, on Solomon's
River, in 1857. He was then a lieutenant in the First United
States Cavalry. Having invented a saber attachment, he had
gone to Washington in 1859 to sell the right to the war department, and was then sent with the forces under Colonel Robert
E. Lee to quell the insurrection at Harpers Ferry and there
identified John Brown. In May, 1861, he resigned from the
regular army and accepted the position of lieutenant colonel of
a regiment of Virginia infantry which had joined the Confederacy. Soon afterward he was made colonel of a regiment of
cavalry which guarded the left flank of Stonewall Jackson's
force at the first battle of Bull Run.

After taking part in several cavalry skirmishes, he was made
brigadier general in September, 1861. He commanded a cavalry
division which guarded the rear of Joseph E. Johnston's army
when it fell back from Yorktown toward Richmond and was
followed by McClellan with the Army of the Potomac in the
Peninsular campaign of 1862. In the middle of June, General
Stuart, with a division of mounted men, moved to the flank
of McClellan's army, and passed entirely around its rear, in
order to ascertain the disposition of the Federal troops. During
the Seven Days' Battle, he was continuously engaged, and for
his military achievements, was made a major general of cavalry.

On August 22, after the Potomac army had moved northward,
Stuart, in a bold raid, penetrated General John Pope's camp at
Catlett's Station, captured his official correspondence and personal effects, and made prisoners of several officers of his staff.
He was present at the second battle of Bull Run and led the
advance of Stonewall Jackson's army on the march toward
Antietam where he guarded Jackson's left in the great battle
which followed, in September, 1862. A few weeks later, with
1,800 picked men, he made a raid into Pennsylvania as far north
as Mercersburg to divert the Potomac army in its pursuit of Lee

in Virginia. He again passed around the rear of McClellan's army, crossing the Potomac below Harpers Ferry.

In May, 1863, at the battle of Chancellorsville he protected Stonewall Jackson's march to the right of the Union army. After Jackson was mortally wounded in this battle Stuart directed its movements on the following day. When it was decided by the Confederate government that Lee should again invade Maryland and Pennsylvania, Stuart was placed in command of the entire cavalry corps composed of six brigades, three of which remained with Lee on the northern movement. With the consent of the commander in chief, leading the other three brigades, he crossed the Potomac at Rowser's Ford to make a bold raid along the right flank of the Army of the Potomac on its movement toward Frederick, Maryland. The story of this movement is told in a preceding narrative. The wisdom of it will always be disputed by military critics.

He commanded the cavalry which attempted to turn the Union right at Gettysburg, but was defeated by Gregg's division on July 3, in what is sometimes called the hardest cavalry fight of the Civil War. He again showed his remarkable ability as a cavalry leader by evading Kilpatrick at Culpeper, then retired from Buford at Jack's Shop, after a severe conflict, but soon afterward forced back the entire Union cavalry in a brilliant saber charge at Brandy Station, Virginia. In the campaign of 1864, when Grant was moving on Richmond from the Rapidan, Stuart protected the flank of Hill's corps. When General Sheridan, in May, 1864, attempted to make a raid into Richmond, he was boldly met by General Stuart who concentrated his force at Yellow Tavern, a few miles from the city. In this battle, Stuart was mortally wounded. Next to the death of Albert Sydney Johnston at Shiloh, and Stonewall Jackson at Chancellorsville, his death was the severest loss inflicted upon the Confederacy during the Civil War. He died at the age of 31.

That Stuart was a soldier of sterling character is unquestioned. Otherwise Lee would not have relied upon him as much as he did. He stood next to Jackson in Lee's esteem. He was deeply religious, temperate in his habits, and neither drank nor used tobacco, yet was socially inclined, and in any gathering proved the life of the party.

In 1855, he married Flora, daughter of Colonel Philip St. George Cooke. For thirty years after the Civil War, Mrs. Stuart conducted a female seminary under the direction of the Episcopal Church at Staunton, Virginia.

## GENERAL WADE HAMPTON

General Wade Hampton, who commanded one of the brigades of Stuart's cavalry at Hanover, was born at Charleston, South Carolina, in 1818. He was a grandson of General Wade Hampton, commander of an American force on the northern frontier in the War of 1812-14, and was later the owner of three thousand slaves, being then rated as the wealthiest southern planter in the United States. His father, Wade Hampton, was inspector general and aide to General Jackson at the battle of New Orleans, in January, 1815. General Wade Hampton was graduated from the University of South Carolina, and at the death of his father in 1858, succeeded to the ownership of the Hampton homestead near Columbia, South Carolina. Early in life he made a speech in the state legislature against the re-opening of the slave trade in America, which the New York Tribune declared to be a "masterpiece of logic directed by the noblest sentiments of the Christian and patriot."

In 1861, he joined the Confederacy and organized Hampton's Legion, composed of artillery, infantry and cavalry. He was present at the first battle of Bull Run, and was under Johnston in the Peninsular campaign, where he lost half his legion at the battle of Seven Pines. In the fall of 1862, Hampton was made a brigadier general of cavalry and placed in command of a brigade in General Stuart's corps. He was famous for his gallantry at the battle of Chancellorsville, and during Stuart's movement through Maryland, on the approach to Hanover, his brigade brought up the rear, guarding the long wagon train which had been captured a few days before. When he arrived he took position southwest of town, and remained there until the Confederate forces withdrew toward Jefferson and Dover. At Gettysburg, his brigade stood the brunt of the fight along the left of the Confederate line, in the contest with Gregg's cavalry, when General Hampton was three times wounded. In this battle, twenty-one out of twenty-three field officers of his brigade were either killed or wounded. For gallantry he was promoted to the rank of major general of cavalry.

In May, 1864, in command of a division, he met and repulsed Sheridan at Trevillian when the latter made a bold dash toward Richmond for the purpose of capturing that city. In twenty-three days of his campaign, General Hampton captured three thousand prisoners, losing 719 of his own men. After the death of General Stuart, he was placed in command of Lee's cavalry with the rank of lieutenant general. Later in the war, he was assigned to Johnston's army, endeavoring to impede the progress of Sherman through the Carolinas. He was one of the ablest soldiers of the Civil War who was not a graduate of West Point.

After the war, General Hampton became reconciled to the situation, and during the reconstruction period, advocated in the south a conciliatory policy. In 1876, he was elected governor of South Carolina, and from 1879 to 1891 served in the United States Senate, of which he was one of the most conspicuous members. From 1893 to 1897, he was United States commissioner of railroads at Washington, D. C. General Hampton was a man of large stature, dignified and courteous manners, and represented the aristocracy of the south during the palmy days before the Civil War. He died on his plantation near Columbia, South Carolina, April 11, 1902, at the age of eighty-four.

---

## GENERAL FITZHUGH LEE

General Fitzhugh Lee, who commanded a Virginia brigade under Stuart in the battle of Hanover, was born November 19, 1835, in Fairfax County, Virginia, and was a grandson of General Lee, known as "Light-Horse Harry," who commanded the Virginia cavalry in the Revolution under Washington. He was graduated at West Point in 1856. He first was assigned to duty in the west, was wounded by the Indians, and then returned to West Point, where he was instructor of cavalry, at the opening of the war. He joined the Confederacy and was made an aide on the staff of General Richard S. Ewell, as a lieutenant colonel and later colonel of the First Virginia Cavalry. He participated in all the campaigns of the Army of Northern Virginia, on the Peninsula, second battle of Bull Run, Fredericksburg and Chancellorsville. July 25, 1862, he was promoted to the rank of brigadier general. During the early part of 1863, General Lee was assigned to the command of a Virginia brigade. He occupied the left of Stuart's forces on the movement from Union Mills to Hanover and took position a short distance west of the town. Late in the afternoon of June 30, a part of his brigade was engaged with Custer's Michigan cavalry southwest of Hanover. After the defeat of the Confederates at Hanover, Lee was sent forward and guarded the captured wagon train in the movement through Jefferson, Dover to Dillsburg, when it was turned over to Hampton's brigade.

Lee was present with Stuart at the great cavalry fight on July 3, at Gettysburg. September 3, 1863, he was made major general. At the battle of Winchester, September 19, 1864, three horses were shot under him and he was disabled by a wound. In March, 1865, he was put in command of the whole cavalry corps of the Army of Northern Virginia, and a month later, surrendered to Meade at Farmville, after which he retired to his home in Stafford County, Virginia.

In 1874, he made a patriotic speech at Bunker Hill which attracted wide attention. He was elected governor of Virginia in 1885. At the opening of the Spanish-American War, he offered his services to President McKinley and was at once commissioned a brigadier general in the regular army. A month later, he was promoted to the rank of major general and placed in charge of the forces at Atlanta, Georgia. When the American forces were ordered by the government to take possession of the island of Cuba, General Lee landed near Havana with an army of 30,000 men, and laid siege to the city, which was evacuated without bloodshed. The entire Spanish army of over 40,000 men was permitted to sail out of the harbor for Spain. His position during the Spanish-American War exercised a beneficial influence on American patriotism. Immediately after Congress declared war, he was earnest in his support of the McKinley administration and the war policy. His attitude during that period, and also that of his former associates in the Confederate army, wielded a remarkable influence toward reuniting the North and the

South. At the request of the President, the grandson of U. S. Grant and the grandson of Robert E. Lee served on Lee's staff during the Spanish-American War. General Lee, who was universally popular in Virginia, died at his home in Richmond, in 1905.

## COLONEL WILLIAM H. PAYNE

Colonel William Henry Payne, who commanded the Second North Carolina at Hanover, was born at Clifton, Fauquier County, Virginia, on June 15, 1830. He was educated at the University of Missouri, University of Virginia and the Virginia Military Academy. At the opening of the Civil War he organized a Virginia company, which became famous as the Black Horse Cavalry, and commanded it at the first battle of Bull Run. Two weeks later he was promoted to major. In 1862, he was made a lieutenant colonel. When Colonel Chambliss took charge of Lee's brigade on its movement toward Hanover, Colonel Payne was assigned to the command of the Second North Carolina, which did the main part of the fighting on the Confederate side in the engagement on the streets and western suburbs of Hanover. Colonel Payne was held as a prisoner of war for several months, and then returned to the army, when he was promoted to the command of a brigade in Fitzhugh Lee's division. With the rank of brigadier general he commanded this brigade during the last year of the war.

In 1865 he resumed the practice of law and later became counsel for the Southern Railway. During the last ten years of his life he resided during the winter season in the city of Washington and during the summer at his home at Warrenton, Virginia. He died at Washington in 1904, at the age of seventy years. General Payne had been wounded three times in battle during the Civil War, the first time at Hanover.

## COLONEL JOHN R. CHAMBLISS

Colonel John R. Chambliss, who commanded the Confederate brigade which was the first to reach Hanover, was born in Greenville County, Virginia, January 23, 1833. He graduated from West Point in 1853. In 1861, he was placed in command of a regiment of Virginia infantry, and in 1862 was made colonel of the Thirteenth Virginia cavalry, which he led in many actions. When Stuart started on his northern movement in June, 1863, Colonel Chambliss succeeded to the command of the brigade of W. F. H. Lee, who was wounded at the battle of Aldie, ten days before the forces reached Hanover. He commanded his brigade on the right of Stuart's line, July 3, at Gettysburg. For gallantry in action and for meritorious services, Colonel Chambliss was promoted to brigadier general. He was killed in a cavalry engagement at Deep Bottom, near Richmond, Virginia, August 16, 1864.

---

## NEWSMEN IN ACTION

Noted war correspondents attached to Meade's headquarters included Whitelow Reid of the Cincinnati Gazette, who accompanied Union forces from Taneytown to Gettysburg through the rich and hospitable Pennsylvania farm lands. Reid was later to be American ambassador to Great Britain.

L. L. Crounse and Samuel Wilkeson represented the New York Times. To the latter fell the painful lot of reporting to the paper the death of his son, the gallant Lieut. Bayard Wilkeson, of the Fourth U. S. Artillery, mortally wounded during the first day's fighting. The newspaperman continued covering the story from the field through the hundred-minute cannonading of the third day and Pickett's Charge to the very end. The reporters used wires when possible and relays of riders to forward their accounts of the campaign.

It was the ambition of every newspaperman to be an eyewitness of the big moments of a battle. It is estimated there were at least thirty or more correspondents of leading papers within the Union lines at Gettysburg, mingling intimately with officers in command and exposing themselves to the same dangers the soldiers faced. Lorenzo Crounse had a horse shot under him when he ventured too close to the front.

Charlie Coffin of the Boston Journal arrived at Hanover July 1 in time to accompany Sykes and his corps from there to the battlefield. Uriah Painter of the Philadelphia Inquirer, William Kent of the New York Tribune, and George W. Hosmer of the

New York Herald were among newsmen covering exciting events of the Gettysburg conflict.

### Trone at Transmitter

A. Homer Byington, of Connecticut, who was a war correspondent of the New York Tribune in 1863, related the following story of his experience at Hanover:

"On my way to Hanover from York in the night of June 30, I encountered some Confederate cavalry, and when I got to Hanover I found that there had been a severe cavalry engagement there during the day. The town had a disorderly appearance, people stayed close to their houses, and the debris of arms and accoutrements lay scattered on the roads. The wounded were gathered in a hall and church. Telegraph wires were broken and strewn around.

"I stopped at the hotel and asked the landlord if there was a telegraph operator in town. 'Yes, there he is,' said he, pointing to Daniel E. Trone. I asked him where his battery was. 'At home under the bed,' he said. 'The wires are all cut and there is no use trying to telegraph.' After considerable parleying I got some men to go out on a handcar and fix the wires, I paying the men and making myself responsible for the value of the car. Then the battery was brought out and we got Baltimore, the operator, Mr. Trone, promising an absolute monopoly of the wire for two days.

### Scoop for Tribune

"I hurried to the battlefield at Gettysburg, thirteen miles off. Before reaching there I met General Howard, and he told me of the first day's fight, of Reynold's death and many other things. I found J. R. Sypher, whom I engaged at Lancaster to follow me, and we sent off by our private telegraph wire from Hanover an account of the fight of the first two days at Gettysburg. It was a magnificent feat. No other accounts got through to New York that night, and between 9:30 and midnight of July 2 the Tribune sold 65,000 copies on the streets of the city.

"Mr. Trone kept getting the strange signal 'K. I.' from his instrument. 'What the dickens does K. I. mean?' he asked. 'I am afraid the rebels have tapped our wire.' Finally he found out that it was the War Department at Washington. 'We have received Byington's first dispatch,' said Secretary of War Stanton to the Hanover operator, 'and it is our first news. Send along more. We are listening.' For two days I sent exclusive dispatches over my wire, giving all particulars of the great battle. The New York Herald was running relays of horses to Westminster and York. I telegraphed that the railroad was whole from Baltimore to Hanover, and the government sent out trains for the wounded. The surgeon told me that that railroad saved General Sickles' life."

---

## COURIERS WHO RISK LIVES

During Lee's invasion of Pennsylvania there was plenty of undercover intrigue going on. Each side had its cloak and dagger men. Not all information regarding troop movements was supplied by spies, however. Ordinary citizens with some intelligence who kept their eyes open could furnish valuable impressions to the military.

So-called couriers were dispatch-bearers if they remained within their own lines, but if they were caught trying to get through enemy lines they might have some explaining to do.

A dispatch from Major General Meade to General in Chief Halleck dated June 28, 1863, and received at Washington at 6:05 p.m. reveals how the Army of the Potomac kept informed with regard to maneuvers of the Confederates: "The following statement has been furnished me. It is confirmed by information gathered from various other sources regarded as reliable.

"Thomas McCamron, blacksmith, a good man, from Hagerstown, left there on horseback at 11 a.m. today. Rebel cavalry came first, a week ago last Monday, General Jenkins having 1,200 mounted infantry said to be picked men from Jackson's men, and three or four hundred cavalry of his own. The cavalry went back and forth out of Pennsylvania, driving horses and cattle. The first infantry came yesterday a week ago—General Ewell's men; he came personally last Saturday, and was at the Catholic church, Sunday, with General Rodes and two other generals. On Monday he left in the direction of Greencastle, in the afternoon, Rodes having left the same morning. Rebel troops have passed every day, more or less, since some days only three or four regiments or a brigade, and some days (yesterday, for instance) all of Longstreet's command passed through, except two brigades. Saw Longstreet yesterday; he and Lee had their headquarters at Mr. Grover's, just beyond town limits, toward Greencastle, last night, and left there this a.m. at 8 o'clock. Think A. P. Hill went through last Tuesday. Heard from James D. Rowan, prominent lawyer and leading Confederate sympathizer, who was talking in the clerk's office last night; said that their officers reported their whole army 100,000 strong, now in Maryland or Pennsylvania, except the cavalry.

### Meade Kept Posted

"Mr. Logan, register of wills, and Mr. Preston, very fine men, in Hagerstown, have taken pains to count the rebels, and could not make them over 80,000. They counted the artillery; made it 275 guns. Some of the regiments have only 175 men; two that I saw, 150 men. Largest regiment that I saw was a Maryland regiment, and that was about 700; don't think their regiments would range 400. Great amount of transportation; great many wagons captured at Winchester; horses in good condition. Ewell rides in a wagon. Two thousand comprise the mounted infantry and cavalry. Saw Wilcox's brigade wagons yesterday or day before. Saw Kershaw's wagons in town yesterday. Kershaw's brigade is in McLaw's division, Longstreet's corps. Know Hood and Armstead; have passed through Hood's division and Armstead's brigade. Pickett's division is in Longstreet's corps. The Union men in Hagerstown would count them and meet at night. Officers and men in good condition; say they are going to Philadelphia. Lots of Confederate money; carry it in flour barrels, and give $5 for cleaning a horse, $5 for two shoes on a horse, rather than fifty cents United States money."

There were another kind of undercover men going the rounds in the sections facing invasion. They claimed to be representatives of the Confederacy who could furnish confidential knowledge—for a price—to farmers that would prevent them from losing their stock to the invaders. They were to make certain cryptic signs to the Rebels and all would be well. There was only one thing wrong with this stunt, and that was the Rebels had not been informed about it. The signs meant nothing to them. They laughed at the bemused Dutchmen making the gesticulations that were to save them from forays and went right ahead confiscating what they wanted.

That same day, June 28, which had so great significance in Meade's fortunes, a person named Harrison, who was later discovered to be known to Longstreet but not to any of the Union officers, moved among the crowds which had poured into Frederick as headquarters of the Army of the Potomac. He was there long enough to learn that Meade had replaced Hooker and that some of Meade's troops extended pretty far west toward the Blue Ridge Mountains. With whatever vital information he could obtain he made his way by horseback through the night with all possible speed to the Confederate lines.

## Spy Brings News for Lee

Early next morning Lee at Chambersburg learned that the Army of the Potomac had crossed the river and that he would face Meade instead of Hooker. But Lee never trusted the hired source of information. He could be in the enemy's pay as well as in Longstreet's. If he only had word from Stuart to confirm the agent's report! Should he move east and meet Meade or north towards Harrisburg? Lee was at his wit's end to find out where his cavalry was.

Meanwhile a solid citizen and merchant of Chambersburg named Jacob Hoke watched with natural curiosity and interest the actions of the Confederate notables visiting his town. He would write a book all about these visitors some day. When he noted that Lee turned his handsome mount Traveller towards the east instead of north, he did something about it. He gave a reliable young man he knew a plug of tobacco and instructed him to find a horse and report to General Couch at Harrisburg. A paper in the chewing tobacco contained important information. Judge F. M. Kimmel was another observant citizen of Chambersburg.

When Major General John F. Reynolds arrived in Gettysburg at 8 a.m., July 1, the first thing he did was consult a local scout,

Peter Culp, for information before he rode out to find Buford. The nondescript fellow Harrison is also believed to have been in Gettysburg that day in the interest of the invaders.

### Farmer Shoots Union Courier

Regular couriers faced danger not only from the enemy but also from ignorant residents of the countryside they were helping to protect.

The death of a dispatch bearer at Green Ridge, in Codorus Township, was one of the unfortunate events of the Confederate invasion of 1863. At 11 a.m. of June 29, General Meade, with his headquarters in the saddle between Frederick and Union Bridge, wrote out an extended report of his plan of operations and the position of his different corps then moving eastward toward Gettysburg, Hanover and Manchester. This courier was entrusted with the important duty of transmitting Meade's dispatches to General Halleck, the head of the army at Washington. He entered the lower end of York County and reached the village of Marburg, four and a half miles southwest of Hanover, at 9 p.m., where he halted for supper. As the telegraph lines had been cut in western Maryland, this dispatch bearer was carrying his message to Glen Rock, where it was supposed a line was still open to Baltimore and Washington.

After leaving Marburg, he moved eastward and seems to have lost his way, when he approached Green Ridge. Not knowing which road to take for Glen Rock, he stopped at the farmhouse of George Bair, and called for the occupants to show him the way. It was now midnight and the affrighted farmer, who did not understand English, thinking the soldier in front of him was one of the enemy, shot and instantly killed the dispatch bearer who fell from his horse. His remains were interred in the burying ground at Stone Church in Codorus Township. A few months afterward, the father arrived and had the remains removed to the home of the soldier in New York state. Mr. Bair, in great distress, surrendered himself to the military authorities and was taken to Hanover and later to Frederick, Maryland, where he was tried by a military court and acquitted of any crime. The dispatches which the soldier carried were found on his person after his death, sent to the War Department at Washington and appear in full in the "War of Rebellion," Series 1, Volume 27, Part 1, pages 66-67.

---

## CARING FOR WOUNDED HERE

Concert Hall, in Center Square, and a small building to the rear of York Street, used by the Marion Rifles at the opening of the war, were turned into hospitals. One of the rooms of Flickinger's foundry on York Street, was used for the same purpose. Before the sun had set, sixty or more wounded soldiers were being cared for by the local physicians, Doctors Smith, Hinkle, Culbertson, Eckert and Alleman. A few days later a United States Hospital was opened by authority of the government. What was then known as Pleasant Hill Hotel on Baltimore Street and used for a private academy, was rented by the government and all the locally wounded soldiers, forty-two in number, were transferred to this place. About twelve thousand wounded men from Gettysburg had been conveyed through Hanover in trains to hospitals at Baltimore, York, Harrisburg and Philadelphia. About 150 were kept at Hanover. Dr. P. Gardner, an army surgeon, was placed in charge of the hospital. W. C. Page served as secretary at the Cavalry Hospital here. It was kept open from July 10 until August 15. In reporting the condition of the hospital, on August 1, Surgeon Gardner said: "Every desired comfort is furnished in great abundance, and every luxury, with which this country abounds in great profusion, is supplied by sympathetic people, and administered to the suffering wounded by devoted women. A heartier response to the calls of humanity, never came from a more generous people than we have witnessed here."

Sergeant J. S. Trowbridge, of the Fifth New York, whose leg was amputated, died at the hospital on July 4. Eberly F. Cady, of Company B, Eighteenth Pennsylvania, died August 4, a few hours after his sister had arrived at his bedside. Generous citizens had the body embalmed and it was sent home for interment. A private named Cowell, under arrest for desertion, escaped from the guard on Carlisle Street, and ran down Chestnut Street. Refusing to stop, the guard fired, the bullet striking

*Concert Hall, southwestern corner of Center Square, was used as hospital after battle. Razed at turn of century. The hall was built by V. C. S. Eckert and served the community as a social, musical and entertainment center for many years.*

him in the heel and coming out at the knee. Cowell died at the hospital a few days later.

In his report to General Lee, Stuart made no mention of his losses at Hanover. General Kilpatrick reported that about fifteen Confederates were killed, and forty-seven captured, including Colonel Payne and one captain. His loss he reported as eleven killed and a number wounded. General Custer's report says the First, Fifth and Seventh Michigan suffered no loss, but the Sixth had fifteen men captured. The list of dead shows one killed in the First Michigan. Battery M, Second United States Artillery, had one man mortally wounded. Major W. B. Darlington reported that the loss in the Eighteenth Pennsylvania was four killed, twenty-seven wounded and fifty missing.

Major John Hammond, of the Fifth New York, reported two officers and two men killed, twenty-five wounded and ten missing.

The first Vermont, Colonel A. W. Preston, lost one killed and sixteen missing. The commander of the First West Virginia did not specify the loss in his regiment (known to have been one killed and at least five wounded), but summarized the loss of Farnsworth's First Brigade as ten killed and sixty-two wounded, besides many slightly injured. Of the wounded, two died at the hospital, making the Union death toll number thirteen.

The bodies of the Union soldiers, who were killed in the engagement, were conveyed to an apartment in the Flickinger Foundry on York Street, now the site of Trinity Reformed Church, where they were prepared for burial. Henry Wirt, a leading citizen of the town, ordered caskets made and at 9 o'clock at night the remains of the gallant dead were placed in these caskets and buried in the graveyard of the Reformed Church near the public school building. The Rev. Dr. W. K. Zieber performed the last rites at this ceremony. The graves were marked for the purpose of identification. Sometime later these bodies were disinterred and removed to the National Cemetery at Gettysburg.

Two well-dressed strangers stopped at the J. W. Gitt store in 1869 and made inquiries as to the whereabouts of the grave of a Confederate officer who was killed by a sharpshooter in the Gitt's Mill section near Hanover. The only clue they had was centered at a blacksmith shop along the Westminster road three

On January 7, 1864, Pennsylvania's Governor Curtin appointed David Wills, Esq., of Gettysburg as agent to purchase a site for "The Soldiers National Cemetery." Mr. Wills employed Samuel Weaver of Gettysburg to superintend the exhuming of bodies, many in unmarked graves. They had to be identified in various ways. In Mr. Weaver's report of March 19, 1864, to Mr. Wills, he said that 3,512 bodies had been exhumed and placed in new graves. Weaver's brother was P. S. Weaver, well-known Hanover photographer. This picture shows the exhuming of the bodies of Union soldiers from the German Reformed Church graveyard, rear York Street, Hanover, for removal to Gettysburg in 1864. Samuel Weaver is shown here with book. The structure in rear is a brick vault.

miles south of town. Mr. Gitt could think of no such place but his youthful son William G. Gitt recalled a soldier had been buried near a barn on the Martin Arnold farm, located just north of the steep Conewago hill. The grave was located and the body shipped South by the soldier's brother*

According to tradition the shot was fired from the William Dresher home on an elevation a couple of hundred yards distant. The Union marksman lay his rifle across the circular well wall of stone bearing windlass and bucket in taking aim.

The surgeon in charge of the Hanover hospital of the Army of the Potomac made the following official report to the government of the engagement at Hanover:

### List of Dead

Adjutant Alexander Gall, Fifth New York; Sergeant Selden Wales, Fifth New York; Sergeant E. S. Dye, Fifth New York; John Laniger, private, Fifth New York; William Crawford, private, Company C, Eighteenth Pennsylvania; David W. Winan, private, Company D, Eighteenth Pennsylvania; Jacob R. Harvey, private, Company M, Eighteenth Pennsylvania; Corporal John Hoffacker, Company E, Eighteenth Pennsylvania; C. Rathburn, private, Fifth Michigan; Sergeant George Collins, First West Virginia; unknown, First Vermont. (Most reports list the name David Winninger in place of Winan.)

### List of Wounded

Eighteenth Pennsylvania—Elisha Jeffries, Company A, gunshot in arm; William Cole, Company A, saber cut; Moses Harrison, Company A, contusion on head; Jesse H. Little, Company B, saber cuts in head and shoulder; John Herrick, Company B, gunshot in back; Alfred W. Stone, Company B, gunshot in temple; M. B. Mikesell, Company D, contusion on back; Joseph Groner, Company D, saber cut in head; Sergeant John Montgomery, Company F, saber cut in head; A. Setterhall, Company F, bruised by fall from horse; Samuel Jones, Company F, gunshot in back; Shadrack M. Sellers, Company G, leg broken;

* Herald—June 30, 1903.

William Smith, Company I, shell wound on hip; Jere Devalan, Company I, saber cut in head; S. Rodebaugh, Company M, bruises in face and head.

Fifth New York—Major White, gunshot, serious; Thomas Richey, Company A, bruise in leg; Bradley Wessart, Company A, saber cut in head; James Hayes, Company A, saber cut in shoulder; George Gardells, Company B, gunshot, serious; Sergeant Owen McNulty, Company C, gunshot in arm and finger; Corporal Kistner, Company C, saber cut in neck, serious; J. B. Updike, Company D, saber cut in head; Corporal S. T. Uptegroat or Updegrove, Company D, wound in hip; P. Schermerhorn, Company D, bruised by carbine blow; Corporal James McGinley, Company D, gunshot in arm and head; H. W. Monroe, Company E, wounded in side, serious; Sgt. B. Alexander, Company E, saber cut in head; Sergeant J. S. Trowbridge, Company E, thigh smashed by shell, leg amputated (died of wound); A. C. Rowe, Company E, saber cut in face; Emile Portier, Company F, gunshot in arm and breast; Corporal McMullen, Company F, saber cuts in head and shoulder; Henry Tuthill, Company F, bruised by horse falling in charge; Corporal N. Barrum, Company G, gunshot in arm and neck; William Sampson, Company H, saber cuts in arm and foot; William Lively, Company H, saber cuts in arm and neck; O. S. Keyes, wounded, captured, died in prison.

First West Virginia—Lieutenant Max Carroll, Company F, wounded in thigh; H. Bucher, Company F, pistol shot in thigh; J. W. Brooks, Company L, bruised by shell; Henry Holman, Company L, gunshot in face; Thomas McGuire, Company M, gunshot in thigh.

Fifth Michigan—Jasper Brown, Company D, shot in breast.

Seventh Michigan—James Livingston, Company F, gunshot.

---

## FIRST VERMONT CAVALRY AT HANOVER

The editor of the St. Albans (Vermont) Daily Messenger, in an 1887 article on "Pennsylvania's Patriotism," after detailing the various appropriations made by the State Legislature for patriotic

(Hanover Herald, May 28, 1887)

purposes growing out of the Civil War gives the following
graphic sketch of the cavalry fight at Hanover:

"With the mention of these matters, vividly return recollections of those scenes of twenty-four years ago to the actors in
them. They see again with eyes undimmed, they hear the spirited clattering of the horses' hoofs on those plains of carnage,
the rattle of the carbine, the clangor of the saber, and the shout
and the cheer of the earnest cavalry charge, as distinctly as
though they were the occurrence of yesterday; and the soul
thrills with emotion, and the blood, fast growing chill with age,
warms up again at the recital. Though peace is restored with
its blessings, and silent and still are the implements and forces
of strife, yet the mind, alone, good-naturedly, will not forget
itself with the rest.

"The first engagement in that State was at Hanover, June 30,
1863, between Stuart's Confederate cavalry and Farnsworth's
brigade of Kilpatrick's division of Union troopers, the day before
the battle commenced at Gettysburg. The army of the Potomac
had been massed at Frederick City, Maryland, from which point
it was moved towards Pennsylvania in three grand columns, the
left led by Buford's cavalry division, the center by Kilpatrick's,
and the right by Gregg's, the cavalry corps being commanded
by General Pleasonton. The cavalry left Frederick City on the
afternoon of June 29, and Kilpatrick's reached Hanover early in
the forenoon of the 30th, the First Vermont Cavalry Regiment
being attached to Kilpatrick's division. Stuart's cavalry had been
raiding in that section, to the great annoyance of the Union
citizens, and the people of Hanover were in ecstacies as the
loyal troopers rode into their town. And what a contrast between
the reception given us that day and the fare and social usage
we had been obliged to put up with in the hostile and desolate
state of old Virginia.

"The doors of the Hanoverians were opened wide, and their
hospitality knew no bounds. Pies, cakes, cigars, pipes and
tobacco, were showered upon the boys, and unrestrained hilarity
prevailed. The Hanover maidens welcomed their protectors, who
at once felt at home; and the boys, out of their saddles, were
dancing numerous jigs with them, when, hissing and crashing,
came a shell into the town and exploded but a short distance

off. Simultaneously with the advent of the Confederate shell came a Confederate yell and a charge into the Eighteenth Pennsylvania regiment, the rear guard of Farnsworth's brigade, which was driven confusedly upon our dismounted regiments in the streets. In a moment, almost, in less time than it takes to tell the story, the streets of Hanover were changed from merriment to the business of war.

"The Fifth New York, the first in the rear of the First Vermont cavalry, received the full force of the shock, which extended some ways into the First Vermont regiment; but little time, however, was lost in facing about and in responding with a counter-charge as furious and as grand, for a spurt, as any made during the war. Stuart's cavalry went out of town livelier by half than the gait they came in on, but leaving a large number of their dead and wounded in the streets. The surprise was well planned by the enemy, but they paid dearly for their intrusion. It is doubtful if the annals of war contain a more sudden transition from gayety to gloom, than was experienced that day at Hanover—from the streets of the dancers to the streets lined with dead and wounded soldiers."

## McSHERRYSTOWN JOHN BURNS

When Historian George R. Prowell visited General David M. Gregg at his residence in Reading in 1904, the Civil War cavalry officer told of the following incidents:

"I have an interesting recollection of my first visit to Hanover forty-one years ago. It was midnight of July 1, 1863, when with two brigades of my division of cavalry, I entered York Street, coming through Jefferson from Hanover Junction. One of the brigades was in command of General McIntosh, and the other of my cousin, General Irvin Grogg, who was then a colonel. My force at Hanover numbered about four thousand men. I had sent my other brigade, commanded by Colonel Huey, to Manchester, Maryland.

"My division of cavalry, composed of nearly six thousand men, arrived at Manchester on June 30 about the time the fight between Kilpatrick and Stuart was taking place at Hanover. At Manchester I received orders from Meade's headquarters at

Frederick to proceed to Hanover Junction, and if Baltimore was protected from the Confederate invaders to go on to York. When I arrived at the Junction I found the station house had been burned, also the bridges along the Northern Central Railway, by Colonel White's battalion of Confederate cavalry a few days before. While I was at Hanover Junction I received orders to move through Hanover toward Gettysburg.

"As I said before, I entered Hanover at midnight and halted in the town for three and one-half hours. When I arrived there I heard for the first time of the cavalry fight that had taken place the day before. The citizens arose from their beds upon our arrival and showed great patriotism by feeding my men and giving them pleanty of good coffee and water to drink. Some of my men slept on the pavement. In fact, the sidewalks on one street (Carlisle) were lined with sleeping men for two hours or more."

Then the famous General here, still strong, vigorous and healthy at the age of seventy-one years, looked over the history of the Fifth Maine Regiment, which served in his command. This book contained a published diary of one of its officers. It stated that the bugle sounded at 3:30 a.m., July 2, for the division to march toward Gettysburg. The battle had opened there the day before. General Gregg talked with interest and enthusiasm of his visit to Hanover, and the movement into the great contest at Gettysburg.

"But," said he reflectively, "there was an incident that occurred just as I entered the village of McSherrystown, west of Hanover. A farmer, in citizens clothes, rode up to me and asked permission to enter my command and fight. He was in real earnest and I turned him over to one of my aides. The man was armed with a large rifle and he rode with us until we approached the enemy in the afternoon of July 2, when we came in contact with Johnson's division of the Confederate army near Gettysburg and the fighting began. I then lost sight of him. And whether he joined us in the fight or not, I do not know. He showed all evidence of being a brave man, a real soldier. Let me know if you find out the man's name. If he is living I would like to hear from him."

General Gregg and General Wilson, of Delaware, were among

the few of the great cavalry leaders of the Civil War then living. It was the latter who captured Jefferson Davis in Georgia in 1865, just as the war ended.

The Rev. Dr. W. K. Zieber, at his home on York Street, Hanover, related the following interesting story of the arrival of Gregg's cavalry on that eventful night of July 1863:

The town had not recovered from the shock of battle that occurred the day before. We were all in a state of uncertainty, not knowing whether Union or Confederate troops would next arrive. I retired about 10 p.m. at my home, the Reformed parsonage on York Street, later the residence of Cornelius Young. Feeling an interest in all the people of Hanover, for I was acting in the capacity of Chairman of the Committee of Safety of the town, I had not gone to sleep. About midnight I heard the tread of many horses coming down York Street toward Center Square. I arose from my bed and looked out through the open window as the advance was passing my residence. The dust on their clothes made it difficult for me to tell whether this large body of mounted men wore the Blue or the Gray. From the top of my house floated a hospital flag, for Marion Hall to the rear was filled with soldiers wounded the day before. My study was occupied by the army surgeon, who attended them. After the advance had passed, I put my head out of the window and called, "What force is this?"

"Gregg's cavalry," was the answer, coming from half a dozen men.

"Why have you a hospital flag on your house?" asked an officer. "Was there fighting here?"

"Yes," I replied, "between Kilpatrick and Stuart."

"Did our side win?" he asked.

When I told them Kilpatrick was victorious they began to cheer as they moved down the street toward the Square.

I remember how manly all these soldiers were, and how they thanked our citizens when they received a glass of water, a cup of coffee, or something to eat, and I also remember how quietly they moved away toward Gettysburg.

It was Gregg's Division that did the hardest cavalry fighting at Gettysburg. His contest with Stuart on the Rummel farm, July 3, was one of the hardest hand to hand engagements of the

Civil War. Custer's brigade of Kilpatrick's division, which fought at Hanover, joined Gregg's division in the battle of Gettysburg.

## CAPTAIN GRAHAM'S WAR HORSE

In 1898 while visiting Charlotte, North Carolina, Historian Prowell met Captain A. W. Graham, of Company F in the Black Horse Cavalry at the fight in Hanover. He related that he lost a valuable horse in the battle of Aldie, just before Stuart's cavalry crossed the Potomac River on the famous Gettysburg campaign.

In 1863 Confederate money was nearly worthless. Governor Graham paid $30,000 in Confederate scrip for another horse which Dr. George W. Graham, a physician at Charlotte, brought to his brother, Captain Graham, five days before the battle at Hanover.

When Colonel Payne charged into Hanover with the North Carolina troops, Graham's company was in the van. In a hand to hand encounter to the rear of the present site of the Methodist Church on Frederick Street, Captain Graham's horse was killed. He quickly mounted another horse which had belonged to a farmer near Hanover. This animal was also killed in the famous cavalry fight which Stuart had with Gregg's cavalry in the battle of Gettysburg.

Captain Graham, who commanded a company of the Second North Carolina Cavalry, communicated to the Historical Society of York County some interesting data relating to the cavalry engagement at Hanover in 1863. He said that his regiment, by order of General Stuart, the Confederate commander, led the second charge into the town after the Virginia Regiment had been repelled with considerable loss. This statement corresponds to that made two years ago by Colonel Payne, who commanded the regiment and who was captured near Winebrenner's tannery at the end of Frederick Street. Colonel Payne and Captain Graham estimated the loss to the Second North Carolina in this charge in killed, wounded and captured at 250 officers and men. The heaviest loss was a short distance west of Hanover.

Captain Graham, who was the senior officer of the regiment,

(Record-Herald, June 30, 1916)

after its commander had been made a prisoner of war, was wounded at Gettysburg. He then returned to his home in North Carolina. After he had recovered from his wound, Governor Vance made him Assistant Adjutant General of his native State. Captain Graham was a son of the late Governor W. A. Graham, who was secretary of the Navy in President Filmore's cabinet.

Captain Graham stated that no official report was made of the part taken by his regiment in the engagement at Hanover. He assigned as a reason for this that Colonel Andrews, who assumed command of the regiment after it returned with Lee into Virginia, had not served in the Gettysburg campaign.

## JOHNNIE CATLIN, BOY BUGLER

One of the happiest men in town during the 50th anniversary week of the battle was "Johnnie" Catlin, the "boy bugler" of the Fifth New York Cavalry, who, upon orders from General Kilpatrick, blew the bugle for the charge on the troopers of "Jeb" Stuart, on Frederick Street, June 30, 1863, which opened the battle of Hanover.

"Johnnie," as stated, was the "boy bugler" fifty years ago, and he is still "some boy." The master mind of a Victor Hugo could weave a romance out of the life of John Catlin which would send the blood to the hair roots of readers of the story.

"Johnnie" Catlin was a "soldier of fortune," and at the age of sixty-four, looked back over a life filled with experiences of a character which would strike terror into the hearts of a weakling, and make a modern Boy Scout glad he was not born on the frontier.

Catlin by fate was destined to be a mortal enemy of the Indians of the plain, and to follow a life of turmoil. Left an orphan in a cabin on the border of California, several years after the "gold craze," his father and mother being killed and scalped by the Indians, he was picked up and brought to New York City, where, fatherless and motherless, he became a street gamin, and naturally would have drifted into a life of crime.

The breaking out of the Civil War was the turning point in the lad's career. On an eventful day in '61, several companies

(Record-Herald, July 2, 1913—Prowell)

of the Fifth New York Cavalry were passing through that city, and following the troopers was a towheaded Irish lad, of twelve years, whose blue eyes and ruddy countenance attracted one of the officers, who playfully asked the boy if he wanted to go to war. "You bet I do," quickly replied the lad, whereupon, a consultation was held, and in a short while arrangements were made and the lad placed on a horse. He was shown a bright brass bugle, which made the eyes of the lad almost pop out of his head. When asked whether he could blow it, the laid replied: "Well, it would be the first thing I couldn't do." And the youth did blow it, and he soon became proficient with the bugle calls.

Thus by fate, "Johnnie" Catlin became the "boy bugler" of the Fifth New York Cavalry, serving with that command through the war, and he was a great favorite with the officers and men, his Irish wit helping many times to cheer up the cavalrymen.

"Johnnie" used to say that the day he joined the cavalrymen was the day of his "adoption as the Fifth N'Yrk was me father and mither. To my comrades I owe all my bravery, fearlessness and patriotism."

And these words bring us to the period of his life following the war. And there is nothing egotistical about the above statement, for if a more fearless, brave or patriotic man ever lived in these United States, let him bring his record and compare it with John Catlin's Civil War veteran, regular army man, Indian fighter, deputy sheriff, Deputy U. S. Marshal, etc.

At the close of the Civil War, "Johnnie" enlisted in the regular army and served for a continuous period of 25 years. He was with Custer in the campaigns against the Indians and was a fearless foe when clashing with the red men on the frontier. His body and limbs bear marks of arrow and pistol wounds, which brought to him pain and suffering untold, but only increased his desire to subdue the savages. He has fought in the West and South, in Mexico, and other territories, and while cut and scarred in many places not one wound was ever inflicted on his back. Several times he was picked up for dead, but after brief periods in hospitals he was back again in the saddle, ready for the next encounter.

After the strenuousness of Indian warfare for so long a time one would imagine that the soldier would seek a vocation offering peace and quietness. Nothing like that for "Johnnie" Catlin, as following his service in the army, he accepted the appointment of deputy sheriff of Linn County, Oregon, and for more than twenty years, he lived at the county seat, Albany, where he was a friend to the peaceful but a terror to the evildoer. As deputy sheriff, he brought his gun in play on a number of occasions. The weapon bore several significant "nicks" on the stock. He was familiarly known as "Dad," giving one a tip as to his character and the esteem in which he was held. In addition to sheriff-deputy, he also served as a Deputy United States Marshal.

The former "drummer boy" had the distinction of being placed in charge of the 80 Union and Confederate veterans which the State of Oregon sent to the reunion at Gettysburg, being selected for this honor by Governor West.

Now back of the visit of Catlin to Hanover lies a romance, which is worth telling, though it was spoiled somewhat by "Johnnie" himself, by reason of putting it off so long, as he has not been here since that memorable day of the battle. A letter was written by the drummer several months ago, in which he stated that he would be here at the 50th anniversary and wondered if the girl who gave him the pie and bowl of milk the morning of the fight here was still living. "Johnnie" never could forget her face, and has ever regretted that the battle of Hanover didn't start five minutes later, for he was compelled to "swallow the pie whole," and leave half the milk in the bowl when the order was given him to sound the charge. The "boy bugler" hastened away and that was the last he saw of the girl on Frederick Street for fifty years.

"Johnnie" told us confidently that he met "the girl" on Monday at the monument oval, as she had read the letter in the paper and was anxiously waiting for him this week. He stated furthermore that she is a widow but her name he wouldn't divulge. "But," said the old bugler, "I'm married and that spoils it all. But I was mighty glad to see her anyway, and we spent a happy hour talking over old times."

It didn't take long for the Oregon veteran to fall in love with Hanover. His Brother Elks first gave him the glad hand of fellowship and though he had only been in town a few days, he became a familiar sight on the street, and everybody spoke to him. On Monday evening he got out his bugle (the same one which he used fifty years ago) and gave a series of calls on the Square and Frederick Street.

This sun-tanned happy-go-lucky, old Irish-American boy declared that when he retired he expected to move to Hanover, which, he said is the "fairest spot on God's footstool, and has the best-hearted people in the world."

His expressed intention to spend his last days in Hanover, alas! never came to pass.

(Herald, December 7, 1903)

Johnny Catlin, who was about eleven years of age when adopted by the Fifth N. Y. Cavalry, had an adventure of note before he took part in the Hanover battle. He was captured July 18, the year before, at Barnett's Ford, Virginia, with 35 Company A troopers, by Jeb Stuart. The general and Colonel Jones of the Seventh Virginia Cavalry said he was too small to imprison. Colonel Jones kept him at headquarters for two weeks, and when he had a furlough took the boy to his sister's home. Being a widower and having no children he planned to adopt Johnny. They returned to the colonel's command at Berryville, in the Shenandoah Valley, by way of Richmond. In that city Johnny drew attention as "the smallest Yankee ever captured."

Mounting a horse was his greatest difficulty but once on the animal's back the youngster was a good rider. As soon as he managed to effect his escape he rejoined the "Fighting Fifth."

## HE FOUGHT AT HANOVER

"I am going to war," said John Trowbridge, as he entered his Vermont home early in September, 1861. "Yes, I have decided to enlist in the army. Captain Jones who is organizing a company to join the First Vermont Cavalry Regiment, delivered a great speech last night. He said it was our duty to defend the flag and the nation, and I have decided to enlist tomorrow. It is nearly three months since Benny Atwood went to the war with the Fifth Vermont Infantry. He was only sixteen years old and I am eighteen."

(Hanover Herald, August 25, 1906—G. R. Prowell)

"You will not leave your mother and me alone here, will you John?" said his sister Mary, who was teaching the district school near his home. Their family was composed of three persons only, and the son was one of the noblest boys in the country round about. He had heard the drums beating in the neighborhood village after Captain Jones had delivered his speech in the school house. This aroused his military ardor. There were few parents in those days who wanted their sons to go to the army, yet they felt that the honor of the nation was at stake and they finally consented. Only persons whose recollections go back to that period remember how frequently parents gave permission to their sons to show their courage and their loyalty to the government over which Abraham Lincoln was then chief executive. Three days later John Trowbridge was wearing a private's uniform, for he had enlisted in Company E of the First Vermont Cavalry. He was a tall, manly fellow, with flaxen hair and wild rose complexion. He was the pride of his home and one of the best known boys of the country surrounding Burlington, Vermont. He owned a horse when he enlisted, Tom was his name. He wanted to take this horse with him to the army, but was finally persuaded to leave him at home. His regiment reached Washington early in October and soon after was assigned to a cavalry brigade in the army under McDowell.

After McClellan had organized the army around Washington into brigades, divisions and corps, the First Vermont joined the expedition, which sailed down the Potomac River in flat boats. McClellan commanded a vast army of one hundred thousand men. They landed at Fort Monroe and then began their march up the peninsula toward Richmond, Virginia. Private Trowbridge riding a fine bay horse did valiant service to this campaign. He followed the fortunes of war and received the recommendations of the Colonel of his regiment for gallant and meritorious service at the battle of Chancellorsville. He was promoted to Sergeant of his company and given a furlough of forty days to return to his home in Vermont. When Trowbridge reached the station at Burlington, he met Benny Atwood, who had enlisted in the Fifth Vermont Infantry. It was Atwood who became famous in the annals of war. He was known to history as "Little Benny," for he was only sixteen when he joined his regiment at Burlington two years before. Early in July 1861, Private Atwood was found sleeping at his post one night when placed on sentinel duty in front of his regiment. The enemy was but a few miles away at Fairfax Court House. The sentence given to a soldier for sleeping at his post when on sentinel duty according to the rules of war required him to be shot. That was the sentence pronounced upon little Benny, but it would have been hard for any authority to have selected the soldiers who would have fired the fatal shot. As the story goes his little sister left her Vermont home and went to Washington to see President Lincoln. When she reached the White House she plead for the life of her brother, telling how young he was and how cruel it would be that such a patriotic boy should lose his life simply because he fell asleep. No accident had resulted from his sleeping for the enemy did not come in sight. The tender heart of the great man was touched; he took the law into his own hands and reprieved the soldier boy, who was permitted to return to his Vermont home for a month. While he was home for a month, on his furlough the people of the neighborhood made a cane out of thirty-three pieces of Vermont wood. When Private Atwood returned to his regiment he sent this cane to the White House, as a gift to the President. Soon after the death of Lincoln in order to show her appreciation of faithful duty, Mrs. Lincoln presented this cane to Lieut. Jameson, who commanded a company of cavalry which acted as a guard around the White House at Washington. His home was near Hanover and shortly after the war he presented the cane to his friend, Davis Garber, of Hanover. Forty years passed by when the owner of this cane presented it to the Historical Society of York County.

Now Corporal Atwood and Sergeant Trowbridge were boon companions while they were home on their furlough during the early summer of 1863. They had both been true soldiers and they were frequently called upon to relate their thrilling experiences in battle down on the plains of Virginia. They both returned to their regiments sometime in June.

Sergeant Trowbridge and his regiment moved northward with the Army of the Potomac during the latter part of June, 1863, to meet the invading army, under Lee then moving northward.

He was a fine singer and popular with all the boys of his company. About 10 a.m., June 30, the First Vermont, in Farnsworth's brigade, moved up Frederick Street, Hanover. A number of young ladies sang patriotic songs and welcomed the boys in blue as they passed through town. After being fed by the citizens of Hanover, the regiment marched on out the turnpike. Soon afterward the booming of cannon was heard in the rear. The enemy's cavalry had attacked the last regiment of Farnsworth's Brigade. Soon after the First Vermont and other regiments of Farnsworth's Brigade came to the rescue. While on a charge through the streets of the town, Trowbridge was struck by a cannon ball which shattered his leg and killed his horse. He was quickly carried away and placed in a hospital on Baltimore Street. His leg was amputated, but his wound seemed to be mortal. He was comforted and taken care of by the hospital surgeon and the people of the town, who nursed him. Several days passed by. There was little hope for his recovery and he asked someone to write to his sister, Mary Trowbridge, and ask her to come and see him. The news was flashed over the wires by Daniel E. Trone, the telegraph operator at Hanover. Two hours later the message was received by the young lady, who the next day left her Vermont home to come to Hanover. Meantime the case of Sergeant Trowbridge grew worse. Anaesthetics were administered early in July, just as the sun was sinking behind the western hills, he breathed his last in the local hospital. A few hours later his sister arrived at Hanover and made all the arrangements to have the remains conveyed to her home in the Green Mountain State. In a village cemetery not far from Burlington stands a marble headstone, bearing the following inscription:

"Sergeant John S. Trowbridge, Company E, First Vermont Regiment, mortally wounded at Hanover, Pennsylvania, June 30, 1863. He died for his country."                    ·

A few years ago while in the state of North Carolina, Mr. Prowell was shown an inscription quite similar. It read as follows:

"Corporal John Eaton, Company D, Second North Carolina Cavalry, killed at Hanover, Pennsylvania, during a cavalry engagement at that place. He was a brave soldier who fought for his country."

## UNION FLAGS WAVE HERE

There were three incidents of the eventful June 30 day at
Hanover worthy of special mention. Some time before the Union
cavalry had entered town, a large flag was stretched across Frederick Street between the residences of Henry Long and John
Rupp. This flag continued to float to the breeze during the contest and throughout the day. It was too high in the air to be
cut down by the Confederate soldiers.

Early in May, 1963, a flag had been placed on a tall pole
near the center of Pennville by John Butt, shoemaker and cigar-
maker. It was here that the fight opened. The enemy had not
time to take it down and it waved proudly to the breeze in the
face of the Confederates during the whole afternoon of June 30,
and it welcomed the Fifth Army Corps, a part of whose men
encamped around it.

Suspended against the wall in the lodge room of Washington
Camp No. 328, P. O. S. of A., is an American flag that is especially interesting to the citizens of Hanover as the flag waved
from a pole in front of The Hanover Spectator office, Frederick
Street, during the battle of Hanover.*

At that time the flag was the property of the family of Senary
Leader, the late editor and proprietor of the Spectator, which
was published in a one-story building, on the site of a residence
erected for Mrs. Emma C. Hafer in later years. After the battle
it came into possession of Mr. Welsh, an antique dealer of
York, and was returned to Hanover and became the property
of Washington Camp No. 328, through the efforts of William
H. Long. The flag measures four by six feet, and is in good
state of preservation.

Attached to the flag is an account in part as follows: "This
flag was raised at the office of The Hanover Spectator in April,
1861, at the outbreak of the Civil War. Two years later, when
Hanover was made historic by being the scene of the first battle
between the North and the South to be fought on Northern soil,
the flag was still waving over the newspaper office.

"On the morning of the memorable June 30, 1863, the flag
was floating in honor of the presence of the Union troops, in

* (Record-Herald, June 30, 1917—Prowell.)

defense of the town, and was the center of conflict for 15 to 20 minutes.

"As the head of the Confederate column, somewhat unexpectedly, charged the town, the brunt of their attack fell upon the rear guard of the Union cavalry, comprising the 18th Pennsylvania, which was halted on Frederick Street while the men were being supplied with refreshments by the ladies and patriotic citizens of the town.

"Great confusion and disorder ensued from the surprise and the suddenness of the attack. The regiment was driven in disorder to Center Square. Here order was quickly restored and the command rallied. They were reinforced by the Fifth New York and First West Virginia; a brilliant and successful countercharge was made, and the partially successful Confederates were driven back in great disorder.

"Much of the fighting was done about the pole from which the flag was suspended, the Confederates making desperate attempts in vain to cut the halyards with their sabers and secure the flag as a trophy."

---

## LINCOLN'S GETTYSBURG ADDRESS

Fourscore and seven years ago our fathers brought forth on this continent a new nation, conceived in liberty, and dedicated to the proposition that all men are created equal. Now we are engaged in a great civil war, testing whether that nation, or any nation so conceived and so dedicated can long endure. We are met on a great battlefield of that war. We have come to dedicate a portion of that field, as a final resting place for those who here gave their lives that that nation might live. It is altogether fitting and proper that we should do this. But in a larger sense we cannot dedicate, we cannot consecrate, we cannot hallow this ground. The brave men, living and dead, who struggled here, have consecrated it far above our poor power to add or detract. The world will little note, nor long remember, what we say here; but it can never forget what they did here. It is for us the living, rather, to be dedicated here to the unfinished work which they who fought here have thus far so nobly advanced. It is rather for us to be dedicated to the

ABRAHAM LINCOLN

*From photograph taken by Alexander Gardner November 15, 1863, four days before Lincoln spoke at Gettysburg. This likeness was widely distributed and is one of the most popular of the Civil War president.*

great task remaining before us—that from these honored dead we take increased devotion to that cause for which they gave the last full measure of devotion—that we here highly resolve that these dead shall not have died in vain—that this nation, under God, shall have a new birth of freedom—and that government of the people, by the people, and for the people, shall not perish from the earth.

## ABRAHAM LINCOLN VISIT

The inscription on the plaque beneath a bust of Lincoln in low relief reads as follows:

### ABRAHAM LINCOLN

On November 18, 1863, addressed the citizens of Hanover from the rear platform of a Hanover Branch Railroad Coach when the train bearing him to Gettysburg for the Dedication of the National Cemetery came down a switch to the station which stood on this site. At the request of Capt. A. W. Eichelberger, President of the railroad, several hundred persons assembled to greet Mr. Lincoln. When Pastor M. J. Alleman, of St. Matthew's Lutheran Church cried out, Father Abraham, your children want to hear you, the President removing his high hat and bending his six feet, four inches of height stepped into view through the low doorway. A few grasped his hand. Jackie (Dr. John A.) Melsheimer, held up by his father, reached him an apple which he smilingly accepted. Referring to the battle fought here June 30 he said: I trust when the enemy was here the citizens of Hanover were loyal to our country and the Stars and Stripes. If you are not all true patriots in support of the Union you should be. Before he could say more the engineer opened the throttle and the train backed out after an eight-minute stop. The next day the President's train again paused here briefly. After the trip Mr. Lincoln gave Conductor John Eckert a silver watch. The car that carried the President from Hanover Junction to Hanover and Gettysburg was built in a railroad shop on this public common.

### Lincoln's Visit Commemorated

Lincoln's brief stop here, almost a century ago was described in the weekly Spectator on November 27, 1863. The account read:

"On Wednesday afternoon last it was reported through our streets that Abraham Lincoln, President of the United States, would pass through our town at about 5 o'clock, and long before the hour we could see men, women and children going hurriedly toward the depot all anxious to get a 'good look' at the President.

(The Evening Sun, Hanover, November 12, 1942)

*Early woodburner locomotive with tender and coach shown in Hanover Branch station at Hanover with lattice-work platform and office building with bell cupola. The bell would be rung when a train arrived or departed.*

"At length the presidential train halted until the track was clear. The people immediately massed themselves around the car containing the President, and gave him cheer after cheer, and asked him to 'come out.' Their wishes were soon gratified and as he appeared he was greeted with cheers and delivered one of the brief quaint speeches for which he is celebrated. He said, 'Well, you have seen me, and according to general experience you have seen less than you expected to see,' and a hearty round of merriment attended the remark. The young ladies then came forward bringing bouquets and presented them to the President, while a beautiful flag was planted in the rear of the car. The whistle screamed, the brakes loosened, the assemblage gave a cheer, and the train rattled up the Gettysburg road."

A marker commemorating the event, erected at the corner of Park Avenue and Railroad Street, and dedicated November 11, 1942, points out that the dramatic appeal of Pastor M. J. Alle-

THE REV. M. J. ALLEMAN
(1820-1897)
*Pastor of St. Matthew's Lutheran Church.*

man of St. Matthew's Lutheran Church, "Father Abraham, your children want to hear you," brought Lincoln through the low doorway of the train, doffing his high hat.

Lincoln is said to have smilingly accepted an apple from small Jackie Melsheimer (later Dr. John A. Melsheimer) and to have referred to the battle of Hanover, which had taken place June 30.

The conductor of the train, John Eckert, Hanover, then thirty-three, had an unforgettable experience during the run to Gettysburg and the return trip the following day.

A statement by his son, Jacob Grant Eckert, preserved in the Western Maryland Railway Company files at Baltimore, reads:

"I was born at Hanover, Pa. My parents were John Eckert and Adeline Eckert.

"My father was a railroad conductor on the Hanover Branch Railroad which afterwards became Hanover Junction, Hanover and Gettysburg Railroad and is now a part of the Western Maryland System.

"My father was conductor of the train which took President Lincoln from Hanover Junction to Gettysburg November 18 and 19, 1863, when he made his famous memorial address at Gettysburg. My father has frequently told me about this occasion. The presidential party was small and did not travel in a private car. They transferred from the Northern Central at Hanover Junction to a special Hanover Branch train. The special train waited (overnight) at Gettysburg for President Lincoln and his party and brought them back to Hanover Junction, where they were turned over to the Northern Central.

"It was at Hanover Junction on the return trip that President Lincoln presented my father with a silver watch and said to him: 'Mr. Conductor, I thank you for returning us safely'; he then handed my father the watch and said 'May God bless you, may you live long and prosper, goodbye,' and walked away."

The Hanover Branch Railroad coach and engine used to convey the presidential party were furnished at the request of David Wills, secretary of the Gettysburg Railroad, by Captain Abdiel W. Eichelberger, president of the Hanover branch.

A recollection of Heber Michael, Hanover tailor, recorded in local data, states that during 1889 the aged Captain Eichelberger asked Mr. Michael to drive him to Hanover Junction, where the captain and President Lincoln had waited under a shade tree for the connecting train. The captain kept ever enshrined in memory his meeting with Lincoln.

---

## DEDICATION OF ABRAHAM LINCOLN MARKER

Alluding to Abraham Lincoln's remark more than eight decades ago that "this government cannot endure permanently half slave and half free," District Attorney Carl B. Shelley of Dauphin County, principal speaker at the exercises November 11, 1942, incident to the unveiling of a marker commemorating Lincoln's Hanover visit, declared that "if it were given to Lincoln to speak through the veil of death, would he not enlarge the scope of the territory referred to in those remarks and say to us: 'I believe that this world cannot endure permanently half slave and half free?'"

"Twenty-one years ago almost to this very minute the body of the Unknown Soldier, representing the nameless dead of the First World War, was returned to his native soil in Arlington Cemetery, overlooking the National Capital," said the speaker. "His funeral procession was the most impressive military ceremonial of our history. The significance of that occasion, however, was not the august formality of reverent tribute. . . . The significance was the thought that he had been willing to die that the American way of life might be perpetuated and that life, liberty and the pursuit of happiness might be the boon of the entire world.

"November 11, 1921, on that third anniversary of Armistice Day, a world's hope was high that the Unknown Soldier had not died in vain. That was before the Black Shirts led by the bellicose Mussolini had marched to Rome. Germany was a struggling young republic and Hitler a petty racketeer, an annoyance only to the local peace officers. Poland was a nation again. China was on her way to stability. The League of Nations and World Court were the promised forms of peace.

"That was 21 years ago. Today, autocracy has supplanted democracy in many lands. Dictators have displaced constitutional guarantees and war lords are on the march. Austria, Czechoslovakia, Poland, Norway, Denmark, Holland, Belgium, France,

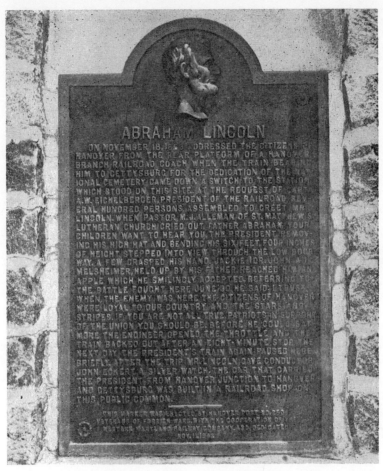

LINCOLN PLAQUE ON RAILROAD STREET

*Commemorating stop of Lincoln train and brief address of the President to Hanoverians when he was en route to Gettysburg, September 18, 1863.*

Yugoslavia, Greece, Rumania, Bulgaria and many other nations have fallen before the weight of Frankenstein war machines and their peoples subjected to conditions worse than slavery.

"Today two opposing theories of government are locked in mortal combat. The Axis powers hold to the belief that all people exist solely for the convenience of the government. The state is supreme and the sanctity of the life, liberty and property of the individual is a mere mockery.

"The United States and her allies are engaged in an all-out struggle to perpetuate and preserve the American way of life which has as its foundation stone the principle that government exists solely and entirely for the benefit of its citizens; that the welfare of the individual is of supreme importance.

"One of these theories of government will succeed and the other one will fail. . . . Time was before the event of modern means of transportation and communication that the world was large enough to allow two such conflicting theories of government to live unto themselves without danger of serious conflict. Today, however, the radio and airplane have made neighbors of people living in the farthermost corners of the earth and therefore two such contrary beliefs respecting the rights of individuals cannot exist. One must succeed, one is doomed to fail."

"Today," continued District Attorney Shelley, "as never before in the history of our country do we have a more urgent need for a review of the life and philosophy of the great martyred president whom we honor here. The seventy-seven years that have passed since the tragic event in Ford's Theater have faded the figures of his contemporaries and Lincoln stands grandly alone. . . . His humility, his self-renunciation and devotion, his patience, his endurance in a great cause of small obstructive minds, and finally his tragic end give him a personality that is as vivid in the hearts of the people as if it were but yesterday. We feel a closer touch with him than with living men. His influence has spread to the four quarters of the globe. The oppressed and lowely peoples, as liberty and free government spread, pronounce his name with awe and cherish his assured personal sympathy as a source of hope."

The orator told how under Lincoln's guidance our forefathers saved the Union, and the nation they saved in 1865 in 1917 saved an imperilled world. "And the end is not yet. The nation which our ancestors led into knowledge, unity and strength, is yet to lead the broken nations of the world into a Promised Land."

"It is fitting and proper," he concluded, "that my comrades of the last war should properly commemorate the great event in the history of this community, and, therefore, citizens of Hanover, in the name and on behalf of Post No. 2506, Veterans of Foreign Wars of the United States of America, I have the honor to deliver into your keeping this memorial commemorating the visit in your community of one of the great men of all time. May it always be your inspiration and faithful guide, remembering always that as you honor yourself you honor the ideals and principles that have made and preserved us a great people."

Mr. Shelley's splendid talk followed the unveiling of the marker erected by the Hanover V.F.W. Post. Miss Mary Joan Alleman, daughter of Mr. and Mrs. Richard B. Alleman, Frederick Street, and great-granddaughter of the Rev. M. J. Alleman, pastor of St. Matthew's Lutheran Church, who acted as spokesman in behalf of the Hanover citizens when they gathered at the little station, which stood on the site of the memorial, 79 years ago to greet the wartime President en route to the battlefield at Gettysburg, performed the simple ceremony of the unveiling.

A large crowd gathered at 2:30 p.m. about the platform erected near the Western Maryland freight office at the northeast corner of Railroad Street and Park Avenue to witness the ceremony and hear the fine program which had been arranged by the committee in charge, headed by Commander Austin V. Lau of the V.F.W. Post.

R. D. Stambaugh, a past commander of the Central Pennsylvania V.F.W. Association, presided as chairman. Following the assembly call by a bugler who stood with the V.F.W. Color Guard at the rear of the platform for the speakers and guests of honor, the Rev. Paul L. Foulk, Past Chaplain General of the V.F.W. of the United States, pronounced the invocation.

The Eichelberger High School choir, composed of about twenty-five young men and women, sang four appropriate selections to good effect under the direction of Miss Eleanor Turner, opening with several stanzas of "America," then following an address of welcome by Burgess J. Oscar Kinneman they presented the hymn "Onward Christian Soldiers."

Presentation of the National Colors and pole given by the Western Maryland Railway Company was made by William E. Dulling, local agent for the company. The flag was raised as Mr. Dulling spoke and fluttered to the breezes during the remainder of the exercises. Mr. Dulling said it would be raised and lowered daily by employes of the railroad company.

C. R. Zarfoos, Baltimore, assistant to the president of the W. M. Railway, who was next introduced, has served as traveling freight agent at York and industrial agent at Baltimore. He thrilled the audience with reports of the latest developments of the war in Europe and Africa, and then launched into an informative discourse on the preparedness of the railroads in America for handling the wartime freight traffic, contrasting the situation here with that in Germany where the railway system was described as failing in adequacy due to neglect under the Hitler regime. He expressed the pleasure of the company in cooperating with the V.F.W. Post by placing the site of the old Hanover Branch line station, now under lease to the W. M. Railway, at the disposal of the veterans for erection of the memorial.

After the unveiling by Miss Alleman, Chairman Stambaugh told the audience that the rugged simplicity of the marker of native granite blocks with granite capstone and plaque bearing a bust of Lincoln in low relief with inscription had been decided upon in keeping with the austerity of the times as well as the rugged character of the man it honored.

The inscription was then read by William Anthony, prime mover in proposing the erection of the marker and active in assembling historical data relative to the event memorialized.

An interesting part of the program was that in which Commander Lau introduced the specially invited guests, asking each to rise as called upon. They included J. Grant Eckert, Baltimore, son of Conductor John Eckert of the Lincoln train, who displayed the selfsame twelve-ounce watch which the President gave Mr. Eckert as a memento upon completion of the trip to and from Gettysburg, and Dr. Gellert Alleman, Wallingford, Pennsylvania, son of Dr. M. J. Alleman, who called Lincoln to the car platform on the memorable November 18, 1863. Mrs. Amelia Melsheimer Ehrehart, also an invited guest and descendant of one who figured in the Lincoln visit, was unable to be present.

Others on the platform presented by Commander Lau had been present as boys on the actual historic occasion. They were J. H. Schmuck and Henry A. Haas, Hanover; Milton Kohler, Hagerstown; and William H. Long, Pikesville, Maryland, all nonagenarians, the eldest being Mr. Haas who was ninety-one. Mr. Long and Mr. Haas spoke briefly. Mr. Kohler, who was born in Hanover, the son of Jeremiah Kohler, a former chief burgess, recalled having heard the Rev. Mr. Alleman call Lincoln to show himself to the citizens assembled. Other guests present were Mrs. Mabel C. Wolcott, public librarian; Robert A. Bagshaw, superintendent of the public schools; C. A. Eckbert, who was responsible for placing the platform and assisting the committee in charge in numerous other details. One member of the audience, George D. Hopkins, it is interesting to note, recalled that as a lad of seven he was taken by his father to see the body of Lincoln as it lay in state in New York City during the course of the trip of the funeral train from Washington to Springfield, Illinois.

The high school choir sang "America the Beautiful" and later "The Star Spangled Banner," in which the assembly joined. The Right Rev. Monsignor Patrick F. McGee, McSherrystown, pronounced the benediction. The sounding of taps by the bugler brought the event to a close.

Handsome programs prepared by Mr. Anthony were distributed. They contained portraits of Captain A. W. Eichelberger, president of the Hanover Branch Railroad, the Rev. M. J. Alleman, Conductor John Eckert, and Lincoln, also a reproduction of a scene at the railroad station here in 1868, showing the old "Conewago" wood-burner locomotive, bell tower and office of the station. The original photograph of the station is from a fine collection of photos owned by the late Charles E. Moul.

The speakers, invited guests, including Mr. and Mrs. Richard B. Alleman, Mrs. Shelley, Acting Chief of Police J. Frank Mulhorn, and press representative were entertained by the V.F.W. committee following the exercises at dinner at the Hotel Richard McAllister. Richard B. Alleman served as toastmaster for this occasion. Reminiscences of earlier days in Hanover were exchanged and historic events discussed.

The committee which had charge of arrangements included, besides Commander Lau, R. D. Stambaugh, Robert Becker, Harry Myers and Robert Gise.

## THE LINCOLN TRAIN

The Lincoln train comprising four coaches left Washington at noon over the Baltimore & Ohio tracks with the intention of arriving at Gettysburg by 6 p.m.

The special train was decorated with flags and red, white, and blue bunting. His secretaries, John G. Nicolay and John Hay, accompanied the President. The rear section of the last car, described as a director's car, was partitioned off into a drawing room. It was here Mr. Lincoln sat. Others on the train came to talk to him from time to time.

The train arrived at Camden station, Baltimore, at 1:20 p.m. President John W. Garrett and Superintendent William Prescott Smith of the B. & O. and President J. D. Cameron of the Northern Central were among those who met Mr. Lincoln there. He was frequently cheered by the crowds as the cars drawn by horses along Howard and Cathedral Streets were transferred to the Bolton station on the Northern Central line. A baggage car was added, fitted up as a dining car for those including the President who had left Washington without lunch. The train left for Hanover Junction at 2 p.m.

According to a letter to The Evening Sun from Mrs. James Wright, Emporium, daughter of James Lilly, engineer on the Lincoln train, she recalled that her father took over the loco- motive at Hanover Junction when the train was about twenty minutes behind schedule. Engineer Lilly promised the President he would reach Gettysburg in time. The train arrived at the depot in Hanover at 5 p.m. and after the brief stop there with Lilly at the throttle pulled into the Gettysburg station at the hour Lincoln had planned.

The Hanover Branch railroad to Hanover Junction was built in 1852, a distance of twelve and a half miles to connect with the Northern Central. Headed by Captain Eichelberger the directorate included Jacob Forney, William Grumbine, John Newman, Peter Flickinger, Jacob Wirt, Hanover, and John Jen- kins, McSherrystown. Jim Lilly was engineer; William Stahl, conductor; John J. Bingley, master mechanic; Charles G. Her- man, machinist; Joseph Leib, passenger agent; Jacob Bange, painter. The railroad had three locomotives by 1865: No. 1,

Gettysburg; No. 2, Conewago; No. 3, Heidelberg. Others later were: No. 4, Hanover; No. 5, Alliance; No. 6, Six Wheeler, until by 1886 the line boasted eleven engines. In September 1886 the Western Maryland absorbed the Hanover Junction, Hanover and Gettysburg Railroad. A round trip Baltimore to Gettysburg and return totaled 142 miles.

Frank G. McKinney, late of Carlisle Street, Hanover, served as conductor on the runs of a combination freight and passenger train from Hanover Junction through Hanover to Littlestown where the road then ended. On the afternoon of November 18, 1863, Conductor McKinney was obliged to run his train on the switch at Porters. He had received notice that a train conveying President Lincoln and a delegation of prominent men from Washington and elsewhere, would pass his train at Porters, moving rapidly to Gettysburg. He reported that this Presidential train was composed of engine, combination car, and four coaches. Every car was filled with passengers.

According to a statement of Captain A. W. Eichelberger, President Lincoln, in company with Secretary Seward, Edward McPherson and others rode in the rear coach. While waiting for the train to leave Hanover Junction, Captain Eichelberger often said that Mr. Lincoln stood beside him at the Junction and talked about the burning of the railroad bridges over the Codorus by the Confederates June 27, 1863.

When the conductor, John Eckert, shouted "All aboard," the President remarked: "I reckon, Captain, we don't want to be left behind." Both then stepped into the car.

On the way to Hanover Captain Eichelberger told the conductor that he should move the train into the station and supply the engine with sufficient water to bring the same excursion train back to Hanover Junction next day. At 6:30 p.m., September 19, the President's train left Gettysburg for Washington. Mr. Lincoln was weary and did little talking. It is said that he "stretched out on one of the side seats in the drawing room and had a wet towel laid across his eyes and forehead."

It was during a brief interval at Hanover on the 18th that President Lincoln, in response to a call for a speech, appeared on the platform of the rear car, where he shook hands with about thirty persons. He was making a few remarks when the

HANOVER JUNCTION, PA., IN 1863

*From Brady photograph. Figure on station platform in front of white shutter and partly obscured by locomotive was claimed to be Lincoln by Miss Helen Nicolay, daughter of the President's secretary, John George Nicolay.*

LINCOLN COACH

*Early Hanover Branch R. R. car claimed by the late William Anthony to be the coach in which Lincoln rode from Hanover Junction to Gettysburg, November 18, 1863. The coach at the time the photograph was taken had been used by the Western Maryland Railroad as a bunkhouse at Port Covington. Mr. Anthony is standing on the car platform.*

conductor signaled the engineer to move the train from the switch onto the main track to Gettysburg.

Pacton Bigham, of Chambersburg, guarded the door in Judge Wills' residence where Lincoln slept the night of November 18. Bigham, then a member of Bell's cavalry, a local military company, said afterward that he saw Lincoln writing at his desk just before he retired for the night. He thought the President may have been copying the speech he was to deliver the next day.

According to testimony of employes in the Western Maryland shops in Hanover after the war, the car in which Lincoln rode to Gettysburg was nearly worn out by 1882, and was knocked to pieces a few years later. No part of it is known to be in existence. It was last used on the road from Hanover to East Berlin. Mr. McKinney remembered seeing and riding in the car when he was conductor on that line.

### Railroad Shops at Hanover

The Hanover Branch line coach which took Lincoln to Gettysburg for the National Cemetery dedication was made in the yards at Hanover. When improved coaches were introduced, the Lincoln coach was sent to Port Covington by the Western Maryland where it was used as a bunk house. No attempt was made to preserve it. The coach is said to have had two long wooden benches, one on each side of the car.

An article in the Hanover Herald 1872 describes a fine new coach built in the Hanover Railroad shops by Master Builder Henry Britcher. The body was finished in red, platform and roof with rounded corners were green, the trucks were a bright green, striped red and white, and wheels buff. The roof extended over front and rear platforms. The interior was in natural finish Hungarian ash. The seats were of white oak—with upholstered back rests. The car weighed 34,000 pounds. J. J. Bingley was machinist; Reuben Sprenkle did the painting; Alexander J. Gitt, the upholstering; David Bixler, the plumbing. Captain Eichelberger was president of the Hanover Branch and H. A. Young superintendent of the road.

*Stone memorial in Mt. Olivet Cemetery marks resting place of Mary Shaw Leader, reporter for the Hanover Spectator who covered the dedication of the National Cemetery at Gettysburg by Abraham Lincoln, November 19, 1863.*

## GIRL REPORTER HONORED

Amid a throng of former neighbors and fellow townsmen Mary Shaw Leader came into her own Sunday, November 16, 1941, as one of the community's historic personages. After resting for twenty-eight years in an unmarked grave at Mt. Olivet Cemetery she was honored for her part in reporting for the community newspaper back in 1863 the address of Abraham Lincoln at the dedication of the Gettysburg National Cemetery in November of that year. With simple but impressive services a

(The Evening Sun, Hanover, November 17, 1941)

handsome granite shaft to her memory was unveiled as autumnal winds swirled the yellowing leaves from towering maples about her resting place. The weather was not unsimilar to that which prevailed when she trudged fifteen miles to Gettysburg to cover the important event there on November 19, 1863, for the Hanover Spectator, and remindful of that occasion the order of exercises yesterday followed closely the program in which Lincoln took a casual but never-to-be-forgotten part.

There were hundreds who gathered at the burial grounds to pay tribute to the girl reporter who "helped the world to remember" Lincoln's appropriate remarks. Most newspapermen at the Battlefield cemetery dedication 78 years ago gave their space to the nearly two-hour flowery oration of principal speaker Edward Everett, and neglected or overlooked the President's words —but not Mary Leader. She brought back to the little Hanover weekly newspaper the President's full three-minute text and printed it all, acclaiming it was a "remarkable speech."

From a platform erected at an intersection of the avenues near the flag-covered memorial, flanked by color guards from the Paul E. Lau Commandery, No. 66, the principal speaker, Dr. Robert Fortenbaugh, professor of history at Gettysburg College, told the story of the intrepid young newspaperwoman who had the courage and insight to recognize the grandeur of the words which Lincoln spoke when others of higher station than she so lamentably failed.

The committee of arrangements used excellent judgment in selecting Dr. Fortenbaugh as the "orator" for the occasion. Not only is he a distinguished historian but he is also a descendant of one of Hanover's first citizens of another day.

To Wirt Crapster, 15-year-old son of Mr. and Mrs. Walter Crapster of Taneytown and a junior in the Taneytown High School, claiming a common ancestry with Mary Leader, went the honor of lifting the American flag from the memorial. A murmur of approbation spread through the crowd as they caught the first glimpse of the stone, bearing a likeness of Miss Leader as she appeared about the time of her journalistic feat and a suitable inscription, beautifully lettered in a style of type that would have appealed to Mary Leader as a member of a printer's family.

Said Professor Fortenbaugh, "This beautiful expression which now stands unveiled before us is a lasting tribute of this community's appreciation of historic interests and a worthy honor to a unique personality. In these days of national stress and strain it is for our better strengthening and encouragement that we well turn to remember heroic days of the past. In face of our present seemingly overwhelming troubles it is good for us to recall other and maybe darker days when true Americans faced their troubles and triumphed over them.

"Seventy-eight years ago was another time of stress and strain, the very future of the American Union was at stake, yes more, the very future of representative government. But the Union was saved, representative government was vindicated, and the Nation went on to grander and greater heights. For in those days we were blessed with a great leader, Abraham Lincoln, a man of courage, of wisdom, of charity, and of conviction. Supporting him were multitudes of lesser men and women. Some of these are remembered; the greater number are forgotten. Among those who are remembered as a worthy follower of the man with a great vision was Mary Shaw Leader.

"The presence and activity of women in business and professional life today is a matter of course, a commonplace circumstance. That was not true in 1863, especially in the field of journalism. An unusual set of conditions, however, put Mary Shaw Leader in a position of responsibility. She bravely took a man's place as a reporter on a Hanover newspaper. That responsibility gave her a great opportunity, and of that opportunity she made the most.

"Present at an event in a nearby town in her capacity as a reporter, she heard a great address. It is to her lasting honor and glory that she recognized the grandeur of the event and the greatness of the address. For this we remember her here today and for her insight and courage to express her convictions we this day dedicate this memorial to her."

With a few bold strokes the speaker gave the setting for the occasion which called Mary Leader to Gettysburg. He quoted from a number of leading newspapers of the day, their views, some few favorable and many unfavorable, upon Lincoln's speech, and as to history's verdict upon that speech, repeated

Henry Eyster Jacobs' words: "Gettysburg will live in history because of its association with Lincoln even more than as the scene of the decisive battle of the Civil War."

Among the few who were quick to discern the true greatness of the address and to evaluate its real significance, Dr. Fortenbaugh continued, was Mary Leader reporting for the Hanover Spectator. "It was not her fault," he said, "that her paper was a weekly and that her next publication was six days later, Wednesday, November 25. Her mind was made up as early as were the minds of other favorable commentators. She gave utterance to that opinion as early as she could:

" 'On Thursday last, the 19th of November, 1863, was a great day in the history of Pennsylvania and the entire nation. The battlefield was dedicated with imposing ceremonies in honor of the great victory which decided the fate of the Nation.

" 'The appearance of the President on the stand was the signal for repeated cheers and enthusiasm.

" 'Then our great President began to deliver a remarkable speech.'

"Thus Mary Shaw Leader correctly discerned the significance of the occasion, and what is more, the superb value of the address. For she discerned what has come to be the common opinion. And to her insight and understanding, this memorial to Mary Shaw Leader is most appropriately dedicated."

Arrangements had been made to broadcast the program through the remote facilities of the Hanover studio of the Monocacy Broadcasting Company and a loud-speaker device enabled those assembled to hear the exercises despite the strong west wind which prevailed.

The services opened with the playing of "America" by the P. O. S. of A. band of Hanover. The Rev. Nevin E. Smith, pastor of Emmanuel Reformed Church, pronounced a prayer. The choir of Emmanuel Reformed Church sang as a dirge "Rock of Ages" under direction of Miss Kathryn O'Boyle with David M. Brown accompanying on a portable organ. Following the oration, the choir sang "Battle Hymn of the Republic" and Dr. Harry Hursh Beidleman, pastor of St. Matthew's Lutheran Church, read the Lincoln address; and the program was concluded with benediction by the Rev. Edward J. O'Flynn, pastor of St. Joseph's Catholic Church, and the playing of "The Star Spangled Banner" by the P. O. S. of A. band.

Present on the platform was Frank E. Cremer, vice president of the Mt. Olivet Cemetery Association, who accepted the monument in behalf of the Mt. Olivet board who announced that the directors had voted to give Mary Leader's grave perpetual care.

Also present on the platform was William Anthony, well known Hanover printer, who conceived the plan of honoring Mary Leader and to whose efforts and perseverance the placing of the suitable memorial has been accomplished. Mr. Anthony learned his trade in the office of The Spectator and has never forgotten the courteous treatment and kindnesses bestowed upon him by Mary Leader during the period of his apprenticeship from 1886 to 1891. The only other surviving apprentice of the Spectator office, Baxter B. Chenoweth, Taneytown, was also on hand for the dedication.

It is to the everlasting credit of the community spirit of Hanover that so many of the families living neighbors to the Leaders when the Spectator office was conducted on Frederick Street were represented at the services. These included members and representatives of the following old Hanover families: Wirts, Naills, Trones, Carvers, Fishers, Stairs, Schmucks, Winebrenners, Anthonys, Rupps, Longs, Groves, Gitts, Forneys, Schwalms, and Eichelbergers.

---

## BOY LISTENER IN NOVEL POST

One of Abraham Lincoln's greatest admirers in Hanover was a life-long Democrat. George D. Gitt, president of the J. W. Gitt Company and the Hanover Glove Company and vice president of the First National Bank, told an Evening Sun reporter that Lincoln had been his boyish ideal and that the older he grew the more highly he regarded this great American.

Mr. Gitt's most cherished memory—and Mr. Gitt, by the way, had a wonderful memory—was his contact with Lincoln at the time of the war president's visit to Pennsylvania for the

(The Evening Sun, Hanover, February 12, 1930)

dedication of the National Cemetery at Gettysburg, November 19, 1863. Any boy will envy Mr. Gitt's experiences on that occasion. The Hanoverian heard Lincoln speak both here and at Gettysburg and he spoke and shook hands with the President at Judge Wills' residence. Moreover, when he listened to the great dedicatory address from the lips of the author, he occupied a point of vantage that was unique, to say the least.

Mr. Gitt was a boy of fourteen at the time—his birthday had been in April—and we are anticipating our story in telling it but the point from which the Hanover youth heard Lincoln's immortal address was lying under the platform directly beneath the speaker whose tall gaunt form clad in black frock coat he glimpsed above him through the spaces between the boards of the platform and whose words came distinctly to him as he lay comfortably on the ground.

He had been standing in a cramped position crushed up against the edge of the platform during Edward Everett's long speech of an hour and ten minutes and the physical relief he had obtained lying beneath the structure was great, Mr. Gitt said. His one boyish regret at the time was that the President made his speech so brief—he felt so comfortable lying there.

### Hears Lincoln at Hanover

All Hanover, men, women and children, was up on the Commons when the Lincoln train stopped here on its way to Gettysburg on November 18, Mr. Gitt recalled. It wasn't the intention to stop here at all but orders had been given by President Eichelberger to take on water for the return trip to the Junction next day. The train pulled off the main line and down the siding toward the lattice-work station located on Railroad Street. The press of the crowd was so great that the people had to be pushed off the tracks in order to let the train through. When it came to a stop, the boy George Gitt found himself at the rear platform of Lincoln's car and could see the President sitting a few seats forward.

The Rev. M. J. Alleman, pastor of St. Matthew's Lutheran Church, who was in the crowd milling about the coach, expressed the impatience of the people who wanted Lincoln to come out and speak to them, when he shouted, "Father Abraham, come out, your children want to see you!" Finally Lincoln made his way to the door, having to remove his hat and stoop in order to get onto the platform. Mr. Gitt expressed the incongruity of the President's size and the smallness of the car by explaining that the coaches then were like toys. Lincoln was about six feet three inches in height and looked taller when he wore his high hat.

The next day George Gitt persuaded his father J. W. Gitt, proprietor of the leading store in this section, to let him have a horse to go to Gettysburg for the dedication which had been heralded up and down the countryside for many days as a big event. A neighbor's son, Harry Anthony, nearly his own age, provided the buggy, and accordingly George Gitt set off early next morning with the Anthony boy and his brother William Gitt, two years younger, for Gettysburg, going the short way through McSherrystown and Bonneauville.

The boys stopped at a farmhouse outside of the town and persuaded the housewife there to allow them to tie their horse to a tree after assuring her that he was a well-trained government animal and would not chew at the bark. Mr. Gitt's father had purchased the horse at a sale of government animals in Baltimore. The woman was the only person at home, the men folks, she said, having all gone to town to see Lincoln. She consented to feed and water the horse. The boys had brought oats along with them.

The three lads, carefree, then set off to see what they could see. The National Cemetery was not the fine level piece of ground with neat lawns and handsome trees it is today, Mr. Gitt declared. In fact, it was so rough and covered with such huge boulders that people wondered what on earth the government meant by picking such a tract of land for a cemetery. It took considerable clearing and grading to put it in its present shape, according to the Hanoverian.

### Crawls Under Platform

The boys got close up to the front of the platform for the exercises, being the kind of boys who were always in the forefront whether it was trouble or pleasure brewing. Mr. Gitt remembers scanning the occupants of the platform, two of whom he recognized. They were the late Mrs. M. O. Smith, York Street, then Miss Louisa Vandersloot, a Gettysburg girl, and Miss Fahnestock, daughter of one of the proprietors of the leading Gettysburg store. Both girls were on the platform by virtue of being members of St. James Lutheran choir which sang during the program.

As previously related Mr. Gitt stood during the long talk by Mr. Everett, but the press of the crowd behind him was so great the edge of the platform was cutting into his chest. So he put his hands against the edge and pushed backward with all his strength and thus made room for himself to slip underneath.

Beneath the platform the boy—he was already assisting in his father's dry goods store—made to him an important discovery. It was that the structure was resting on what was known in store parlance as long "W" cases from the Fahnestock store. The youth counted the boxes and made a mental calculation as to their value. The new cases cost $2.50 apiece and secondhand ones 50 cents each. The merchants then, whenever possible, made it their business to have the goods shipped to them in used instead of new boxes as there was a difference of $2 in the cost.

### Meets Lincoln at Wills House

Following the dedicatory exercises the three boys made a dash down town before the crowds and they were in time to see the barouche bearing Lincoln and Judge Wills stop at the latter's home. Boylike they peered into the hall after the President and watched him standing there at the foot of the staircase with his arm on the newel post. Judge Wills spied the trio and recognizing George D.—his father and the judge were good friends—he motioned them to come forward and introduced them to Mr. Lincoln as "three York County boys from Hanover." He shook hands with them saying, with a humorous twinkle lighting his careworn and tired face:

"You boys had a lively time just recently. How did you like it?" He referred to the engagement fought at Hanover on June 30.

"Not so well," the boys replied.

# To the Citizens of Hanover!

"The funeral ceremonies of the late lamented **Chief** Magistrate. Abraham Lincoln, will take place on **Wednesday, the 19th** inst., at 12 o'clock. The various religious denominations **throughout** the country are invited to meet in their respective places of **worship at** that hour for the purpose of solemnizing the occasion **with appropriate** ceremonies."

In ~~consequence~~ with the above request from the Acting Secretary of State, the citizens of Hanover are respectfully requested to suspend all business on said occasion from 11 to 2 o'clock.

At a meeting of the Burgess & Town Council of Hanover, held last evening, the following programme was agreed upon :

Bells to commence tolling at 11 o'clock---continue tolling one hour. Citizens to meet on the Public Square at half-past eleven o'clock, form into procession and proceed to German Reformed Church, where services appropriate to the occasion are to be held.

The Soldiers all who have been in service, will lead the procession, with Martial Music.

Ministers of different denominations.

Borough Authorities.

Citizens.

It is expected that the citizens generally will join in the procession. A Great, a Good Man has been taken away from us---and as Americans, as Patriots, it becomes us to honor the Upright Magistrate, the Honest Man, the Faithful Servant.

By Order of the Council.

## DAVID S. TANGER,
### CHIEF BURGESS.

L. F. MELSHEIMER, Secretary.

## Hanover, April 18, 1865.

*Following the assassination of President Lincoln above notice was issued by Burgess David S. Tanger. It was printed on 10 by 12-inch sheets at The Spectator office. A copy owned by Miss Fannie Hostetter, Broadway, granddaughter of Burgess Tanger, was loaned for this reproduction.*

"It looks as if some of you young people will have to get into it yet," he went on.

Then as he turned to mount the steps slowly he said to the judge, "Do not let any one disturb me for the next hour."

And so he disappeared from view going to the upstairs room which had been assigned to him.

The three boys spent part of the day going over the battlefield which was, of course, unmarked in those days and still littered with the debris of battle. They picked up some of the smaller souvenirs—shell fragments, Minie balls, even bayonets and the like, then discarded them as they found other articles that pleased them better.

Mr. Gitt had visited the battlefield soon after the conflict and hardly a year passed since that time that he had not taken parties of friends on sightseeing trips over the field. On an early visit after the battle the youth accompanied a group of Hanover citizens when dead horses still lay unburied beside their batteries. They had been covered with some chemical like the product used in tanning, he said, and were all of a uniform "dun" color, making some people believe that the government had used only dun-colored horses.

One other incident in regard to Lincoln is recalled by Mr. Gitt. That was when word reached Hanover of his assassination and death and when Hanover with the rest of the country was plunged into deepest mourning. They had just received at the store a fifty-yard bolt of black print or calico, worth at the close of the war on account of the scarcity of cotton 65 cents a yard. The youth proposed that they use this black print to drape the front of the store, and after gaining his father's consent this was done. The J. W. Gitt dry goods store was the first in this section to honor the martyred president.

## MARION RIFLES AND OTHER MILITIA

Presently housing the E. S. Stambaugh Auto Parts Co., Marion Hall stands on East Walnut Street, almost directly opposite the elementary school building. A century ago it served as drill headquarters for the Marion Rifles and later as a hospital for casualties in the "first engagement of importance on free soil in the War of the Rebellion," the battle of Hanover.

Marion Hall, East Walnut Street, erected in 1860 as armory for the Marion Rifles. Used as hospital after Hanover battle, and later as school. Now an auto parts store.

The lot on which the brick building stands was deeded June 10, 1763, by the town's founder, Richard M'Calister and his wife, Mary, to George White. On the part of the site facing the Monocacy Trail, now York Street, was erected the Weiss (White) Tavern, later the home of Mr. and Mrs. Stambaugh.

The Hanover Spectator recorded June 5, 1857: "We are pleased to see that a military spirit is beginning to take hold of our citizens and the prospect of raising a fine company is very favorable. Some forty have already joined and we think it will not be long till they have as many more, as there is material enough in our midst to raise two of the largest companies in the state."

On July 10, 1857, according to the newspaper:

"The Marion Riflemen under command of Captain R. J. Winterode now found their formation. (It is proper to state here, perhaps, that this company is about organizing, but are not as yet uniformed.) After marching around the various streets they were finally brought to the market square and there drilled in the presence of a large number of citizens who appeared to be much delighted. . . ."

In a second deed, dated August 30, 1859, the site of the armory was sold to the Marion Hall Association by William Barnitz.

### Marion Hall Cornerstone Laid

The ceremony of laying the cornerstone of the Infantry Armory took place on Saturday, June 30, 1860. The parchment on which was written the history of the building and the principal purpose for which it was to be devoted, the names of the President of the U. S., the Governor of Pennsylvania, and chief burgess of Hanover, names of members of the corps, the designer and contractor, with the usual records and some coins, was placed in a bottle which was sealed and deposited in a metallic box with borough papers. The ceremony of laying the stone was performed by Major Fred Metzger, the oldest soldier of the town and gallant commander of the Hanover volunteers at the battle of North Point. The major died June 24, 1868, in his ninety-third year.

## Hanover Infantry Organized

The military corps was organized in Hanover on the Public Square July 1, 1860. Election of officers resulted as follows: Captain, F. M. Baughman; first lieutenant, Stephen Keefer; second lieutenant, John Busbey, Jr. The following non-commissioned officers were chosen: First sergeant, Jacob Britcher; second, William B. Woods; third, Reuben Sprenkle; fourth, Joseph Jenkins; corporals, Pius Smith, Isaac Wagner, Samuel Trone, and William Beard. Dr. Charles Humbach was named surgeon; Jere Kohler, pioneer; Henry S. Sherman, ensign; and John Forrest, quartermaster sergeant. William B. Woods was chosen secretary of the company and Jeremiah Kohler treasurer.

The muster roll of the riflemen, who reportedly took their name from Francis Marion, the "Swamp Fox" hero of Revolutionary War days, included:

Horatio G. Myers, captain; Joseph A. Renaut, first lieutenant; Jacob W. Bender, second lieutenant; Alfred McKinney, first sergeant; William Troup, second sergeant; George Kohler, third sergeant; Henry Houser, fourth sergeant; Adam Klunk, first corporal; Abraham Becker, second corporal; Henry Trone, third corporal; Andrew Miller, fourth corporal; Silas Yingling and Lewis Renaut, musicians.

Privates William Klunk, Henry Carr, Adam McKinney, Henry F. Constine, Rolandus Roland, Jeremiah Carbaugh, Adam Rebeling, William Stamm, Adam Reiling, Jacob D. and Pius Neiderer, Edward C. Slagle, Thomas Brown, John Gross, Lewis Cline, Martin Diehl, William Allwood, P. Henry Bittinger, William Bair, Charles Fiscus, Alexander Parr, Jackson Wintrode, Jacob Doll, Daniel Lookabaugh, John Martin, Adam Soule, Ruben Stonesifer, Israel Boblitz, John Low, George Colbea, Calvin Simpson, William White, James Grimes, Daniel Keeser, William Rhinedolar, John McClroy, Anthony Klunk, George Warner, Jerome Adams, Nicholas Hartz, Benjamine Shonston, John Wheeler, Daniel Witmyer, Peter Shuck, George W. Brigg, Andrew Brubaker, George K. Yinger, George Whitaker, Clinton W. Keister, Charles March, Lewis Burns, Michael F. Mulgrew, Daniel L. Stoud, Charles F. M'Creary, Ruben P. Struminger, John Foust, Isaac M'Creary, John A. Walters, Joseph Mannock, Nicholas Hahn, William G. Little, William McFarland and Daniel Weaver.

Later deeds show that the hall was sold to the directors of the association April 1, 1865, and resold in 1867 to Cyrus Diller, who had served as a colonel in the Pennsylvania Volunteers.

The Marion Rifles as Company F, with Horatio Gates Myers as captain, and the Hanover Infantry as Company G, with Cyrus Diller as captain, served in the Sixteenth Regiment, Pennsylvania Volunteers organized at Harrisburg May 3, 1861, in answer to President Lincoln's first call for troops. Thomas A. Ziegle, York, was elected colonel of the regiment. It trained at Camp Scott in York. It was mustered out of service July 30. It missed taking part in the first battle at Bull Run July 21, 1861.

Many of the men re-enlisted for three years' services in the Seventy-sixth Regiment, Pennsylvania Volunteers, in August 1861, forming Company D with Cyrus Diller as captain. When he was promoted to major, William S. Diller and Charles L. Bittinger succeeded as captains.

History reveals that Hanover was hardly ever without a military quota in training or in active service from the time of Captain Richard McCalister during the Revolution on down through the second war with Britain and the Mexican War. The Warren Greys with a company of sixty men, Luther R. Skinner, captain, was organized in 1830; the United Blues of sixty men, A. W. Eichelberger, captain, 1842; and the Fourth Dragoons, cavalry corps of fifty, 1849, A. W. Eichelberger, captain; Cyrus Diller, first lieutenant; A. G. Schmidt, second lieutenant; and Dr. W. H. Bange, first sergeant.

During the battle of Hanover, June 30, 1863, an event still considered by some to have been the turning point of the campaign, Union and Confederate troops fought hand to hand in Center Square. About a score of the injured were taken to Marion Hall where they were treated by local doctors. Those who died were buried that night across the alley in the old Emmanuel Reformed churchyard.

Around the turn of the century the hall served as a schoolhouse. The sturdy little brick building, which has had such a busy existence, started its second hundred years somewhat expanded but in good basic condition and its original windows still intact.

## Home Guard Formed

Hanover citizens met at the Market House on the Square April 3, 1861, at the instance of Jacob Wirt and Lucian F. Melsheimer, to organize armed Border Guards for protection of the town, according to The Spectator. Jeremiah Kohler was named commander in chief; Jacob Wirt, captain; lieutenants, L. F. Melsheimer, William Bange, and Joseph C. Holland. They established what we would call now a curfew law. Any persons found on the streets after 10 o'clock would be hailed and required to give an account of themselves. It was estimated from eight hundred to one thousand men under arms could be called upon in an emergency. A flag raising was held. The flag was suspended across Baltimore Street from the Pleasant Hill Academy to the residence of Adam Forney. That was then considered the entrance to the borough.

For use of the Border or Home Guard in defense of the town the following supplies were secured September 8, 1862: 260 muskets and their accoutrements, 50 cavalry pistols of .44 caliber with holsters, 50 cavalry sabers, and two brass cannon of 6-pound type.

The subject of paying for substitutes to make up the draft requisite for which the Hanover borough was liable occupied much of town council's attention May 12, 1864, and following meetings that year and in 1865. From $250 to $300 was paid for each substitute.

Borough officials for the Civil War period included the following: 1862—Chief burgess, Jeremiah Kohler; town council, Allowies Smith, Edward Bair, John R. Stine, John Rupp, William Bange, and Davis Garber; high constable, David S. Tanger; auditor, David Slagle; council organized with Allowies Smith as assistant burgess; L. F. Melsheimer, secretary; Daniel Q. Albright, treasurer.

1864—Chief burgess, Stephen Keefer; town council, Edward Etzler, John Aulabaugh, David S. Tanger, N. B. Carver, Luther Weigle, William Shultz, and John Grove; high constable, Henry Heusner; council organized with David S. Tanger, assistant burgess; L. F. Melsheimer, secretary; and Daniel Q. Albright, treasurer.

EQUESTRIAN STATUE OF "THE PICKET," CYRUS E. DALLIN, SCULPTOR

# THE PICKET:
## YESTERDAY AND TODAY

*Picket, I greet you, and I greet*
*Your simple faith and honest fame;*
*To me it seems not all unmeet*
*That glory spell your only name.*
*Again a startled summer morn*
*Thrills on the heart with dreadful pride,*
*And hostile feet trample the corn,*
*And Custer and Kilpatrick ride.*

*Down Frederick street where horsemen clash,*
*Ere Gettysburg is fought and won,*
*On hot steel glint and saber flash*
*The steep rays of the noonday sun.*
*Stuart will flaunt his beard in vain*
*When Freedom breathes her native air;*
*The town is free and shall remain,*
*A picket guards the crimsoned square.*

*Still in the busy market place*
*A picket and his charger stand;*
*Now undivided, by God's grace,*
*Hail North and South, one mighty land!*
*Undaunted as of old each stood,*
*Cast not in bronze nor carved in stone,*
*Blood loyal to their fathers' blood,*
*Of kindred flesh and selfsame bone.*

*Here is the challenge, here the cause:*
*Free peoples sharing from above*
*Liberty's sovereign rights and laws,*
*God's conscience with us and His love.*
*Our rights to take and ours to give,*
*Our laws to make and to obey!*
*For less those fathers scorned to live—*
*Truth's altar, are we less than they?*

## UNVEILING OF THE PICKET

After two previous fruitless attempts had been made to have the Commonwealth provide funds for erection of a battle monument, the earliest by I. C. Dellone when a member of the state legislature and later efforts of Assemblyman William H. Long, finally in 1903 John R. Bittinger, residing near Hanover and then a member of the state legislature, proved successful in getting a measure passed, signed by the governor, and securing an appropriation of $7,500. Under this act, Governor Samuel W. Pennypacker became chairman of the commission, to be composed of three persons. He appointed Colonel John P. Nicholson, president of the Gettysburg Battlefield Association, and the Rev. Daniel Eberly, D.D., of Hanover, to serve with him on this commission. They selected Cyrus E. Dallin, a noted sculptor, of Boston, to design and execute the monument. The commission decided to have made an equestrian statue in bronze of a mounted cavalryman on picket duty resting on a pedestal of granite. Authority was given by the borough council and the citizens to erect the monument in the oval on Center Square.

### First Markers of Battle

On June 30, 1900, the thirty-seventh anniversary of the battle was celebrated at Hanover by an imposing demonstration. On this occasion two Civil War cannon and two iron markers, with appropriate inscriptions, were unveiled within the oval in Center Square by Major Jenkins Post 99, Grand Army of the Republic. At the same time Camp 328, Patriotic Order Sons of America, erected a tall flagpole, and the Gettysburg Battlefield Commission, under direction of the United States Government, placed two iron tablets within the oval to mark the positions of the different army corps when the engagement opened at Hanover, on June 30, 1863.

Through courtesy of Post No. 2 of Philadelphia the local G.A.R. post secured the cannon which saw much service during the war. A tablet bore the following inscription:

Battle of Hanover
June 30, 1863
Fought in these streets between 5,000 Union cavalry,

(Hanover Herald, October 7, 1905)

under General Kilpatrick, and 6,000 Confederate cavalry
under General Stuart.

The prelude to the battle of Gettysburg July 1, 2,
and 3, 1863, and a great factor in making the battle a
Union Victory. Erected under auspices of Post 99,
G.A.R., of Hanover, Pa.

The center of the oval then contained a fountain erected by
prominent citizens in 1874. This fountain with its rows of
spouting elves and dolphins surmounted by a figure of Hebe,
cupbearer of the gods, was removed to Wirt Park to make way
for "The Picket." Sold later by town council the fountain is
now privately owned and located in a Florida resort.

When the bronze equestrian figure was completed and placed
upon its base, September 28, 1905, was the date set for the unveiling and dedication. A double-arched canopy wrapped with
red, white and blue bunting was erected over the monument.
Throughout the town the Stars and Stripes were unfurled from
flag staffs and windows. Special trains over both the Northern
Central and Western Maryland railroads brought visitors in
large numbers and holiday mood to witness the parade and
exercises. Strains of martial music were heard from an early
hour as visiting organizations accompanied by bands arrived.
The community was honored by having as guests a remnant of
the boys in blue, including survivors of the Fifth New York and
Eighteenth Pennsylvania Cavalry who had taken part in the
battle of Hanover.

Chief Marshal Daniel L. Slagle led the morning procession
which traversed the streets lined by ten thousand cheering
citizens and visitors. The parade was made up of Grand Army
posts, fire companies, and fraternal organizations. The Eichelberger Cadet Corps served as escorts for the Governor. Many
special guests rode in carriages. The various groups and bands
wore colorful uniforms.

The unveiling ceremonies at 2 p.m. were held on the Square
before the battle monument. A large stand had been erected
for the speakers, choir and survivors of the battle, at the Frederick Street entrance to the Square.

*Reviewing stand on Baltimore Street for the procession preceding unveiling of "The Picket." Governor Pennypacker wearing high silk hat is standing in front row.*

### Governor Pennypacker Present

On the speakers' platform were seated Governor Pennypacker, Colonel John P. Nicholson and the Rev. Dr. Daniel Eberly, members of the monument commission; Colonel A. M. Gherst, of Reading, the orator of the day; General E. D. Dimmick, U. S. A., Washington, D. C.; Major H. C. Potter, Philadelphia; Lieutenant C. T. S. Pierce, Vergennes, Vermont; John Francis, of Allegheny, Pennsylvania, member of the Legislature; Andres Bridgemen of Mt. Vernon, New York; the Rev. Dr. C. M. Stock, the Rev. Ellis S. Hay; Dr. J. H. Bittinger, T. J. O'Neill, S. A. Hammond, of Gettysburg; W. H. Shenton, of Philadelphia; representatives of the press and others. D. D. Ehrhart, chairman of the dedication committee, presided.

After a selection by the Glen Rock Band, prayer was offered by the Rev. Dr. Stock, after which the choir of 200 voices under the direction of Professor W. H. Newborough, of York, accompanied by the band, sang "The Star Spangled Banner."

The monument was then unveiled by Miss Edna Florence

Bittinger, daughter of John R. Bittinger who, as a member of the Legislature, was instrumental in having the bill for erection of the monument pass that body in the session of 1903. While the band played a patriotic selection the cord which held the two large American flags draping the monument, was released and the Stars and Stripes falling gracefully revealed the handsome equestrian statue of "The Picket," the noble gift of the Commonwealth of Pennsylvania in commemoration of the battle of Hanover. As the flags dropped the national salute was fired by the G.A.R. Post cannon.

"The Picket" is a fine example of the work of Cyrus E. Dallin, noted Boston sculptor. It adds distinction to the town and compares favorably with the equestrian statues on the Gettysburg battlefield.

The transfer of the monument to the care of Hanover Borough was then made by Governor Samuel W. Pennypacker, who said in part:

"I am not here to make a speech but as one of this vast assembly to participate in the exercises on this occasion, ride in the parade in an automobile with Dr. Eberly, to sit in this old chair made in 1430, illustrating the stability of your people. I am here as the Executive of the Commonwealth to indicate by his presence the great interest which the state has in this demonstration. I well remember the first day upon which I ever saw the town of Hanover. It was on the 24th of June, 1863, as a private in a regiment on my way to Gettysburg, one company of which had come from this town, whose lieutenant colonel was a citizen (Major Joseph S. Jenkins). We stopped here for half an hour. It was time of great excitement. A crowd had gathered at the depot to welcome us and the first question we asked was 'Are there any Confederates in the neighborhood?' The answer was 'None.' We then went on our way to Gettysburg. The town made its impression on me as one of a simple, earnest, honest set of people, the basis of which was the stock we know as 'Pennsylvania Dutch.' Here in 1807, a citizen of your town, Frederick Melsheimer by name, had written and published a book which was the beginning of Science of Entomology in America, and made his name known the world over.

"But you are about to have another claim. A succession of events gathered around you, out of which you emerged famous forevermore. On the day that our regiment passed through Hanover, Stuart's cavalry left Lee to attempt to ride around the Army of the Potomac.

"The Commonwealth has erected this beautiful monument. You have the representation of the private soldier—the men in the ranks who won that war. The Commonwealth recognizes that this monument could not have been erected without you. We know the sacrifice you made in giving up a town ornament for placing the monument on the most suitable site. I feel that you will ever be satisfied with what you have done and see the wisdom of our choice.

"Now the Commonwealth delivers it into your charge with the assurance that you will care for it as a fitting tribute to the courage, bravery, rigor and patriotism of the American soldier."

The massive antique chair occupied by the governor was brought from Yorkshire, England, by John J. Bingley, Western Maryland Railroad mechanic. English oak inlaid with various kinds of wood was used in its construction.

Attorney John J. Bollinger spoke in acceptance of the trust as follows:

"To the Honorable Samuel W. Pennypacker, Governor of the Commonwealth of Pennsylvania, Colonel John P. Nicholson, and our worthy fellow citizens, the Rev. Dr. Daniel Eberly, members of the Monument Commission under whose supervision was erected this peaceful and beautiful memento commemorating a bloody engagement fought on our streets over forty years ago, on behalf of the Chief Burgess, the Town Council and all the citizens of the Borough of Hanover, I come with good cheer and hearty congratulations.

"Love of this land and nation has been born in every American and has been with us a cardinal principle since the foundation of the Republic. Never has the patriotism of the citizens of this vicinity been challenged that there has not been a noble response not only in spirit but in volunteers who were willing to seal their faith with their blood on the field of battle. Just two weeks before the engagement fought on these streets, at the call of our great war Governor, fifty-eight volunteered in one day, many of whom are here today to attest to their loyalty as they stand in the ranks of Grand Army Post No. 99, whose name and character has carried fame to all parts of this great Commonwealth as one of its very finest. The patriotism of my fellow-citizens of Hanover needs no substantial memorial; the commemoration of their deeds is its own sweet reward and is as enduring as bronze and marble. The patriotic virtues of the people of Hanover are only mentioned that you may be enabled to judge the better as to the fitness of the hands into which you have placed for keeping this magnificent memorial of patriotism. Judging of their faithfulness by their glorious past, you cannot but have assurance that they will preserve, defend and protect it upon this spot as a sacred trust, not only for thirty years but for thirty times thirty years.

### Accepts Monument for Borough

"In accepting this monument, I hope to be pardoned for making personal reference to a few out of the many who have interested themselves in accomplishing this work. To the Honorable John R. Bittinger, a former townsman but now a citizen of Adams County, belongs great credit; he richly deserves our thanks in a special manner. His untiring efforts attracted the attention of his fellow legislators and merited the aid of our Governor who favored the project. He took with him to the capitol, the Rev. Daniel Eberly, M. O. Smith, T. J. O'Neill, Dr. J. H. Bittinger, George R. Prowell and others whose solicitous activities influenced favorably the Committee on Appropriations, the Governor's signature eventually assuring the erection of the monument. It was the lack of the signature of Governor Beaver that caused the failure of the erection of a monument cn this site a quarter of a century ago after the project had been worked up to that point by the indefatigable labor of I. C. Dellone, then a member of the legislature from this town. Honor to his name and peace to his ashes. We do not overlook the work of R. M. Wirt and George D. Gitt, the Burgess and the Town Council in moving the fountain to Wirt Park, giving this site upon which to place this production of fine art. To each member of the Grand Army of the Republic and all others who in any way contributed to this great success, on behalf of the Burgess and Town Council, I return sincere thanks. And now, in the name of all the good citizens of my native town, I accept this monument from your hands and I pledge this town and all its people as its faithful guardians and protectors for all time."

Major Gherst addressed the assembled citizens in part as follows: "As at Gettysburg the Confederacy received a blow from which she never recovered and her star of destiny had set to go down later beyond the horizon of Appomattox, so we come to Hanover today to consider the importance of the engagement here which too was a Union victory and had its effect upon the issue at Gettysburg. The cause of the Confederacy was changed when the troops of Stuart struck the Eighteenth Pennsylvania, Kilpatrick's rear guard, then and there the destiny of Gettysburg was decided as Stuart was on his way to join Early at that place. Here the conflict lasted from 10 a.m. to late in the afternoon—seven or eight hours of valuable time lost to Stuart's army and the Confederate cause. He was forced to go by way of Jefferson, Dover, Dillsburg and Carlisle to Gettysburg and did not reach his chieftain until the night of the second of July. Had Stuart reached there on the first day, which he would have done had he not met Kilpatrick here the result might have been different. Was it a battle? Indeed it was a battle—fourteen men of the Union cavalry shot down in a few minutes. Kilpatrick's reported loss was 197. Lee said: 'Stuart had a severe engagement at Hanover.' What did it mean to Lee? Without the cavalry the intention of the enemy could not be discovered."

General E. D. Dimmick, U.S.A. retired, formerly a Captain of Company M, Fifth N. Y. Cavalry, who participated in the fight, was then called upon and gave a brief account of the battle as he recalls it in part as follows:

"On the night of the 29th of June, 1863, Companies L and M of our Fifth N. Y. Regiment were encamped at Littlestown. In the morning I received orders from General Kilpatrick to recall outposts, form into a squadron and march north. We were proceeding in perfect security until about three miles had been covered when we saw some men in a field to our right. We captured two and brought them in. They belonged to Wade Hampton's division of Stuart's cavalry. We moved on carefully and as we approached were fired upon. We returned the fire. When about 150 yards distant, the Confederates charged on our rear. We took to the fence and made a circuit of the fields. When we reached your town the fighting was about over. I know from the records that the Fifth N. Y. acquitted themselves with great credit."

## Potter Among Speakers

Major H. C. Potter, of the Eighteenth Pennsylvania spoke as follows: "Kilpatrick's Division, consisting of two brigades, left Littlestown early on the morning of June 30 in the following order— Kilpatrick, staff and body guard, the First Ohio; Custer with the First, Fifth, Sixth, and Seventh Michigan Cavalry, in which were three new companies armed with Spencer repeating (seven-shooter) rifles; then came Elder and Pennington with the artillery; Farnsworth followed with the First Vermont; First West Virginia, Fifth New York and Eighteenth Pennsylvania, with the ambulances, wagons, pack mules and horses in the rear.

"Colonel Brinton ordered me to pick my men and stay about a mile in the rear, which made a line eight to ten miles long. When we came to a small stream (Plum Creek), we stopped to water our horses. About fifty mounted men of the Thirteenth Virginia crossed over the road at this time and called for surrender. We refused and charged through the Confederate lines . . . and fired into them, driving them back and scattering them like chaff. A second charge was made. At this time we were joined by Adjutant Gall of the Fifth New York, who a moment later dropped mortally wounded from his horse."

Other speakers included Lieutenant C. T. S. Pierce, secretary and historian of the Fifth N. Y. Cavalry Association; Assemblyman John Francis, Allegheny, a member of the legislature who assisted in passage of the monument bill; and Andrew Bridgeman, ex-president of the Fifth Cavalry Association. Selections by the choir included "Tramp, Tramp, the Boys Are Marching," "Just Before the Battle Mother," and concluding with the hymn "America." The Rev. Ellis S. Hay pronounced the benediction.

*Soldiers' Monument, Mt. Olivet Cemetery, with plaques bearing names of Civil War soldiers from Hanover and vicinity.*

## SOLDIERS' MEMORIAL AT MT. OLIVET

More than fifty years have passed since the people of Hanover dedicated the Soldiers' Monument in Mt. Olivet Cemetery, which has been the terminal ceremonies center for the community's Memorial Day parades for many years. The community's representatives gather around the monument each May 30 in annual renewal of the custom inaugurated in 1868 of memorial-

(The Evening Sun, Hanover, 1951, and Hanover Herald, August 5, 1911)

izing the war dead and decorating their graves with floral tributes.

Due to a delay at the granite quarry in Guilford, Maryland, source of the material which forms the base of the monument, original plans for the dedication on Memorial Day of 1911 had to be postponed, the ceremony was put off until July 28 of the same year—another date of historical consequence from a strictly community viewpoint. That date was the 50th anniversary of the mustering out of Hanover's first volunteers in the Civil War.

Erected on the soldiers' plot near the original cemetery gates, the monument stands beneath majestic trees and is flanked by iron field pieces of the Civil War type. The main pedestal supports the bronze figure of an infantryman in the uniform of the period.

It was mostly a Hanover production. The design and working drawings were prepared by E. Leonard Koller, a son of the Rev. Dr. J. C. Koller, pastor of St. Matthew's Lutheran Church from 1877 to 1906 and a veteran of the Civil War. Leonard Koller was principal of the arts and crafts department of the International Correspondence Schools, Scranton. Charles F. Redding, the Baltimore Street stone cutter, erected the monument.

M. O. Smith, local newspaper editor and a former commander of Post 99, Grand Army of the Republic, with the assistance of J. D. Zouck and J. H. Bucher, was responsible for the original planning of the monument. Additional support and active interest were given through the combined efforts of the citizens of Hanover and the Major Jenkins G.A.R. Post, named in honor of Joseph S. Jenkins, who was killed at Petersburg when major of the 184th Regiment.

The Philadelphia foundry which cast the bronze work was the same firm that had provided similar service for the Commonwealth's monument, "The Picket," erected in Center Square in 1904.

During the 1911 ceremonies at the cemetery, it was pointed out that no town of its size had been more patriotic than Hanover in times of national peril. McAllistertown, one of Hanover's earliest names, was recorded as having furnished many soldiers for the Revolutionary army, and Hanover had sent two full companies to the assistance of Baltimore when that city was assailed by the British in 1814.

Hanover sent at least 317 citizens into the Union army in the Civil War to serve in many different commands. No less than thirty-six regiments of Pennsylvania infantry, seven regiments of cavalry and three batteries of artillery listed in their ranks from one to ninety-three Hanoverians. The largest number were registered in the Sixteenth Pennsylvania Regiment. A few were in the regular army and navy.

Family records in the community show that John Stahl and his five sons served the North at one time. The Diller and the Beard families each furnished four brothers, and three Stine brothers were under arms at one time.

Dedicatory exercises for the monument in 1911 began with a parade to the cemetery, led by members of the Grand Army of the Republic and the Sons of Veterans.

The joy that infected the village a half-century earlier was evidenced by an account in The Spectator August 1, 1861, although the homecoming was not complete. All who had left on that Sunday in April were not in the ranks of the occasion. Five had died during their brief term of service.

The Marion Riflemen had lost three—David Shull at York on May 21, Henry F. Constine at his home in Hanover, July 8, and Thomas Brannon at Hagerstown, July 17. From the ranks of the Hanover infantry two had died, Alexander Parr at York, May 28, and Daniel Heidler at York, July 26. Captain H. Gates Myers, commander of the Marion Rifles, had been left behind at Hagerstown, sick in a hospital, where he died the following August 8.

### Homecoming Welcome

The Spectator's description of the homecoming:

"We know of no more pleasing duty than that of chronicling the return—the safe arrival of our bold boys. When the clarion notes of the trumpet of war but a few months ago sounded throughout the length and breadth of this land, calling upon all the loyal citizens to rally around the standard of their country, these were the first to volunteer their services in defense of that standard.

"That was the darkest hour in this, our national crisis, and nobly did our soldiers come forward and declare themselves ready for the duty and the times.

"They have done their duty—they have discharged it faithfully in the camp and on the march—they have driven the traitors before them and compelled treason to hide its head behind masked batteries, and they come back to us now in the full enjoyment of life and health.

"All hail to Hanover for the joyous reception she gave them upon their arrival on Tuesday evening.

"Nothing can adequately describe the confusion that took place. Men, women and children rushed into the ranks to grasp some loved and respected one by the hand.

"Finally they got them in order, and, preceded by the Silver Band and Border Guard, they marched them up Carlisle Street to the Public Square, halting in front of the Central.

"Here they were addressed by the Rev. Mr. Swanger on behalf of the citizens and Lieutenant Diller on the part of the Border Guard.

"The wear and tear of camp life has made an impression on them, bronzing their features and making their imperfect clothing, as it was, still more imperfect. Our boys are certainly the lions of the day in Hanover, now. Every one has a group of eager listeners around him as he relates the pleasures and perils of the soldier's life."

The principal speaker at the dedication was Major M. A. Gherst of Reading. Miss E. Louise Jenkins, Philadelphia, granddaughter of Major Jenkins, released a cord unveiling the monument which was accepted for the borough by Burgess J. A. Sheely and for the cemetery by Dr. C. M. Stock. The memorial is of Guilford, Maryland, granite. The main base rests on a concrete foundation six feet deep. On this a stylobate of flat granite slabs supports three pedestals, connected by parapets. The main pedestal in the center, eight feet high, supports a bronze figure of an infantryman, in the service uniform of the war period, standing at rest. It shows a young man of earnest mien, typical of the boys in blue. On the side pedestals each six feet high are mounted bronze lamps of ancient Greek design with flames symbolic of eternal life. The face of the main pedestal bears a dedicatory bronze tablet inscribed as follows: "Erected 1911 by the People of Hanover in Grateful Memory of Their Fellow Citizens Who Served In the War For the Union 1861-1865."

Attached to the face of each of the smaller pedestals are four bronze tablets, each 16 by 30 inches, bearing 364 names. On two are inscribed the roster of G.A.R. Post members and on the other two names of nonmembers, many of whom died in the service or before the G.A.R. was organized.

## G.A.R. Post Members

Henry Abels, R. M. Adams, Vincent Adams, Geo. W. Adams, William Alwood, Albert Anthony, John Arntz. Silas Beard, Geo. F. Beard, Wm. A. Beard, William Bair, Daniel L. Baker, Wm. J. Backmaster, Peter C. Bollinger, Emanuel Bunty, A. M. Bucher, P. H. Bittinger, R. F. Baughman, Jacob W. Bender, Louis N. Brady, Rudolf Brown, Abraham Baker, Geo. H. Baker, Esau Bailey, J. H. Baughman, Jacob H. Bange, Thomas W. Brown, Wm. Bodein, J. F. Blair, Charles Bunty. N. B. Carver, Henry L. Carr, George W. Carl, Daniel Carter, Andrew Chambers, John Cline, Jacob Cline, John W. Craumer, Amos Carbaugh, Jeremiah Carbaugh, Joseph H. Chambers, John A. Cremer, R. M. Chenoweth, Herman S. Cook, John Culp.

Cyrus Diller, L. Y. Diller, Simon J. Diller, John Donnely, William Dresher, John W. Davis, Peter Duce. Henry Ernst, Fred Eigelke, Daniel Eberly, Wm. F. Eckert, O. T. Everhart. John L. Forrest, David F. Forney, Benj. F. Flegle, Daniel W. Fink, E. K. Foreman, George F. Felty. Elias W. Garrett, Oliver W. Garrett, Jacob Gundrum, J. H. Gobrecht, Alex. Gleason, James F. Gordon. Henry L. Hamme, Jose Henry, Joseph Hinkle, William Hertz, Warren T. Hoyt, William Howe. James Irving. Chas. W. Johnson, Lewis B. Johns, Samuel Jacobs. Charles T. Kump, J. C. Koller, Jeremiah Kohler, A. D. Kohler, Henry Kohler, John R. Kessler, Peter A. Keller, John Krichten, Elias Kemper, Daniel M. Krout, J. Nich. Kremer, Peter Krichten, F. X. Keffer, Edwin R. Kessler, Philip Kretz, George Koehler, Joseph Kuhn, N. F. Klinefelter, Hiram Kepner, Sam. A. Kendig.

Jas. A. Lawrence, Michael Lawrence, Lewis Lau, William

Low, Jacob Low, Isaac Loucks, John Lauchman, James A. Long, Wm. H. Little, C. Laukermann, Frederick Louth. William Mathias, Aloysius Marshall, Alfred McKinney, John McKinney, Jos. G. McKinney, Sol. McMaster, John McMann, Pius D. Miller, Henry L. Miller, William Miller, James Miller, Geo. C. Myers, Amos Meckley, William Mummert, Andrew Mummert, J. J. Morningstar, James K. Montes, Charles Myers. Mahlon H. Naill, Leo B. Nace, Jacob D. Neiderer, Francis Noll, Chas. C. Newman. W. H. Overbaugh, L. C. Overbaugh, Francis Overbaugh, S. P. Orwig, W. H. Pensinger, Michael Poet. Joseph A. Renaut, Louis I. Renaut, Jacob Rusher, Fred Ridinger, Adam Reiling, Adam Rebling, Frank M. Roberts, John H. Russ, John Rebel, Hezekiah Rickrode, John Roth.

Edw. H. Snyder, Daniel F. Stair, Andrew J. Snively, Jacob N. Slagle, Calvin Stahl, Howard Stahl, John Stahl, George W. Stahl, Jeremiah Small, David Small, William H. Small, Joseph B. Sanders, John J. Staub, Nathaniel Stambaugh, F. Shanabrough, Charles Swartz, Jacob Shultz, William D. Sell, James Stonesifer, John A. Sipe, Daniel R. Snyder, M. O. Smith, Eph. J. Stegner, Edward Steffy, D. P. Stonesifer, Wm. H. Sterner, James Switzer, Thaddeus Smith, Cornelius Smith, John E. Smith, Henry Smith, Daniel Stine. Charles Z. Thomas, Geo. W. Thomas, Henry L. Trone, Samuel E. Trone, Geo. A. Trone. Isaac Wagner, Wm. H. Wagner, Wm. W. Wagner, J. H. Waltman, David H. Weaver, J. Henry Wiest, Henry K. Wentz, D. E. Winebrenner, Alex. Wilhelm, Daniel Withers, Ephraim Wilt, Chas. P. Weissig, John H. Wolford, Joseph Wizotskie. Charles Young, Henry Yeager, John F. Yake. Frank Zeigler, J. George Zuern (Zinn), John M. Zurn (Zinn).

## Nonmembers of G.A.R.

Jerome Adams, Wm. Althoff, John Anthony, H. Backmaster, Walter F. Beard, J. Emory Bair, Wm. E. Bair, Wm. Bair, Theodore N. Bair, John Bare, Louis I. Bargelt, Alex. T. Barnes, Daniel J. Barnitz, Web. R. Barnitz, Henry Beard, John Beard, Chas. L. Bittinger, D. N. Bittinger, Emanuel Bowers, Fred M. Boyer, Augustus Britcher, John Britcher, H. C. Bucher, Jacob Burns. Eli Cisler, Howard M. Clark, Emanuel Cline, Lewis

Cline, Anthony Clunk, William Clunk, Jackson Craumer, Andrew Creager, Geo. L. Creager, Charles Cremer, John H. Crook, H. F. Constine, Valentine Cook. John Deiner, Martin L. Diehl, Alex. Deitz, Wm. S. Diller, Jacob Dull, Fred Dome. V. C. S. Eckert, H. A. Eckenrode, John A. Eline. John Ferdinand, Charles Fiscus, Fred. Fritz, John Fitz, Samuel Fitz, Wm. C. Forney, Geo. Frederick. James E. Gordon, Henry Gotwalt, Sebastian Grimm, Wm. Grimm, John Groff, Henry S. Grove, Joseph Grupp.

Wm. Hampton, Jerome Hare, Joseph Hare, Michael Harman, Addison Herman, Henry H. Heusner, Henry Heisner, Barthabas Hines, John H. Hinkle, Michael Hoke, Lewis G. Halter, Wm. H. Halter, Geo. Holtzman, Henry Houser, John Houser, Jos. S. Jenkins, J. W. Johnson. John Keller, Isadore Keever, Adam King, A. F. Klinefelter, Adam Klunk, Lewis F. Kraft, John Kouk, Henry J. Kountz. Wm. Leader, Amos F. Leschey, Lewis C. Leschey, Geo. Livingston, Henry Low, John Low. Mathias Mann, W. H. McCausland, A. H. McFarland, Wm. McFarland, A. S. Mc-Kinney, Joseph McKinney, L. I. McKinney, Jer. McWilliams, H. C. Metzger, Jacob Michael, Andrew Miller, John Miller, Lewis of J. Miller, Lewis of Y. Miller, A. Morningstar, H. Morningstar, H. Gates Myers, Wm. A. Myers, Wm. Myers. Charles Neuman, Wm. Neuman, Pius Neiderer, Henry Norwig. Alex Parr, Samuel Petry, John Petry, Rufus Parr, Hezekiah Ports, Samuel W. Parks. John Reed, Peter Reever, Rolandus Roland.

Jacob Sanders, Sol. Scheivert, Alex. Schuerer, Eman. Schuerer, James R. Schmidt, Jacob H. Schriver, L. N. Schriver, John H. Serff, Edward Shaffer, Sam. G. Shaeffer, Henry Stine, Geo. E. Sherwood, And. G. Scholl, David Scholl, Henry Shyltz, Valentine Shultz, Wm. Shuman, Edward C. Slagle, John D. Slagle, Joseph A. Slagle, Eli Snyder, Daniel J. Snyder, Henry Snyder, John Snyder, Wm. H. Snyder, Adam Sohl, John Sponangle, John Shaunessy, Geo. W. Stine, Obediah Stahl, Wm. Stahl, Reuben Stonesifer, Augustus Swartz, Fred Schmidt, Thos. Sneeringer. Abraham Test, Geo. E. Trone, Gustavus Trone, Louis A. Trone, Samuel D. Trone, Oliver Trone, Jacob Troup, Wm. Troup, Sr., Wm. Troup, Jr. Wesley Wagner, N. V. Waltersdorff, Daniel Weaver, Samuel Weigel, Geo. W. Welsh, Jacob Wendel, Wm. White, John Willing, Geo. W. Wilson, John A. Wilt, Jacob J. Wintrode, Rufus S. Wintrode, Calvin C. Wirt, Thomas L. Wirt,

Michael Wise, John Winsore, William Wolff, Emanuel Wolford, Pius Wonner. Geo. E. Yingling, Silas C. Yingling, Cornelius Young, John M. Young.

---

## EIGHTY-SEVENTH PENNSYLVANIA VOLUNTEERS

When the Hanover Infantry, Marion Rifles, and other York and Adams County groups returned from three months' service, recruiting took place in August, 1861, to form the Eighty-seventh Regiment of Pennsylvania Volunteers. The regiment numbered thirty-eight commissioned officers and one thousand enlisted men in ten companies, eight from York County and two from Adams. Company G was recruited from Hanover by Vincent C. S. Eckert and Henry Morningstar; Company F from Gettysburg by Captain Charles H. Buehler, William J. Martin, and James Adair; and Company I from a nucleus of men drilled by Thaddeus Stevens Pfeiffer, who assisted his father as instructor at New Oxford College. On August 19 Captain George Hay of York was commissioned as colonel of the regiment; Lieutenant John W. Schall was chosen lieutenant colonel; and Captain Charles H. Buehler, of Gettysburg, major. Major Buehler married Anna Fahnestock of Gettysburg in 1860.

The first task set for the regiment was to perform guard duty along the Northern Central Railway from the Mason and Dixon line to Baltimore. Company A, the Zouaves, and four other companies were assigned five miles each to patrol. The remaining companies including Company G left for Cockeysville, regimental headquarters, and received training. The camp was named Camp Dix in honor of General John A. Dix in command of the Middle Department. After shooting several cows as "bridge burners," the drill squads and sentinels settled down to serious work.

The big Harpers Ferry muskets which weighed fifteen pounds and kicked like small cannon were exchanged for the Austrian rifle, shorter and lighter. The following year Enfield rifles were supplied, and later the famous Springfield muskets.

A detachment of forty men from Company K in command of Captain John W. Albright and Lieutenant John McIlvain went to Westminster Saturday night, September 29 and surprised a

*Hanover Branch Railroad Engine No. 3 with tender and two coaches from photograph taken about 1870 at Emory Grove station near Glyndon, Md., after the road was taken over by the W. M. Railroad. The engineer is John Reed; fireman, Edward Colgan; conductor, Reuben Kessler; brakeman, Addison Eckert.*

company recruiting for the Confederate service. They entered by a rear door the armory where the recruits were drilling and disarmed them. The guns were taken to company headquarters at Relay House. About two weeks later the same number of men went by train to Westminster and marched eighteen miles to another village where they captured thirty Springfield rifles in Confederate hands. Four miles farther on they stopped over night at the home of a physician at Liberty and the next day went through the manual of arms to the delight of the citizens. Another group of thirty Southern sympathizers were compelled to surrender their Springfield rifles.

The regiment was relieved of guard duty May 18, 1862. They went into camp at McKim's Hill, east of the present site of Union Station, Baltimore. While there they were visited by crowds of Baltimoreans who admired their drilling exercises. On June 22 the regiment with all its equipment left from the Baltimore & Ohio station for West Virginia where they were assigned to General R. H. Milroy's division. He reviewed them at Clarksburg. From then on the Eighty-seventh participated in twenty-eight engagements including Carter's Woods, Winchester, the Wilderness, Monocacy, Cold Harbor, and Petersburg.

Vincent Eckert, who was chosen captain of Company G, retired from the service September 1, 1863, Lieutenant Henry Morningstar, who was captured at Winchester June 15, 1863, remained a prisoner until March, 1865, and Lieutenant Robert A. Daniel of Ohio, who was a teacher in York County when the company was organized, commanded the company in most of the engagements, Lewis I. Renaut of Company G became principal musician of the regiment. Howard Stahl was also a musician. Sergeants were William F. Eckert, Charles F. Ropp, and Isaac Wagner. William Waldman was promoted from sergeant to second lieutenant.

The Eighty-seventh Regiment lost 104 men in front of Petersburg and seventy-four men in the battle of Monocacy. Gloom pervaded York when news of the casualties at Monocacy reached there. Flags were at half-mast for two days. The dead included Sergeant Daniel L. Welsh, of Company G, who was pierced by a ball near the heart, and Adjutant Anthony M. Martin.

The Eighty-seventh formed part of Sheridan's command at

the battle of Opequon Creek, Virginia, driving Early out of Winchester. This battle was one of the hardest in which the Eighty-seventh fought, losing fifty men in killed and wounded. Sheridan carried the Rebel position capturing 2,500 prisoners, five pieces of artillery and nine battle flags. Major General Rodes, C.S.A., was killed, and Fitzhugh Lee was wounded. Company G dead included Privates John L. Kunkle, Sylvester Gelding, William Wagner, and Owen Bishop.

David N. Thomas, of Company I, was the first man of the regiment to reach the enemy's breastworks in the charge at Fisher's Hill which was carried between sundown and dark with the capture of sixteen of Early's guns. This was the last engagement in which the Eighty-seventh participated. The three-year enlistment period had expired.

## CAMPAIGNING IN MARYLAND

When Lee made his second invasion north in 1863, Hooker established headquarters for the Army of the Potomac near Frederick June 27 and here Meade took over June 28. A bronze plaque indicating place of headquarters has been set up west of Frederick on U. S. 340. Meade moved his headquarters the following day to Middleburg, and on July 6 following Gettysburg he directed the concentration of the army from there, and ordered the movement of wagons to Frederick from Westminster. A year later Frederick paid Jubal Early $200,000 to keep him from burning the town. In 1862 Stonewall Jackson led his troops through en route to Harpers Ferry. It was at this time that the Barbara Fritchie incident occurred.

Westminster was occupied three times by Confederates during the war. The first time by Colonel T. L. Rosser with his Fifth Virginia Cavalry September 11, 1862, when he spent the night at the home of John B. Boyle, on the corner of Main and Carroll streets.

Major Napoleon B. Knight entered Westminster over the Baltimore road June 28, 1863, and camped along the Littlestown road on property now owned by Western Maryland College. The next afternoon his First Delaware Volunteer Cavalry clashed with Jeb Stuart, who drove him in flight toward Baltimore.

Another account of the action with Stuart relates that Captain Churchman and a provost guard of eighteen men under command of a lieutenant had been in camp for a week or more on Paris Ridge in the western part of the town, with Captain Churchman having headquarters in a hotel near the railroad station. A false alarm Sunday night brought the Union cavalry to the open space in front of Yingling's store, where the Littlestown pike runs into Main Street. The next afternoon, June 29, an apparently small body of Gray riders were entering Westminster, when the Delaware Cavalry rode to the attack. The enemy had stopped at Baughman's blacksmith shop. The forces met at the Washington road entrance to the town. Hand to hand fighting took place. The few Rebels turned out to be Stuart's whole army. Most of the Delawareans were captured and the others fled. Lieutenants Murray and Gibson of the Confederates and two of the Union men were killed and about a dozen on each side wounded. The two Southerners were temporarily buried in the Episcopal Church cemetery.

Gregg's Second cavalry division of the Union army en route to Manchester captured some of Stuart's stragglers. Union supplies from Baltimore piled up in Westminster and Stuart picked up some of these at the local station. During the battle wounded and prisoners from Gettysburg and Hanover were routed through Westminster to Baltimore.

During Jubal Early's thrust towards Washington Colonel Harry Gilmor of Bradley T. Johnson's brigade appeared in Westminster July 9, 1864, charging through the streets at night on a foray to destroy bridges and cut telegraph wires. It was on the occasion of the battle of Monocacy when Major General Lew Wallace delayed Early's forces. Early gave up the attempt to capture Washington fearing Sixth Corps troops had been sent to defend the capital.

General Meade had his headquarters briefly at Middleburg June 29, 1863, before setting up general headquarters at Taneytown where Sickles' Third Corps had encamped on the farms of Jacob Null, John Thomson, and Benjamin Shunk. Meade's tent was pitched on the Shunk (later the Charles W. Eckard) farm when on the 30th Sickles moved on to Bridgeport, three miles to the northwest and then to Emmitsburg. The Twelfth

Corps moved through Taneytown to Littlestown. General Hancock's Second Corps bivouacked on the Swope farm west of Taneytown July 1. He left his corps there when called to take command at Gettysburg. Headquarters for the Signal Corps were established at Taneytown June 30. During the battle at Gettysburg the tower of the Lutheran church was used to display flags by day and flares by night.

New Windsor residents were aroused the night of June 29 when a regiment of General Gregg's Second Cavalry Division marched through to join his forces at Westminster from where he planned to go in pursuit of Stuart. Part of Gregg's men were located around Ridgeville before joining the main body at Westminster.

From June 29 to July 1 Hancock had his headquarters on the John Babylon (currently the Harry Haines) farm, a mile east of Uniontown.

---

## THE CUSTER MAPLE

Josiah W. Gitt (1821-1898), prominent merchant of Hanover, planted a maple tree in 1860 along the sidewalk, near the entrance to his private residence at the southwest angle of Center Square. The tree grew rapidly and with spreading branches furnished shade for the family and friends who sat on the doorstep in front of the Gitt home summer days. By 1863 the tree had grown to considerable size with a trunk about four inches thick.

Following the first stage of the battle here General Kilpatrick made his headquarters in the Central Hotel. When General Custer visited headquarters to confer with the Union commander, he selected the Gitt tree as a convenient place to tie his horse and directed his colored servant to stand near and be ready for any emergency. Naturally Custer's action was noted by citizens standing about at the time. In the course of years the maple became known as the "Custer Tree." The association surrounding the tree endeared it to members of the family, and as Mr. Gitt's business grew, the tree also flourished and grew in size.

(Record-Herald, March 22, 1924—Prowell)

Fifteen years after the battle at Hanover, General Kilpatrick visited the town and delivered a lecture in Concert Hall on the Square nearby. When his attention was called to the maple where Custer's horse had been tied, he said that his own mount had been placed in a stable at the rear of the hotel, with orders to his colored groom to be ready at a given signal to bring the animal to the front of his headquarters.

The Gitt store building eventually occupied that whole corner of the Square. Mr. Gitt's eldest son, George D. Gitt, who succeeded his father as head of the firm, continued bestowing a careful interest in the tree. After sixty-four years the maple began to show signs of decay and the branches no longer put forth buds. It was eventually removed in 1924 while Mr. Gitt was absent in Florida. Later a special square design was placed in the pavement to mark the spot where the tree stood. A six-inch star was sunk in the center and a two-foot circle marks the position and circumference of the tree. A bronze tablet with likeness of Custer and inscription has been placed beside the entrance to the store building now occupied by the J. C. Penney Company.

---

## MIDDLE GROUND

### New Oxford

New Oxford's preparations for defense of the country had its beginnings in the activities of Dr. Michael Diedrich Gottlob Pfeiffer, a native of Germany who had received military training during the Napoleonic wars. He arrived in Baltimore from abroad and afterward went to Manchester, Maryland, where he married Miss Foltz. In 1840 he established the New Oxford College and Medical Institute. He was the first postmaster of New Oxford, and a close friend of Thaddeus Stevens. A military company of forty men, known as the Oxford Fencibles, was organized in March, 1859. The fall of Fort Sumter touched off a wave of patriotic excitement. Dr. Pfeiffer and his son Thaddeus Stevens Pfeiffer formed a new company of young men, known as the New Oxford National Guards, from the college and surrounding territory including New Oxford, Hanover, Conewago, Littlestown, Gettysburg, Irishtown, Mt. Rock, Hunterstown, Abbottstown, East Berlin, McSherrystown, New Chester, Dover, and even Harrisburg. Reports of Dr. Pfeiffer's military know-how had spread widely. His son, then aged twenty-one, was an instructor in the school. The company of about fifty eager youths was the pride of the town. In showy uniforms of blue jackets, red trousers and caps, they drilled weekly.

When word was received that a regiment was being organized at York, the services of the company captained by young Pfeiffer were offered at unanimous request of the members. Anthony M. Martin, also of New Oxford, afterward adjutant of the Eighty-seventh Regiment of Pennsylvania Volunteers, was first lieutenant, and James M. Hersh, who became regimental quartermaster, was second lieutenant. Findlay J. Thomas, who afterward became major of the Eighty-seventh Regiment, was one of the corporals.

Other officers in order of rank included Sergeants William H. Lanius, York, Christian W. Kehm, New Oxford, Edward F. Coe, Littlestown, George Dosh, Abbottstown, T. J. Montgomery, Hopewell; Corporals Robert K. Slagle, New Oxford, Charles Crosta, New Oxford, F. J. Thomas and Daniel Decker, New Oxford, Alexander McManus, Harrisburg, Adolph Rahter, Littlestown, Edward D. Stough, Oxford township, W. D. Hombach, McSherrystown; musicians, Henry Miller and D. A. Yount, both of Littlestown.

The entire community turned out the end of August, 1861, when the "boys" entrained for York, where they took up quarters at the old fairgrounds. More recruits were received bringing the company up to the full quota of one hundred, as Company I. They drilled in squads and by company twice a day until their uniforms were furnished. Captain Baldwin of the regular army mustered the volunteers into service for three years early in September. Two weeks of camp life on the York Public Commons followed.

The first assignment of Company I was to guard a five-mile stretch of Northern Central Railroad from Parkton to Monkton, Maryland, with headquarters at White Hall. They went on to participate in many of the twenty-eight engagements of the regiment during the next three years. Company I suffered many casualties, and some languished for months in Southern prisons.

But seventeen re-enlisted at the expiration of their three-year term of service and remained in the army until the end of the war. They were with Grant when Lee surrendered at Appomattox April 9, 1865, and soon thereafter were mustered out of service.

Captain Pfeiffer was killed just after going on picket duty with fifty men, at the battle of Cold Harbor, June 3, 1864. He was buried under a tree, the grave was marked and later his remains were removed to New Oxford. John D. Keith had the original letter written by Thaddeus Stevens securing a pass for John Quincy Adams Pfeiffer to enter the Union lines to recover the body of his brother Thaddeus and bring it to New Oxford for interment. The letter was to Lincoln's Secretary of War Stanton and Stanton indorsed the pass. Lieutenant Anthony M. Martin, who became adjutant, died of wounds received at Monocacy, a hard fought battle which took place near Frederick, July 9, 1864, when General Lew Wallace checked Early's invaders and helped save the National Capital. He is buried in Conewago Chapel Cemetery.

Captain W. H. Lanius, of York, who became a staff aide, commanded the company in several engagements. When reforming his men in line of battle after the repulse at Locust Grove in November, 1863, a Minie ball or a piece of shell cut in two places the leather strap that supported his haversack, which then fell to the ground. A mounted officer of an Ohio regiment, observing this miraculous escape, turned the incident into a joke by saying, "Captain, you had better retreat at once; your base of supplies is cut off." Lanius later was wounded at Monocacy. Lieutenant Robert A. Daniel commanded in the field in his place.

The body of Captain Thaddeus Pfeiffer was brought home Monday, November 13, 1865, according to the Hanover Spectator, by his brother, Captain Quincy Pfeiffer, for burial with the honors of war. The Rev. Dr. D. J. Hauer gave the funeral discourse in the Lutheran church. Interment took place in the Lutheran church cemetery by the side of his brother John Theodore Pfeiffer, regimental bugler of the 202nd Pennsylvania Volunteers, who died of wounds received the previous year at White Plains, Virginia. Death took place in a hospital in Grace Church, Alexandria, Virginia. All three of Dr. Pfeiffer's sons served in the Union armies; two of them gave their lives for their country.

The troops of General George Gordon, C.S.A., went through New Oxford en route from Gettysburg to York, and some of Stuart's cavalry were seen on the way to New Chester and Hunterstown before arriving at Gettysburg. Custer's Fifth New York outfit also passed through.

Residents of Conewago formed a home guard to protect their properties from Rebel "bushwackers" raiding the countryside.

Lewis Miller of New Oxford lost a valuable horse to Rebel raiders, and after the Gettysburg battle he went to the field to see if he could find the animal among the captured horses, and sure enough he did. But thereafter, according to the story, it never amounted to a hill of beans. The terror and turmoil of battle had affected the horse's spirit.

Charles S. Diller, Hanover R. D. 1, relates that his great-grandfather, Peter Diehl, had a tannery on West High Street in New Oxford, and in connection with this business ran a wagon freight line to Baltimore to haul his products to market and bring back groceries and other supplies. Upon hearing of the approach of Confederate forces he sent his son, Charles A. Diehl, and Amos Lough, who later married his daughter Louisa, with his horses to cross the Susquehanna into Lancaster County to save them from capture. Stuart's cavalry detouring after the battle at Hanover caught up with them at Ziegler's Church, near Seven Valley, took their horses and made them prisoners. The two young men were put to work carrying water from a big spring near the church and helping to care for the wounded. Toward evening they were released and provided with a couple of worn-out plugs to return home. Certificates were issued later by the state to reimburse owners for horses taken by the Confederates. Due to the legislature failing to appropriate funds the certificates were never redeemed.

## Abbottstown

The Gettysburg-York and Hanover-East Berlin pikes intersect at Abbottstown, formerly known as Berwick borough. General Gordon's brigade of Ewell's corps was directed to travel over the hard road from Gettysburg through New Oxford and

Abbottstown to York. Among the residents who watched the invaders march through was George Jordy, aged immigrant and founder of the American Jordy family. When General Gordon tried to impress him with the size of the Confederate army, Jordy told him he had seen greater armies during Napoleon's Russian campaign. Traces of earthwork where Gordon planted a battery of cannon north of the town may still be seen. Many of the men stopped for water at Sara Steffan's pump on the Square. She buried the begrimed tin cup after their departure. John M. Wolf, recruiting agent and opponent of subversive organizations, was sought out by the Confederates with the intention of making him a prisoner when informers gave word to the enemy. He was warned in time, however, and escaped capture.

A caisson chest exploded near Hartman's Mill when Kilpatrick's Union forces were returning through Abbottstown to Hanover June 30 as word reached them that a battle had started there. James Moran of Battery M, Second U. S. Artillery, attached to Custer's First Michigan Cavalry Brigade, was mortally wounded and two horses were killed in the explosion. The injured man was removed to a house along the road where he was cared for until his death a day or two later. He was one of the most popular men in his command. His body was buried in the old Lutheran church cemetery in Abbottstown, the Rev. Dr. Daniel J. Hauer officiating. Two months later at the request of Private Moran's friends the body was removed to the Paradise Catholic church cemetery.

After the battle at Hanover Kilpatrick's men spent the night along the pike between Hanover and Abbottstown. Scouts were sent out. On July 1 at 11 a.m. the First Brigade of the Third Cavalry Division moved to Abbottstown and East Berlin in pursuit of the enemy. The Fifth New York and a section of Elder's battery were sent on a reconnaissance towards York, taking some prisoners and returning to East Berlin by midnight, where they bivouacked till morning.

## Hunterstown

Thursday, July 2, the division marched rapidly toward Gettysburg by way of Abbottstown and New Oxford. When within four miles of Gettysburg, the division moved to Hunterstown where they were engaged with Stuart's cavalry in a hard and bloody fight which lasted till dark. Charges and countercharges were made and the artillery did not cease to fire until long after the infantry in front of Gettysburg laid down to rest.

Hunterstown, Straban Township, a crossroads cluster of houses in a wooded section, along a narrow dirt road not far from the 1787 stone Great Conewago Presbyterian Church, was once considered for the county seat of Adams County. Here the Sixth Michigan Cavalry, which had fought at Hanover, late in the evening of July 2 met some of Stuart's troopers on the way to Gettysburg. The First Cavalry Regiment under Colonel Towne formed on the right of the road near the town. Other regiments of the Sixth Brigade included Fifth under Colonel Alger, Sixth under Colonel Gray and Seventh under Colonel Mann. Captain H. A. Thompson's Company A charged the enemy suffering great loss but checked the Rebels so as to enable a battery to be placed in position, when other squadrons drove the enemy back and the guns caused them to surrender the field. As squadron leader, Captain A. W. Duggan participated in the action.

Kilpatrick's troopers also struck the rear of Ewell's division at Hampton, ten miles north of Hanover, when Lee's men were hurrying back to Gettysburg. During the night about 1 a.m. Kilpatrick's division moved from the extreme right to the extreme left of the Union line, arriving near the Round Tops at 9 a.m., July 3.

---

## TRIBUTE TO GEORGE R. PROWELL

Full credit for the basic narrative of this history of the battle of Hanover, June 30, 1863, and original research used in connection with its preparation is due the late George R. Prowell, historian and educator. The present Chamber of Commerce committee in charge of the production of this volume has drawn freely from Mr. Prowell's writings on this subject in his "History of York County," Volume I, published in 1907, in various pamphlets, and in contributions to local newspapers. In numerous cases his information was derived from actual interviews with

GEORGE R. PROWELL
(1849-1928)

Civil War officers from the North and South participating in the events described. It has been the effort of the present editors to arrange, expand, and clarify Mr. Prowell's cherished records only in the light of later and fuller information.

George Reeser Prowell was born in Fairview Township, York County, Pennsylvania, December 12, 1849. He obtained his education in the public schools, the State Normal School at Millersville, Pennsylvania, and the University of Wooster, Wayne County, Ohio. After teaching in a private academy for a brief time at Goldsboro, he was elected assistant principal of the York City High School, and later served as principal of the High School at Wooster, Ohio, instructor in the York County Academy, and superintendent of public schools at Hanover.

While residing at Wooster, he studied law with Solicitor Martin Welker, who during that time was appointed United States Judge for the Northern District of Ohio. He acted as private secretary for Judge Welker at Cleveland, and during his residence there engaged in newspaper work. He continued writing for the press while filling positions as teacher and school supervisor. He served on the staff of the Philadelphia Press. He spent six years in Washington and four at Philadelphia in newspaper and literary work.

Mr. Prowell became associated with John Gibson in 1884-85 in the compiling of a comprehensive history of York County. He also prepared histories of several Pennsylvania communities published by L. H. Evarts & Co., Philadelphia. In 1887 he wrote and published a "History of Camden County, N. J.," in a large octavo volume which included the history of what was originally known as the Province of West Jersey based on original research in early New Jersey records.

At the request of the Historical Society of York County he began in 1902 the collection of historical documents, books, portraits, and early products and art of first settlers. The third floor of the courthouse at York was turned into a museum, and contributions came in from various sections. He became curator and librarian of the project. He continued his historical researches and contributed to various publications. Starting in 1904 and continuing until 1921 he was principal and owner of the York School of Business.

Mr. Prowell was married at Stamford, Connecticut, in October, 1878, to Virginia, daughter of Colonel John and Sarah (Tillman) Dean. They had three children, Nellie B., Edna D., and Dean. Colonel Samuel Dean, grandfather of Mrs. Dean, commanded a regiment of militia from Connecticut, during the Revolution, and participated in the battles of Long Island, White Plains, Trenton, Princeton, and Monmouth. Mrs. Dean died May 22, 1925.

Mr. Prowell was of Welsh descent. His first American ancestor, James Prowell, came to Pennsylvania with the early Welsh immigrants and settled in Chester County, near Philadelphia. For the last twenty years of his life Historian Prowell was blind. He continued his work up to the end with the aid of a secretary. Death took place February 23, 1928, from a stroke of apoplexy, at the home of his son-in-law and daughter, Mr. and Mrs. Maurice Trone, 61 Frederick Street, Hanover. He was seventy-nine years of age. His daughter Edna preceded him in death. His son died in January, 1962.

Funeral services for Mr. Prowell were held at the Frederick Street residence with the Rev. Henry I. Stahr officiating, and burial was in Mt. Olivet Cemetery, Hanover.

He prepared a "History of Wilmington" in 1888, and the chapters relating to the early settlements appeared in the "History of Delaware," published by L. H. Evarts in 1889. He served as associate editor of the "National Cyclopedia of American Biography," published in twelve volumes in 1890-94. It fell to his duty to prepare sketches of the lives of several U. S. presidents and their cabinets, all the justices of the Supreme Court of the U. S., and members of the U. S. Senate from the foundation of the republic to 1894. He also wrote the lives of all the governors of half a dozen states, including Pennsylvania, and the history of the University of Pennsylvania in the lives of its heads and faculty members.

Returning to the field of education he served three years as superintendent of the Hanover public schools. While engaged as contributor in 1898-99 to "Lamb's Dictionary of American Biography," he spent eight months in New England and the Southern States in preparing data on the growth and development of the U. S. cotton manufacturing industry. During the next two years he published the "History of the 87th Pennsylvania Volunteers," a regiment composed of York County troops who served a three-year period in the Civil War, and another story of the "71st Pennsylvania," known in Civil War annals as the "California Regiment."

---

## MEMORABILIA

### Grant Stops at Hanover

General U. S. Grant in 1868, during the first year of his presidency, stopped at Hanover. He was then on his way to Gettysburg for the first time. No provision was made for him to stop, but owing to a defective engine, another one was attached to the train and the President remained for a period of fifteen minutes sitting in the center of the car. Few people knew of his presence at Hanover. Grant was accompanied by a part of his Cabinet for a two-day tour of the battlefield. The only

MAJOR GENERAL U. S. GRANT
*As he appeared on arrival in Wash-*
*ington from campaigning in the West*
*to take over supreme command of*
*the U. S. Army.*

remarks that he is known to have made were in reference to
the cavalry duel at Hanover:

"So far as I know Kilpatrick, commanding the third division
of Meade's cavalry corps, displayed military genius in the contest at Hanover. He was supported by such able men as George
A. Custer and E. J. Farnsworth, two of the best brigade commanders of the Civil War. Sad to relate Farnsworth lost his life
while gallantly leading his men the third day of the battle at
Gettysburg. Kilpatrick won fame and distinction under Sheridan
in front of Richmond and as the leader of the cavalry corps in
Sherman's triumphant march from Atlanta to the Sea, in 1864.
I cannot speak in too high terms of the military genius of Custer
in the many engagements in which he took part in the Army
of the Potomac. Custer was rated by Sheridan as one of the
most capable cavalry leaders of the Potomac army."

It should be recalled that while the battle of Gettysburg was in progress Grant was negotiating for the surrender of thirty-five thousand Confederates, the same number of muskets and rifles and sixty cannon at Vicksburg, Mississippi. (1915 Centennial Program—Prowell.)

## General Howard Inspects Field

Almost unnoticed Major General Oliver O. Howard, distinguished Civil War officer and Gettysburg veteran, arrived in Hanover June 30, 1903, over the Pennsylvania Railroad, according to the Hanover Herald. He walked from the station down Carlisle Street to the Hotel Barker, corner Carlisle and Chestnut streets, and continued to Center Square where he read the tablets and inspected the cannon. He spoke to a bystander, asking which was Frederick Street from which the Confederates entered the town and saying he didn't quite get here in '63. He walked alone out to Forney Field examining the topography as he went along. On his return he stopped at the Emlet & Jenkins drugstore where he ordered an egg phosphate, a popular soft drink of the period. Howard was noted for his strong stand for temperance. The clerk recognized him by his armless sleeve and a portrait he had seen in the Christian Herald. The visitor took a bus from the hotel to the station and continued on his way to Gettysburg where he took part in the exercises July 1. He was with Sherman and Slocum on the March from Atlanta to the Sea. Upon the death of McPherson he took over command of the Fifteenth and Seventeenth Corps.

## Mrs. Thorn Serves as Guide

Mrs. Peter Thorn, Gettysburg, lived in the house at the entrance to Greenmount Cemetery. The dwelling was used as headquarters by General O. O. Howard. Mrs. Thorn's husband was away from home at that time (serving in the 148th regiment of Pennsylvania volunteers and then stationed in Virginia), leaving her with two young children. During the first day of the fight General Howard wanted some one to show him and tell about various roads leading from Gettysburg, and asked a number of men and boys who were in the cellar of the house to go with him and point them out. These persons were too full of fear to go. Then Mrs. Thorn showed her courage and patriotism by voluntarily offering to show the roads. This offer was at first refused by the general, but Mrs. Thorn persisted in her offer, saying: "Somebody must show you, and I can do it; I was born and brought up here, and know the roads as well as anybody." Her offer was accepted, and with the officer and horse between her and the fire of the enemy, Mrs. Thorn went from one spot to another pointing out the different roads. Some soldiers they passed spoke up: "This is no place for a woman." "I know it," said the general, "but I couldn't get a man to come; they were all afraid." This answer started cheers for Mrs. Thorn, showing that the soldiers admired the courage shown at such a time. (Popular History, World Co., 1880.)

### Engaged to Jennie Wade

One of the members of Company F, Eighty-seventh Pennsylvania Volunteers, was Corporal Johnston H. Skelly of Gettysburg, who was engaged to marry Jennie Wade, only citizen of the town to be killed during the three-day battle. A bullet coming through the door of the kitchen where she was engaged in baking bread for Union soldiers resulted in her death. A picture of Corporal Skelly was found in her pocket. The corporal's father was a tailor, but the corporal was working as a granite cutter when he enlisted in Company E, Second Regiment of Volunteers, for three months. In August, 1861, he joined Company F. He was mortally wounded at Winchester, June 14, 1863, and died at Winchester the following July 12, a little over a week after Jennie's death. The girl was just twenty years of age. Her christened name was Mary Virginia Wade. She was buried in a coffin which had been made for a Confederate officer. Her fiance had a brother, Charles E. Skelly, also a member of Company F, and his father served in Company K, 101st Pennsylvania Regiment. (87th Pennsylvania Volunteers—Prowell.)

### Peter Markle, Wagon Driver

Peter Markle and Joe Carl, two youths of the Abbottstown area, were rejected as too young when they went to Washington and endeavored to enlist in the Union army, but were told that their services could be utilized as drivers at the government arsenal in the national capital. The wagon trains supplying armies in the field with munitions, food and other supplies were made up there in units of twenty-five wagons to a unit. Any number of units would comprise a train. They were employed as drivers until the end of the war.

It so happened that young Markle was present the night of April 14, 1865, at a performance of the popular comedy, "Our American Cousin," in Ford's Theater, occupying an orchestra seat not far from the stage. The seats or chairs were cane-bottomed. Like many other members of the capacity audience of about 1,700 he had come especially to see the President and General Grant who was expected to be present also. The general, however, had another engagement out of town. The President and Mrs. Lincoln were late in arriving, but when they occupied their box, the orchestra leader signaled for "Hail to the Chief," and the audience rose in a body to cheer the war-time executive again and again.

After the audience had settled down the actors resumed their presentation of the play until about 10:15 p.m. when a pistol shot rang out and a figure waving a dagger tumbled out of the president's box and staggered across the stage shrieking the motto of the Virginia coat-of-arms, "Sic Semper Tyrannis." All was in a turmoil. Nobody knew just what had happened. Presently the word spread that the President had been assassinated. Anger and sadness were mingled in the minds of the witnesses of this great catastrophe, among them the youth from Abbotts-town.

When Peter Markle returned home he took up various means to earn a living. He worked at the Alwine brickyards and then at the Wolf Bros. tannery, off the Hanover road, but he is best recalled as having been associated with the East Berlin rail-road. He was a member of G.A.R. Post 409, a Civil War veteran who had never enlisted. A son Raymond Markle resides here on Broadway.

John M. Wolf, well-known teacher in Adams and York counties schools, held clerical posts in Washington during the war. He was present at both of the Lincoln inaugurals. Squire Wolf and

Sergeant Boston Corbett, who shot John Wilkes Booth when he was cornered in a barn on the Richard H. Garrett farm, near Front Royal, Virginia, boarded at the same home. He heard Corbett often retell the story of Booth being dragged from the burning shed, and made charcoal drawings of the scene from the sergeant's descriptions.

### Lincoln Society Dedicates Marker

One of the Pennsylvania Railroad's fast express trains which usually whizzes by the now unused Hanover Junction railway station stopped the afternoon of May 31, 1953, to let out Miss Helen Nicolay, eighty-seven-year-old authoress, and a group of Washington visitors.

Before a crowd of several hundred persons in front of the station Miss Nicolay, daughter of Abraham Lincoln's personal secretary, John George Nicolay, unveiled a marker erected by the Pennsylvania Historical and Museum Commission and inscribed with these words:

"Hanover Junction—Here, November 18, 1863, a special train carrying Abraham Lincoln and party to Gettysburg for dedication of National Cemetery changed railroads. Earlier in that year, wounded soldiers were transported from Gettysburg battlefield to this Junction, thence to distant hospitals. It was a chief point on the Military Telegraph line, 1863."

It was the high point of the celebration staged by the Lincoln Society of Hanover Junction, which began Friday night at the Seven Valleys Community Hall.

Hanover Junction had a remarkable apprentice operator in John H. Shearer, only sixteen years of age, who transmitted telegraphic messages from Gettysburg and Hanover through Hanover Junction to the President and the War Department at Washington during the battle of Gettysburg.

### Gettysburg Losses

Estimating the number of troops engaged in any Civil War campaign and the losses involved pose difficult problems. A given figure will not show the actual number of front line fighters, it will include many who have tasks to perform in the rear and many stragglers who fall by the wayside during the arduous marches. Conservative estimates place the strength of the Army of the Potomac at 93,000 in round numbers at the start of the Gettysburg campaign and the Army of Virginia at 78,000. Meade's losses are placed at 23,000 killed, wounded and missing; Lee's at 21,000 killed, wounded and missing; Meade's killed alone, 3,000: Lee's killed, 2,600; Meade's wounded, 14,500; Lee's wounded, 13,000. How many of the missing and the wounded became captives is mere guesswork.

L. L. Crounse of the New York Times reported from Gettysburg and Abbottstown that the work of burying the dead began July 5. The field, he wrote, presented an appalling sight before the center and right of the Union line. He had seen about all the battlefields in the east and declared never was there evidence of carnage as at Gettysburg.

## Lincoln Has Joke on Meade

Editor Byington of the Norwalk (Connecticut) Gazette was among those who criticized Meade for not following up his victory by crushing the Army of Virginia before it returned to its home grounds. Lincoln had also expressed his disappointment over Meade's over-cautious stand.

Byington was at Washington, he said, when Meade came to report after the battle of Gettysburg. He asked Gideon Wells, Secretary of the Navy, about the interview. "I was present in the Cabinet," Wells told the editor, "when General Meade came to tell about the battle, and take counsel about the situation. 'Do you know, General,' Mr. Lincoln suddenly broke out, with a laugh, 'what your attitude toward Lee for a week after the battle of Gettysburg reminded me of?' 'No, Mr. President, what is it?' asked Meade. 'I could think of nothing else,' replied Lincoln, 'than an old woman trying to shoo her geese across the creek!' After that Meade never quite recovered confidence." (Popular History, World Co., 1880.)

## Aftermath of Battle

Many wheat fields in the area remained uncut and considerable damage was done by both Rebel and Union forces. Kilpatrick pitched camp on the farms of Andrew Rudisill and others along the Abbottstown road. Wheat was trodden down and rail fences burned for the campfires. Corn was confiscated for the horses. Damage was estimated at $1,800, but the government never repaid the farmers for damage done. Much of their stock had been removed to the hills but any stock remaining in the barns was taken. When the cavalry moved on crates of hard-tack left behind were fed to the hogs and unexploded shells dumped in Beaver Creek at Hartman's mill. It was at the George Wertz property along the Abbottstown road that a caisson exploded causing the death of a private and two horses.

A cleanup detail was left behind by General Sykes when he hurriedly vacated his camp near Pennville. They burned the beef carcasses remaining from the interrupted evening meal in a nearby stone quarry. Horses killed in the battle were also pulled to the quarry and destroyed.

### Returning Veterans Get Lost

Corporal Nelson G. Madden, who had been with the Sixth Michigan Cavalry and Sergeant Theodora N. Berry of the 44th New York Regiment but then residing in Michigan, on returning to Hanover in October, 1902, thirty-nine years after the battle, were quite lost. They were trying to find the spring where the corporal had filled his canteen in 1863. After going in several wrong directions they finally located the spring on the Samuel Forney place out Frederick Street. They had pitched their shelter tents opposite the Forney residence the evening of June 30 and were preparing food for the Fifth Corps when the call to battle upset their plans.*

### Reads Paper on Battle

At a reception tendered visiting veterans of the Fifth New York Cavalry in the Arcadian Club rooms, Captain Jabez. Chambers, Brooklyn, New York, read a paper on the part taken by the Fifth at Hanover and Gettysburg in '63. The paper had been prepared by C. B. Thomas, Chicago, late commissary sergeant of the Fifth Volunteers. Captain Chambers said he came

*(Hanover Herald, October 13, 1903)

to Hanover first because it was here on June 30, 1863, that the greatest of battles really started. At the first gunshot Major John Hammond, who commanded the regiment, directed his men out Abbottstown Street and passed down side streets to the open Commons where they reformed into line, drew sabers, and breaking off into fours, charged against the enemy. Sergeant Thomas estimated the enemy dead at twenty-five and the wounded far exceeded that number. Seventy-five prisoners were taken.

## Kilpatrick Gives Lectures

General Hugh Judson Kilpatrick returned to Hanover twice after the battle in which he commanded the Third Division of the Army of Potomac Cavalry. Under the auspices of G.A.R. Post 99, he delivered a lecture in Concert Hall, Center Square, the evening of February 8, 1879. His subject was on Sherman's March from Atlanta to the Sea. His talk proved so popular that he was asked to return. He delivered his second lecture about a month later.

## Out of the Mouths of Children

After the battle at Hanover Stuart's forces marched southward and most of them crossed the Baltimore turnpike at Centre schoolhouse, near the Brockley farm, and moved toward Jefferson. A hundred yards east of this schoolhouse a small squad of Union cavalry was concealed in the woods watching the movements of the enemy. They had dashed down the pike from Hanover after the fight.

A farmer in the vicinity knew that the Union troops were in the woods. When Stuart's rear guard passed his house, an officer asked if there were any Yanks in the vicinity. The farmer could speak but little English. He didn't want to betray a trust and shook his head negatively, but his little son of twelve years, who stood nearby taking it all in, stepped up briskly with a knowing look in his eyes and corrected his father; then pointing in the direction of the woods, indicated that Federal soldiers were stationed there. About a hundred Confederates charged toward the scouts who fell back. Shots were exchanged. One soldier was

wounded and two or three horses were killed in this little skirmish in West Manheim Township.

(George R. Prowell)

## CAPTAIN POTTER'S MEMOIRS

The committee preparing the account of the battle at Hanover
has been privileged to consult those parts of the Civil War Memoirs of Captain Henry Clay Potter (1841-1912) dealing with the
Gettysburg campaign. The original memoirs are still in manuscript form in the possession of the captain's son, William Woodburn Potter, who has placed them at the committee's disposal.

Captain Potter was born in Philadelphia in 1841. His military
service began at Fort Delaware in April, 1861. He eventually
enrolled in the cavalry and was transferred in April, 1863, to
Kilpatrick's Cavalry Division in time to participate in the Gettysburg campaign with rank of captain in the Eighteenth Pennsylvania Cavalry. He took part in Farnsworth's charge July 3

CAPTAIN HENRY CLAY POTTER
*His troopers in first clash at
Hanover.*

and in pursuit of Lee's retreating army. In a skirmish near Hagerstown July 6 he was captured, and underwent internment in various Southern prisons until exchanged. He was discharged at Harrisburg November 7, 1865.

Captain Potter prefaced his account by saying he wrote only of what he personally saw or participated in. His narrative differs in many respects from the words of the leading officers who figured prominently in the various events recorded in history. His story of the unfortunate sally of Farnsworth in the vicinity of the Round Tops especially refers to accounts from other sources which claim that an argument between Kilpatrick and Farnsworth was carried on in language so loud that it was heard by enemy scouts in the vicinity. We think our readers may be interested in the Potter story for what it is worth:

We were under General Hooker when we crossed the Potomac. It had to be forded and some of the horses had to swim part of the distance and some were drowned, owing to poor handling by their riders, and boats had to be put out to save the men. We rested a while to dry off and went to Poolsville (sic) and then soon to Frederick. On Sunday morning, June 28, 1863, we changed Commanders and had a Review. General Hooker was replaced by General Meade. At the time we considered this a matter of routine. After the Review we started off right away and reached Littlestown about sunrise Tuesday morning, June 30, where we got plenty to eat from the people as we passed through.

At the outside of the town and near a creek we halted at 8:30 A.M. The column then started in changed formation, my Regiment being the last to leave. Kilpatrick went first with Custer's Brigade, 1st, 5th, 6th, 7th Michigan 3,000 strong, Pennington's Battery six guns, then Farnsworth with the 1st Vermont, 1st West Virginia, 5th New York, Elder's Battery, pack horses, mules, ambulances, etc. and last the 18th Pennsylvania Cavalry.

Before leaving Littlestown, while the column was moving, Lt. Col. Wm. P. Brinton told me to take my men, about 40, and stay in the rear about a mile, and to keep a sharp look-out for the enemy; but from all inquiries no rebels had been seen. Then while on the march I was joined by Capt. Freeland with a few men. He was under arrest being the worst forager I ever knew. He rode with me a little ways and then took a road to the right where a barn was in sight as he wanted to steal something. We proceeded until we came to a stream that crossed the road where we halted to water our horses. Up to this time no Rebs had been seen or heard from. While waiting, a man came out from a farm house close by saying that the Rebs had run off with all his horses and cows and he called to me to get them back. I went with him to his barn which I found to be empty of livestock. He then pointed to a group of men in the distance saying 'There they are." As I looked I saw blue overcoats; and thinking they were Freeland's group, told the farmer I would have his stock brought back and I went on. As I approached and looked at them closer, the group appeared to increase in numbers and their flag seemed too suspiciously red so I sent Corporals Street and Dannehauer over the fields to see who they were. They did not get far but came back saying it was Freeland who had captured an old Conestoga wagon. However, I did not credit this as the group must have numbered a hundred men, whereas Freeland, when he left me, did not have over ten men, so I told our men to unsling carbines and load.

While we were watching this questionable group some of them appeared on my front calling out for us not to shoot and that they would not shoot and for us to surrender, also saying that they had just captured a lot of our men and for us not to make a noise. I was carrying a carbine then and told my men what to do but to wait until I gave the word. We were walking toward them all this time and they thought we were going to surrender as there seemed nothing else to be done. When we got to about 300 feet from them I gave the order to "Fire" and then "Charge," which we did. They flew without firing a shot into a lane from which they had come. We followed and were under full headway towards the town of Hanover and as we neared the town, our boys of the 18th Pennsylvania Cavalry Rear Guard were getting into the saddle. I shouted "Right about." We turned, being joined by about 150 of my regiment. As we righted about, I was on the right of the first set of fours. Lt. Gall, apparently detached from the 5th New York, dashed up to my side asking all sorts of questions as to

how it started etc., when he fell from his saddle, apparently
mortally wounded. We drove the Rebs up the lane for over a
mile. Stuart with all his staff was in a field beyond a fence.
They stood their ground until we got close to them when they
stampeded, some of them clearing the creek, others going head
foremost into it horse and all. If we had had support here we
could have had them all; but no one came to our help, notwithstanding false reports that have gotten into history and
statements that have been put into records and printed to the
contrary. We, the 18th Pennsylvania Cavalry fought hand to
hand with Chambler's (sic) men fully a mile from the town
until the Rebs opened up on us with one gun that caused us
to give way. In the melee Corporal Harvey was shot. He fell
over my horse and I had to push him off and he slid to the
ground between the horses. He was either killed outright or
was tramped to death by the horses. In giving way and nearing
the town again after about three-quarters of an hour of fighting, the 5th New York Cavalry came to our support which was
at the end of the fight. At the start of the fight Kilpatrick was
eight miles away and he and his staff got the news from excited
stragglers etc. who had been in the fight. When Kilpatrick arrived with Elder's Battery he went on the roof of a tavern on
the square of the town to watch events but the enemy in the
meantime was getting away as fast as possible having probably
some other basic mission to perform. The only prominent military men there was Custer who had stopped in the town to get
something to eat, his command being seven miles away. Farnsworth did not get up in time to take part in the fighting, nor
did he make the charge credited to him. The men who could
have reported the skirmish correctly were Custer and W. P.
Brinton, neither of whom mentioned it. Darlington also was not
there, being at his home in Harrisburg, and his report was
made up from hearsay after he came back. Kilpatrick's report
was not made until two months after June 30th and then only
from accounts from people who were not engaged. The only
troops engaged were the 18th Pennsylvania who did all the
fighting and Gall of the 5th New York when Gall was killed.

The official report of the large number of troops killed in the
action is not correct. Most of those lost were stragglers who

were rounded up as prisoners. The only men killed on our side were Gall, Harvey and one other by an accidental shell. Darlington's report is decidedly not correct and the Lieutenant he mentions was not in the action. The 18th Pennsylvania Cavalry killed one Reb Colonel and five men out near the creek and Lt. Colonel Payne was rescued after he had fallen into a tan vat and taken prisoner by my regiment.

After our skirmish at Hanover we started off on the road to go to York to intercept Stuart's Cavalry Regiment (who were probably paving the way for a march on Harrisburg by Lee's army). We met Stuart in the night of July 1st on the same road and not wanting to force our way through we turned around. They followed us until we came together again on the afternoon of July 2nd when we had quite a brisk skirmish. We staid (sic) in contact with them until about 1 A.M. (July 3rd) when we quietly moved off to go to the Round Tops to protect the extreme left flank of our Army concentrated at Gettysburg which Confederate General Lee was threatening to turn. We halted at Two-Taverns, cooked some coffee and got into battle position about 9 A.M. July 3rd.

We had only the 1st Brigade of Kilpatrick's Division composed of the 5th New York, the 18th Pennsylvania, the 1st Vermont, the 1st West Virginia Cavalry and Elder's Battery, having lost Custer's command during the night. Our Cavalry were dismounted and part of the 5th New York and the 18th Pennsylvania were deployed forward as skirmishers and were about a thousand yards in front of us where they lay all day. Many of the men of the battery took the horses from the guns and dragged the field pieces into position.

After Elder had fired a shot and located the enemy, it became an artillery duel between him and Robinson's (I think it was Robinson) Battery, more or less all day. Kilpatrick wanted to have the enemy battery charged and captured, believing it to be unprotected, so at about one o'clock Captain H. C. Parsons with some of his troops the 1st Vermont was ordered to reconnoiter to our right and front. They closed in and I did not see them return. Then Capt. Wells of the same regiment also went in and did come back with a few of his men and reported that the ground was not feasible for cavalry and that the enemy guns were on a hill behind a high stone wall in a very strong position. Nothing more was said about it until about four o'clock when we were getting a very severe and uncomfortable shelling. At this time Kilpatrick, Farnsworth, myself and the bugler were dismounted in the rear of Elder's guns close together among a pile of rocks. Kilpatrick was talking to Farnsworth about charging the enemy battery in front of us, that it was in an isolated position and could be captured. Farnsworth contended that the enemy guns, being on a high hill, could not be reached with cavalry which could not maneuver among the stone walls. The conversation continued for a long while and in a quiet and friendly manner until about the height of Picket's (sic) charge which I think was about 3:30 or 4 P.M. Kilpatrick jumped up and impatiently but in a low voice said, "Farnsworth, if you don't charge that Battery, I will." No one except myself and the bugler could possibly have heard the conversation between Kilpatrick and Farnsworth, and all stories about other people having heard it are pure imagination and not true. There was no order given to charge; but as soon as Kilpatrick made the remark, Farnsworth got up, passed me and beckoned to his orderly to bring up his horse, met it half way, mounted and ordered the troops to file out. The 1st Vermont went first by fours followed by the 1st West Virginia. I went to my horse and mounted waiting for things to shape up expecting trouble. By this time Farnsworth's men were cheering and shooting when Kilpatrick came rushing at us shouting, "Why in h — and d — don't you move those troops out?" In a few seconds we, the 18th Pennsylvania and the 1st New York, were under way with the rest. All of a sudden the Rebs in our front appeared by the thousands. They seemed to come out of the ground like bees and they gave us such a rattling fire we all gave way and retreated toward the woods. Here I called to the men to dismount and, getting behind trees, gave them a rattling fire which sent them flying and left us a clear field. In the meantime, Farnsworth was out on the meadow, leading a straggly charging mass of cavalry. He fell at the head of the line near Devil's Den. At about this time the fighting on our section of the army in the Battle of Gettysburg was practically over. During the night of Friday, July 3rd, 1863, Lee's army was in full retreat.

Captain Potter describes the first clash at Hanover in a letter to the Philadelphia Ledger as follows:

When about a mile from the town the road they (the enemy) were on turned sharply into the road we were on and about sixty of them came out directly in front of us . . . we fired . . . they scattered and we went through them. It did not take long for them to recover and come after. As we ran towards the town a bend in the road brought into view the rear of my regiment dismounted. Hearing the firing in their rear they were mounting their horses and some of them joined us in driving them back. It was here I was joined by Adjutant Gall of the Fifth New York. He rode with me in the first set of fours. He did not get far when he fell from his horse. We were again driven back, and this time the whole regiment joined in and we drove them to a standstill. It was here up a lane with a high stiff post and rail fence on each side, the cutting and slashing was done, and for a few in the very front it was a fist fight.

It was here General Custer came dashing up in the field behind us, shouting "Drive them!" but for a short time neither side would give way. Custer went back for more troops, but before they arrived the enemy dropped a shell (the first fired) in our midst, when we gave way and fell back to the edge of town, when the Fifth New York came to our assistance. This practically ended the affair . . . the "rebs" at no time had over 700 or 800 troops and but one gun that they used.

We lost no wagons or ambulance, and the enemy were never near them. . . . We killed a Confederate colonel and buried him, with three or four men, where they fell inside the fence and not far from th creek.

(Philadelphia Public Ledger, December 31, 1903. H. C. Potter)

The Hanover paper recalls Captain Potter's visit at the time of the dedication of The Picket when his remarks were misquoted:

Major H. C. Potter, of Philadelphia, a survivor of the 18th Pennsylvania Cavalry, and a participant in the battle of Hanover, June 30, 1863, visited Hanover, September 28th, 1905, on the occasion of the dedication of the monument, and made a brief speech during the ceremonies. His remarks were incorrectly reported, in several particulars, he says. The papers made him say there was a bridge over the stream near where the fight began and a toll-gate also, while there was at that time neither bridge nor toll-gate. There was a house close by the creek and one about half-way between the creek and the town, which house stood a little back, on the left side of the road, with a railing and gate. The only other building, he says, was a stone one on the same side, without a roof, and in front of this Adjutant Gall was killed.

(Hanover Herald, August 18, 1906.—Prowell)

## HELPED NURSE WOUNDED SOLDIERS

Mrs. Mary C. Fisher, of York, had a very interesting story to tell of her experience in going from York through Hanover to Gettysburg, the day after the great battle in 1863.

Mrs. Fisher was the widow of Robert J. Fisher, who served for a period of thirty years as President Judge of the Courts of York County; twenty of those years he also presided over the courts of Adams County. Mrs. Fisher said when her husband heard that the enemy approached Gettysburg he feared that they might destroy the County Records. When he heard after the battle was over that the courthouse was not injured and that the books and legal documents were undisturbed he was very much gratified.

When General Early, with his nine thousand Confederate troops arrived at York on Sunday morning, July 28, 1863, he demanded that York should pay him one hundred thousand dollars in money and forty thousand dollars in shoes, hats and clothing for his men. The people of York raised twenty-eight thousand dollars in paper money, then known as "Greenbacks," for that was the name given to the National currency. Early wanted the balance of the one hundred thousand dollars, but they couldn't raise it, for the money in the banks had been sent to Philadelphia and New York to places of safety. General Early sent word to Judge Fisher to come to the courthouse. When the Judge arrived, Early said: "I want the keys to all the offices in the courthouse, for I expect to burn the records. The Yankees burned the courthouse of Fairfax County, Virginia, some time ago, and I am going to burn the records of your courthouse unless I get the balance of the one hundred thousand dollars." "Two wrongs would not make a right," said Judge Fisher, and then the judge pleaded with General Early not to burn the Records. Soon afterward a courier came from Carlisle with a dispatch from General Ewell, ordering Early to retreat with his nine thousand men toward Gettysburg, where the battle would soon be opened.

William Woods, of York Street, Hanover, was Recorder of Deeds at York when General Early came into the courthouse on Sunday morning, June 28, 1863, and took up his headquarters in the Sheriff's office.

"Some days before the Confederates came," said Mr. Woods, "the Register of Wills and myself carried all the valuable documents, books and records down into the cellar of the courthouse. The records of the Recorder's office were in one corner of the cellar, and those belonging to the Register's office in another corner. We covered them with straw and big sheets of paper so as to conceal them. Judge Fisher had ordered us to do this so that they might be saved if the Confederate soldiers were ordered to destroy them."

General Early did not get more than twenty-eight thousand dollars in York. The balance of the one hundred thousand dollars is what he wanted. It is hardly probable that he intended to destroy the County Records, but he threatened it in order to get the money. He had to leave York before he could compel the citizens to pay the balance.

The great battle of Gettysburg followed the next three days and the second day of the fight a brigade of Early's troops, commanded by General Hayes, then known as the "Louisiana Tigers," lost heavily; in fact the entire brigade ceased to be an organization after the retreat from Gettysburg.

Mrs. Fisher described her experience at Gettysburg and her trip to the battlefield, where she served for eleven days as a volunteer nurse in the field hospitals. At three o'clock in the afternoon, in company with a gentleman and two other women, she started from Center Square, York, on a mission of love and mercy. News had come to York that the Union army had won the battle and that thousands of suffering men were lying wounded on the field or in the hospitals. She arrived at Hanover late on the evening of July 4. A train of forty wagons loaded with provisions, clothing, lint and anything that would be needed to comfort the wounded soldiers, who needed the attention of surgeons and nurses, was also dispatched.

It rained all day July 4, for a big rain always follows heavy cannonading. Rainstorms succeed every great battle. The cannon discharges affect the meteorological condition of the atmosphere, which causes rain. The forty wagons passed on from Hanover to Gettysburg and arrived there during the night of July 4. Most of them did not go up the turnpike, because there were so many straggling soldiers on that road, so they came around through Hanover, where they stopped for a brief time and then moved onward. Lee's army had begun the retreat across the South Mountain on the way to the heart of Virginia, from whence it had come. A train of ambulance wagons, seventeen miles in length, followed the Confederate army across the mountains and across the Potomac. This was one of the saddest sights of the Civil War. This train of wagons carrying wounded Confederates moved westward in a deluge of rain.

Mrs. Fisher and her companions started from Hanover late in the night of July 4. The rain had ceased and they moved towards New Oxford in the starlight; the moon was still behind the Eastern hills. When the wagons reached a point beyond New Oxford they came in the lines of Kilpatrick's Union cavalry. It was this division of cavalry that had engaged in battle with Stuart's cavalry on the streets of Hanover a few days before.

"Unload the wagons," said General Kilpatrick, "and use them to carry wounded officers to Littlestown."

"At first," said Mrs. Fisher, "I thought Kilpatrick's order must be obeyed, but at this juncture, early in the morning and before daylight of July 5, the leading chaplain of the Twelfth Army Corps under Howard demanded that the suffering soldiers needed the provisions and the goods on those wagons. He wanted them to move onward at once to the field hospitals, and his request was obeyed."

It would make a long story to relate all the experiences that

*Pleasant Hill Hotel, Baltimore Street, was taken over by the government as a U. S. Cavalry Hospital in July and August, 1863. An Academy was conducted here at one time.*

Mrs. Fisher had as a volunteer nurse during the succeeding ten days. They first stopped at a barn near the town of Gettysburg. Four hundred wounded men were in this barn; some had received the attention of the army surgeons and some had not, for there were many thousands of Union and Confederate soldiers who had been wounded in this battle. Some of them had been taken away on trains to hospitals at Baltimore, York, Lancaster, Harrisburg and Philadelphia. The large building on Baltimore Street, Hanover, then known as Pleasant Hill Hotel, was also used for a hospital.

On Sunday, July 6, Mrs. Fisher and companions were sent to a field hospital southwest of Gettysburg. Most of the troops belonged to Sickles' corps. General Sickles had been kept here for several hours after his leg had been amputated. There were many touching incidents that came to the attention of Mrs. Fisher during the succeeding days that she remained in that hospital. Her devotion to the interest of the wounded men received the highest commendation from the surgeon in chief and other officers who were present. She had the consolation that through her devoted efforts she helped to save the lives of a number of men and comforted hundreds of them in their deep distress.

(The Hanover Herald, January 10, 1885—Rev. Cyrus Cort)

## THE BALTIMORE ROWDIES SCARE

The so-called "Baltimore Rowdies Scare" took place at Hanover Monday afternoon, April 22, 1861. It became a sort of legend, and like legends was added to from time to time according to the imagination of the narrator. Here's one of the accounts as told by the Rev. Cyrus Cort, Greencastle, Pennsylvania, in the Hanover Herald, January 10, 1885:

The community was in a state of ferment at the time. Hostilities had commenced, Sumter had been fired on, and Massachusetts troops had been assailed by a mob on the streets of Baltimore a few days previous. The bridges had been burned on the line of the Northern Central Railway and regular communication between Washington and the North had been interrupted.

Two companies of volunteers under Captains Myers and Diller had left Hanover for York on the previous day (Sunday), amid exciting scenes. A Home Guard containing several hundred members had been organized and they had just passed through the first drill on Monday afternoon when Captain W. H. Jenifer came riding into town on horseback from Carlisle Barracks. He belonged to the Second Cavalry Regiment of the regular United States army lately arrived from Texas. Its regimental officers were no less a trio than Albert Sidney Johnston, Robert E. Lee and George H. Thomas. The chief burgess had received a telegram from Governor Curtin requesting the arrest of Captain Jenifer under the belief that he was deserting to the secessionists with valuable information. Jenifer was not a deserter, but had lately resigned his commission, to take effect April 30, and had received leave of absence from Major Geo. H. Thomas to visit friends in Maryland and Virginia, whither he was proceeding on horseback because of the interruption of railroad travel.

To allay the angry and excited feelings of the crowd, some of whose members had begun to threaten personal violence, Captain Jenifer was permitted to address the people from a window of the Central Hotel which he did in a way that was satisfactory for the time being. But shortly afterward the burgess was handed a letter from a homesick member of one of the volunteer companies written from York to his father, condemning the action of the state authorities in taking them away from their homes where they might soon be needed to defend their families against an expected attack of Baltimore rowdies.

"To arms! To arms! The Baltimore rowdies are coming to destroy the town and Jenifer is to lead them," was the cry then suddenly heard from the window.

This was like applying a lighted match to gunpowder. A panic ensued. With incredible swiftness the unfounded rumor spread through the town and to the regions beyond. It is said that the report that the Baltimore rowdies were destroying Hanover reached Gettysburg by horseback, a distance of fourteen miles, and badly demoralized a town meeting two hours after the unfounded rumor was recklessly started in Hanover. In fact it

went all along the Pennsylvania Border like a galvanic shock,
reaching far beyond the mountains. A lady at New Oxford or
East Berlin died of fright and a company started out from
Carlisle to help repel the invasion. The writer was stopping
temporarily in Hanover at the home of Stephen Keefer, along
with J. Spangler Kieffer, nephew of Mr. Keefer and later a
Doctor of Divinity and pastor of the First Reformed Church
in Hagerstown, Maryland. Our host, like many other citizens
of Hanover, had gone to York in the interest of the two volunteer
companies that had left town the day before. We had set down
to supper about 5 p.m. when the maid of the house rushed in
with the startling report that the Baltimore rowdies were coming to destroy the town. We ridiculed the report as absurd and
preposterous. She begged us to come to the front door and see
for ourselves. We went and sure enough the "rumors of wars"
were such that we felt it our duty to arm ourselves for the
coming fray. We got a gun in the wareroom attached to the
premises and a lot of ammunition out of the store and hastened
to the market house where the people were massing to resist
the invaders.

Horsemen galloped to and fro warning the people of the
impending danger. Stores and dwellings were closed up. Women
and children, terror stricken, were screaming, fainting and fleeing to the country. Men were shouting, firing alarm guns and
tolling bells. Some very ludicrous as well as distressing scenes
occurred. One woman seized a large feather bed and fled from
her house toward the country, leaving articles of far greater
value and much less bulk and weight behind. A young woman
snatched up her child and hastened several squares when its
screams attracted the attention of persons less excited, who discovered that its frightened mother was carrying it with its
head downwards. One old gentleman was short of ammunition.
Mounting his old horse, in woman fashion, with his gun in one
hand, he dashed up and down the street shouting in Pennsylvania German, "Wo kann ich koogla griega? Wo kann ich
koogla griega?" (Where can I get bullets?) Another one got
down his flint-lock shotgun and in his haste to load it and light
his pipe to calm his nerves at the same time, he put the tobacco
into the gun and the powder into his pipe. Having occasion to

use the pipe first, he discovered his mistake by the explosion which seriously damaged his eyes.

John W. Love, pastor of the Reformed Church in Greensburg, was coming toward town in a buggy when he met an old female acquaintance a mile or two out. In reply to his query: "Why, Aunt Polly, what's the matter?" she exclaimed: "For God's sake, turn back! the Baltimore rowdies are burning the town, and killing off the people, men, women and children, just like flies!"

The old market house then stood in the center of the town where the fountain is now located. This was the rallying point and here the excitement and confusion were intense. An old sailor had loaded a small swivel with slugs and it was pointed down Baltimore Street ready to deal out destruction to the rowdies who were momentarily expected to rush into town. Those who had no guns were equipped with such formidable weapons as dung forks, pitch forks, corn cutters and even scythes. In the midst of the panic some of the infuriated people resolved to put Captain Jenifer out of the way before his rowdy Baltimore accomplices would make their assault.

A rush was made towards the hotel where he was closely confined under guard. Captain A. W. Eichelberger bravely threw himself in front of the mob and motioned them with both hands to stand back, exclaiming that they would have to go over his dead body before they could kill a prisoner of war. It was a critical moment and Jenifer's doom seemed to be sealed. The writer and his friend Kieffer together with several Gettysburg College students, and some sensible citizens of Hanover, rushed forward and gave three cheers for Captain Eichelberger. The Rev. Dr. Zieber, who had ascertained the unfounded origin of the rumor, came along, and mounting a meat block in the market house, counseled calmness and consideration or they would be forever disgraced as a community.

The burgess concluded to send the prisoner to York for safe keeping. To this end Jenifer's legs were bound with chains and handcuffs were sent for. Captain Eichelberger who knew Jenifer's father by reputation as a worthy man who had been for many years a Whig Congressman from Charles County, Maryland, and U. S. Minister to Austria, protested against the indignity and insisted that as a gentleman and an officer of the army,

Captain Jenifer must not be chained or handcuffed. The prisoner gave assurance that he would not attempt to escape. The chains were removed and under guard of the burgess and two other armed persons Captain Janifer was conveyed in a closed carriage to York, where he was placed in the jail at midnight. Next day he was placed in a stronger cell and heavily ironed. Through the efforts of Lieutenant Wells of the Navy, and Major George H. Thomas, Captain Pentz and others of his regiment which had quite recently been transferred from Carlisle to York, Judge Fisher was induced to release Captain Jenifer after consulting by telegraph with the Governor. His fellow officers insisted that he should be lodged at their headquarters instead of remaining in jail. Another order coming from Harrisburg to re-arrest him, it was arranged that Jenifer should go to Harrisburg and see the Governor in person which he did in company of Captain Pentz of his regiment and Lieutenant Jones recently in command at Harpers Ferry. After hearing the statement of Jenifer, Governor Curtin remarked: "These are exciting times and we have to be on our guard." He was then allowed to depart and proceeded to Baltimore.

Jenifer's resignation was accepted and he afterwards entered the Confederate service where he became a colonel and was noted for his daring reconnaissances on horseback. He figured prominently in the battle of Ball's Bluff—mounted on his white charger, he seemed to bear a charmed life, as he galloped along the picket lines at times amid a shower of bullets from sharpshooters.

After the Civil War was over he became chief of staff to the Khedive of Egypt for several years and finally returned to America with a splendid stud of Arabian horses which were exhibited in York at the Fair and elsewhere. He died in the spring of 1878.

# EPILOGUE

## HANOVER TODAY VS. HANOVER TOMORROW!

We told of Richard McAllister founding the town two centuries ago at the beginning of this book and of one important phase of American history that it survived. We thought it but proper that after several other wars, including two World Wars, we should mention at the end the town still exists and is flourishing to a greater degree than ever before.

Tanning buckskins and turning out gloves, shoes and jackets was one of our leading industries at the start. Our forebears were handy with guns and got the bucks, which abounded, in the woods right around them. They established gristmills to turn the wheat and rye they grew into flour and sawmills to produce lumber from the oak and hickory trees flourishing in the same woods. Water was the main source of power.

Carriage and wagon making became a leading industry down to the Civil War period. After the war the community lost the trade which progressive citizens like Abdiel W. Eichelberger had built up in Georgia and elsewhere in the South. For a period of fifty years cigarmaking then furnished employment to men and women as the area's mainstay, together with agricultural products.

During the present century the manufacture of shoes, gloves, heels and soles has revived the leather industry to so great a degree that 1,949 of the residents are engaged in the leather and leather goods category—more than in any other single industry. During this period also gainful pursuits have become greatly diversified. In 1920 the town had twenty-eight industrial establishments. Today there are a hundred covering many fields. The principal products are shoes, books, garments, potato chips, wirecloth, and canned goods.

During the Revolutionary War Mary Ann Furnace turned out rifle bullets, grapeshot and cannon balls for Minute Men and fireplace fixtures for homes; blacksmiths shod horses, put tires on wheels, and wrought other iron parts for vehicles. Today

Hanover has twenty or more firms with 978 hands producing metal articles and machinery. Six textile firms with 824 employes today replace the handful of individual carpet and coverlet weavers of a century and more ago. Seventeen firms manufacture furniture as successors to the few cabinet workers and clock-makers who toiled for months on a single cherished piece. Wood products here today range from penholders to pre-fabricated houses.

Two large packing plants and one of the country's largest potato chip producers with other firms preserve and market the products of surrounding fertile farm lands.

Among the firsts the Hanover Shoe Farms rate as the world's largest standard-bred nursery. It is natural that Hanover, a half-dozen miles north of the Mason and Dixon line, should share with the South a love of fine horses. One of the main plants of Doubleday & Co., world's largest book publishers, is located in Hanover.

The population of the metropolitan area is placed at 35,795, of whom 97 per cent are native born and over 8,300 are wage earners. Wages and salaries in 1960 in the industrial establishments totaled $18,761,700 and products made had a value of $66,250,700. The four banks in Hanover have total deposits of $53,565,088; assets of $61,142,996; and total capital of $6,686,518.

In the Hanover area thirty-one largely attended churches are to be found, including the famed Conewago Chapel. The Hanover Public Library with its 68,000 volumes has an outstanding genealogical department and is nationally known for its children's section, with 2,402 members in the Vacation Reading Club. The Library was opened in 1911 after many years of keen anticipation. The population has tripled since then. It is putting it mildly to point out expansion of facilities is long overdue.

Four national service clubs and four welfare organizations are active. Three Veterans' groups are handsomely housed. A score or more of clubs and lodges fill the fraternal need, and if you can't find the kind you want, you will have no trouble in starting one to suit your taste.

Hanoverians are consumers as well as producers. There are five supermarkets within the borough limits. The eighty automotive dealers employ 382 helpers. There are sixty-six retail eating places, twenty-seven furniture stores, and fifteen general merchandise stores, including three branches of nationwide establishments, handling TV sets, refrigerators, and the like.

Electricity, gas, and oil furnish heat, light, and power in due measure. Numbers and quantities, statistics for today, have little meaning. They are ever-changing, ever-increasing before the ink on these pages is dry.

The Hanover General Hospital has one hundred beds—a million dollar addition nearing completion will bring it to 145-bed capacity by tomorrow. There are ten fire companies with engine houses, tomorrow there will be eleven. The area boasts two high schools, a junior high, and a dozen grade schools. A new four-year secondary school to accommodate one thousand pupils is under way at a cost of two million dollars. One hundred and fifty acres are devoted to athletic fields and playgrounds. A new modern high school and two grade schools are located in Penn Township just across the borough boundary line. Yesterday's little red schoolhouse is a museum piece.

Hanover's water supply, with over seventy-five miles of mains, is municipally owned and operated. The average daily consumption is two million gallons. The impounding dam has a capacity of 217 million gallons. A new impounding dam with a capacity of 1,700,000,000 gallons will soon be constructed as part of the Hanover Municipal Water Works plans to insure an adequate supply of water for the next forty years. The borough's thirty-two miles of sanitary sewers with complete disposal plant will too be expanded to meet increasing needs.

Ever moving onward and upward—there is no Hanover Today. There is only a Hanover Tomorrow!

## LOCAL HISTORIANS

Joseph S. Gitt (1815-1901), editor and publisher of the earlier Hanover Herald, The Democrat, and The Regulator, surveyor for the Hanover Junction, Hanover and Gettysburg Railroad, and Mt. Olivet Cemetery. He contributed a narrative of the History of Hanover to the Hanover Spectator starting in 1872. Spent his last years in New Oxford vicinity.

Malcolm Orlando Smith (1846-1916), co-founder with P. H. Bittinger and editor of the weekly Hanover Herald; later president of Record-Herald Publishing Company. Contributed to Herald The Annals of Hanover from July 6, 1872, to May 24, 1873.

John Timon Riley (1856-1924), Hanover and McSherrystown, wrote and published eight volumes on The Collections and Recollections of the Life and Times of Cardinal Gibbons, the last volume being a memorial to Pope Leo XIII and to the author's wife. He also issued a History and Directory of the boroughs of Adams County in 1880 and Conewago—a collection of Catholic Local History in 1885. At the time of his death he was working on an Anthology "Beauties of Mary" in homage of the Virgin Mary in two volumes. A handsome marker has recently been placed at his grave in Conewago Chapel cemetery.

William Lenhart Hoffheins (1858-1921), former high school principal, contributed section on Civil War to Prowell's History of York County.

Jesse Bollinger (1843-1907), member of G.A.R. Post 99 of Hanover, a former councilman and assistant burgess, issued a brochure on Hanover battle September 28, 1905. Father of late attorney John J. Bollinger, of Mrs. Paul W. Koller, and Mrs. Jacob Rebert.

William Anthony (1875-1958), printer, native citizen and descendant of early Hanover families, compiled and published a history of the battle of Hanover in 1945. Best known for his activitiy in promoting the erection of markers commemorating local historic shrines.

Robert E. Spangler (1867-1955), collector of mementoes of local interest and compiler of early Hanover history left in manuscript form at the time of his death.

Willis W. Eisenhart, Abbottstown, a retired school supervisor, is the author of a History of Abbottstown, 1953, which is the definitive work on the subject. He has also published a family genealogy.

# BIBLIOGRAPHY

References to the battle at Hanover, York County, Pennsylvania, the first battle in the state since the Battle of Germantown in 1777 and frequently called the first battle on free soil, are found in the following books:

Anthony's History of the Battle of Hanover, Hanover, Pa., 1945 (out of print), Hanover B.P.O.E. sponsor.

"War Years With Jeb Stuart," by W. W. Blackford, Charles Scribner's Sons, New York, 1945.

"High Tide at Gettysburg," by Glenn Tucker, the Bobbs-Merrill Company, Inc., New York, 1958.

"They Met at Gettysburg," by Edward J. Stackpole, The Stackpole Company, Harrisburg, Pa., 1956.

"The Great Invasion of 1863, or General Lee in Pennsylvania," by Jacob Hoke, 1887.

"Meade of Gettysburg," by Freeman Cleaves, University of Oklahoma, 1860.

"Yankee Reporters 1861-65," by Emmet Crozier, Oxford University Press, 1956.

"The Life and Campaigns of Major General J. E. B. Stuart," by H. B. McClellan, Boston, 1885.

"History of York County, Pennsylvania," by George R. Prowell, J. H. Beers & Company, Chicago, 1907.

New York Monument Commission Report, Vol. III, Albany, 1900.

Pennsylvania at Gettysburg, Vol. II.

Michigan in the War, compiled by John Robertson, Lansing, 1882.

John Gibson's History of York County, Pa., F. A. Battey Publishing Co., Chicago, 1886.

Congressional Report on Conduct of the War, Washington, D. C., 1865.

"Bullet and Shell," by George F. Williams, Fords, Howard & Hulbert, New York.

The Popular History of the Civil War, Vol. 3, Mammoth Cyclopaedia, The World Co., New York, 1880.

Century Magazine, November 1886, "First Day at Gettysburg," by General Henry F. Hunt, Chief of Artillery, Army of Potomac.

"Gettysburg," edited by Earl Schenck Miers and Richard A. Brown, Rutgers University Press, New Brunswick, 1948.

"The Union Reader," edited by Richard B. Harwell, Longmans, Green & Co., 1958.

"Gettysburg, the Pivotal Battle," by Capt. R. K. Beecham, A. C. McClurg & Co., Chicago, 1911.

"History of 87th Pennsylvania Volunteers," by George R. Prowell, York, Pa., 1901.

"Pictorial Field Book of the Civil War," by Benson J. Lossing, Vol. III, Hartford, Conn., Thomas Belknap, Publisher, 1881.

"Bohemian Brigade," by Louis M. Starr, Alfred Knopf, publisher, 1954.

"Union Mills, the Shriver Homestead Since 1797," by Frederic Shriver Klein in Maryland Historical Magazine, December, 1957.

"Meade's Pipe Creek Line," by Frederic Shriver Klein in Maryland Historical Magazine, June, 1962.